The World Makers

The Past in the Present

The World Makers

Scientists of the Restoration and the Search for the Origins of the Earth

William Poole

Peter Lang Oxford

First published in 2010 by

Peter Lang Ltd
International Academic Publishers
Evenlode Court, Main Road, Long Hanborough, Witney
Oxfordshire OX29 8SZ
United Kingdom

www.peterlang.com

William Poole has asserted his moral right under the Copyright, Designs
and Patents Act of 1988 to be identified as the Author of this Work.

A catalogue record for this book is available from the British Library

ISBN 978-1-906165-08-6

COVER ILLUSTRATIONS:
Cover designed by Dan Mogford.
Top: engraving from *De magnete* (On the magnet) by William Gilbert (1540–1603), published in
Stettin, Poland, in 1628. Courtesy of the Science Museum/Science & Society Picture Library.
Bottom: photo collage by Dan Mogford.

Every effort has been made to trace copyright holders and to obtain their permission
for the use of copyright material. The publisher apologises for any errors or omissions
in the above list and would be grateful for notification of any corrections that
should be incorporated in future reprints or editions of this book.

Printed in the United Kingdom
by the MPG Books Group

Contents

vi

Illustrations

Acknowledgments

This short book has arisen out of a number of fairly recent, but formative intellectual encounters. First among these is the research I did with Ludmilla Jordanova and especially Felicity Henderson on our AHRC-funded project, 'Language-Planning and Free-Thinking in Late Seventeenth Century London' (2004–7), initially created out of a friendship struck up when I was a research fellow at Downing College, Cambridge. I thank them both. Next, and more generally, I thank those scholars whose methods and interests, from near and from afar, have awoken me over the last six years or so from the lazy parochialism of the literary department, and pointed me in new directions. I cannot name them all, but here I would like to mention in particular Mordechai Feingold, Rhodri Lewis, Noel Malcolm, Scott Mandelbrote, and Richard Serjeantson, who have all in their different ways decisively changed how I think. Lewis in particular has been both a good reader and a good friend. In terms of working spaces, I have spent many hundreds of hours musing over old books and manuscripts in the finest working geography in the country, the Duke Humfrey's Library in the Bodleian; I thank its staff past and present, and intone woe unto those who would meddle with this unique space. At Peter Lang Publishing Group my editors, formerly Alexis Kirschbaum and latterly Nick Reynolds, have been alike helpful and patient, and I thank too my anonymous readers for amiably insisting on the rewriting of a prior, messier manuscript. My typescript was excellently copy-edited by Jennifer Speake and formatted by Gemma Lewis. At a trying time, my old Oxford friend and comrade Richard Scholar and I were, I hope, mutually supportive. Institutionally, I owe profound thanks to New College, Oxford, where I am fortunate to be a fellow of a society that sometimes seems a university unto itself. In New College I would like to single out my subject colleague the Anglo-Saxonist Mark Griffith for his almost daily company and conversation over the last five years. I would also wave at my New College undergraduate pupils, who will hopefully be somewhat intrigued by this revelation – if they notice – of what their literature tutor gets up to in his spare time. I have many more debts, both scholarly and personal. I hope that the former are at least partially recorded in my notes and bibliography, and I plead only that this is an introductory work, and as such synthesises rather than surpasses a great deal of prior labour that I can only partially acknowledge. My personal debts are not interesting to the majority of readers, but I would especially thank my family for their continued concern over their maverick youngest. I dedicate this book to three old friends, the Interesting Times Gang: Anthony Gent, Jake Wadham, and Jack Wakefield.

Introduction

… the most popular pretences of the Atheists of our Age, have been the irreconcileableness of the account of Times in Scripture, with that of the learned and ancient Heathen Nations; the inconsistency of the belief of the Scriptures with the principles of reason; and the account which may be given of the Origine of things from principles of Philosophy without the Scriptures.

— EDWARD STILLINGFLEET (1662)

This book is an introduction to a series of closely connected intellectual debates that took place in late seventeenth-century England. The subject was the Earth itself, and the early history of its inhabitants. These were the questions asked. How and when had the world come into existence? When and where had people originated, and how had they spread? Had the surface of the earth changed significantly over this time? What is the current state of the earth and how is this known? Will it change again? How will the world end? The answers to these questions were sought in both of God's 'two books', that of his Word, and that of his works – what we would today term respectively 'the Bible' and 'science'. My subject is the interaction of these two sources in the work of late seventeenth-century natural philosophers and scholars.

This set of debates was at the time digested into a detailed compendium for the general scholar by a young cleric in a hurry: Edward Stillingfleet (1635–99), in his 1662 book, *Origines Sacræ, or a Rational Account of the Grounds of Christian Faith, as to the Truth and Divine Authority of the Scriptures.* Stillingfleet's stout quarto, in which he systematically assessed over some six hundred pages the merits of pagan historical accounts of the origin and age of the world, ancient and modern philosophical explanations of the physics of Creation, theological arguments about God and the problem of evil, the dangers of the new Cartesian philosophy, and the pious conclusions to be drawn from the researches of the new experimental philosophers, was a huge success, going through five editions in under two decades, and still in print two centuries later. In a much shorter compass, this book revisits Stillingfleet's subject some three and a half centuries later, although my approach is historical rather than apologetical, and I largely exclude from consideration Stillingfleet's strictly theological discussions on the existence of God, the problem of evil, and so forth.

For reasons we will later investigate, Stillingfleet changed his mind about how to organise the *Origines Sacræ*. Late in life he attempted to rewrite his book, commencing now not with the problems posed by long-dead pagan historians and philosophers, but with the discoveries of the new experimentalists and what he portrayed as the increasing threats posed by the rise of modern atheism and deism. Stillingfleet's purpose was, as we noted, apologetic: he wanted to defend the Christian religion and the Mosaic accounts of Creation and Flood against ancient and modern impugners, and he evidently grew to feel that the Moderns were overtaking the Ancients as the more potent adversaries. This book is an essay in intellectual history, as opposed to the genre of religious apologetic, and I have had to find a different principle of organisation. I have chosen to organise matters by (seventeenth-century) chronology of topic. So I move from ideas about the Creation through to the Flood, the subsequent history of humankind, and then of the natural world, problems about geomorphology and the nature of fossils, theories and descriptions of the geocosm as it existed in Stillingfleet's day, and finally discussions of its dissolution at the Apocalypse, and the potential Millennium. Not every development can be covered in a short book, but these are the ones that seem most important to me.

Stillingfleet's central thesis was that Christianity was true, and that patient, rational examination of both ancient and modern scholarship on his subject supported no other conclusion. This short book sets out to perform a different task, indeed two. The first is to affirm the centrality of the Bible in certain branches of English science in the rough period 1660–1700, though I hope to show too that this centrality was controversial, and that Stillingfleet was right to suspect that there were developments both within biblical criticism, and within what we would today term the earth sciences, that were querying both the accuracy and the relevance of biblical evidence in such discussions. The second task is to correct the popular interpretation of the scientific revolution in England as the triumph primarily of the exact sciences, in particular mathematics and astronomy – the 'Newtonian Revolution'. While it is true that following the publication of Isaac Newton's *Principia Mathematica* in 1687 Newtonianism started its rise to dominance, it is also true that the 'mathematicians' were a small clique in English science, working in a language of numbers that was rapidly becoming unintelligible to non-specialists. This inevitably prompted a mixture of irritation and jealousy among the greater group of 'naturalists', who either struggled to use or shunned the mathematical dialect, and who had formerly assumed arbitration of natural philosophical questions. Subsequent popular historiography has tended to give the impression that the 'scientific revolution' as experienced in England was essentially mathematical in character, that Newton (1642–1727) was in charge of it, and that no one objected much to that hegemony. Yet after Newton's death in 1727 and a long power struggle, the presidency of the Royal Society passed to the king of the naturalists, Sir Hans Sloane (1660–1753), whose vast collections were upon his death to found the British Museum, today split into the modern British Museum and British Library. Sloane and Newton happened to be friends, but the majority opinion of the Society was that the 'philomat' cabal had to be smashed. The frustrations that this governing dynamic could cause over the opening decades of the Society's history are captured in a grumble made by the FRS and Astronomer Royal, John Flamsteed (1646–1719), who had an exceptionally stormy relation with the Society, especially with his astronomical rivals Newton and Edmond Halley (1656–1742). In 1704 Flamsteed complained that the Royal Society 'understand little but vegetables'. The Newton of these pages is correspondingly a background, if powerful, presence, one who speculated on the chemistry implied by the opening chapters of Genesis; and the Halley seen here is a brilliant meteorologist and magnetician, who suspected that the interior of the planet was inhabited by an alien race. Halley is set in dialogue not with Newton, but with his friend Robert Hooke (1635–1703), whose researches in what became the earth sciences we will often have occasion to discuss; indeed Hooke will be a more dominant presence than either Halley or Newton. To some this will appear a perverse inversion of the 'intrinsic' importance of these three men. But if we want to restore to rightful prominence the burgeoning research in – to use for now modern terminology – geography, meteorology, oceanography, cartography, geology, palaeontology, magnetism, archaeology, ethnology, chemistry, even comparative linguistics, and textual and biblical criticism, then we will need to cede space to the naturalists and philologists who discussed these matters, and who not coincidentally bulked out the rank and file of the Royal Society itself.[1]

This leads me to an explanation of both the geographical and chronological range of this book. I consider some continental texts, and chronologically I often range before 1660 and sometimes after 1700, but in the main remain within that bracket of four decades. The geographical excuse is simply that continental texts influenced English writers, and are hence indispensable; Scottish and Irish input has proved largely incidental.

The chronological apology is harder to make. It is obvious that the 1690s represented the culmination in the debates on cosmogony in England, for instance; but it is less obvious why 1660 is a good starting-point. Although I have largely based my enquiries around the newly founded Royal Society of London, the founding of the Royal Society, first unofficially in 1660 and officially in 1662 and again in 1663, is in intellectual terms merely coincident with the Restoration. Its direct origins lie in certain Oxford and London clubs of the 1640s and 1650s, and its indirect origins in the larger European phenomenon of the growth of the learned society. As Mordechai Feingold has recently argued, the traditional narrative constructed by the truculent mathematician John Wallis (1616–1703) of the Royal Society's origin in a specific earlier London meeting is unreliable polemic, and it is better to understand the incorporation of the Royal Society as the culmination of a range of formal and informal gatherings, with continental and earlier English examples. Many of the older Restoration experimentalists too had participated in the 'Hartlib Circle', as it is today termed, that pan-European network of medical, educational, technological, and religious reformers, whose interchanges were orchestrated by the London-based Prussian Samuel Hartlib (1600–62) throughout the middle decades of the century. The political significance of such continuities has been much debated and is not my topic, but I heed the cautions of Feingold, Michael Hunter, and Noel Malcolm that we should not over-interrogate the political allegiances of given natural philosophers in the period when discussing natural philosophy itself. No political or religious consensus was shared by the first Fellows of the Royal Society. Indeed, scientific endeavour was seen by many as an escape from the turbulence of the age, and public religious orthodoxy often arose because the Church was effectively the only large-scale employer of the intellectual without private means, or because open heterodoxy within the clerisy would attract unwonted attention. In such a situation it is likely that we will experience tensions between the public and private utterances of intellectuals, and it is notable how many experimentalists both composed and suppressed from public view religiously sensitive theories, many of which we will encounter. Again, it has recently been noted that the term 'club' in the civil war bore the military sense of a politically neutral band of men, keeping the peace against Royalist and Parliamentarian alike, but often with slight Royalist sympathies. The scientific 'clubs', especially the one operating in Commonwealth Oxford, were intellectual analogues, and their members at the time were quickly dubbed 'Club-men'. Their operations certainly fed into the ones privileged here, and the academic influence, bringing with it various suppositions about how intellectual labour should be categorised and apportioned, shall also be represented here.[2]

Yet the formation of the Royal Society was an important enough watershed to justify treating it as a rough *terminus a quo*. This is because the Society regularised and then legally incorporated a set of formerly at best semi-organised habits, and in its first decade the Society made almost three hundred elections, albeit the number of core participants was of course much more modest. The importance of the November 1660 meeting is pragmatic too: from this time forward the Society's modest secretariat implemented a standard of documentation that bequeathed to subsequent scientists and historians organised access to communal scientific endeavour. As the Society's apologist Thomas Sprat (1635–1713) wrote in 1667, 'Their purpose is, in short, to make faithful *Records*, of all the Works of *Nature*, or *Art*, which can come within their reach.' This attitude to minute documentation was soon offered to the book-buying world through the hugely successful publications of Robert Boyle (1627–91) and his assistant Robert Hooke. Boyle himself, ever sensitive to the literary dimension of scientific publication, published an essay on the new form of the lab report in order to justify 'this naked way of writing'. The Society next established an even more important literary organ, the learned journal: the *Philosophical Transactions*, edited and personally published from 1665 by their Secretary, Henry Oldenburg (c. 1619–77), promulgated signed and often dated scientific papers, a profound innovation in intellectual history. Oldenburg's journal continues to this day. The French *Journal des Sçavans* founded in the same year, in contrast, was generically much more unfocused, politically more engaged, and its papers often undated and unattributed.[3]

Finally, an explanation of some terms I use to describe the intellectual disciplines addressed in this book. No two commentators in the period agreed entirely on how to divide, descriptively or prescriptively, the disciplines, and as with any lexicographical venture destabilisation pursues the heels of codification. In order to avoid misunderstanding in what follows, however, we may note the following contemporary conventions. *Physics* in the early-modern sense referred to one of the three sciences that made up the theoretical or contemplative part of *philosophy*. It addressed material substances, as opposed to *mathematics*, which dealt with quantities abstracted from matter, or *metaphysics*, which treated subjects abstracted from both quantity and matter. Physics (adjective *physical*), also known as *physiology*, or *natural philosophy*, was itself divided into two parts, *general* and *special*, the former dealing with principles common to all matter, the latter with specific applications of the former principles. *Geology* was not a word used in the period, but its content was a recognisable branch of special physics, as was *meteorology*, a word that was starting to appear in English. *Geography*, like *astronomy*, was a branch of *mixed mathematics*, which like mathematics dealt with quantities, but reassigned to physical bodies. It too generated *general* and *special* wings. *Philosophy* therefore contained what we would today call science, and philosophy was itself a part of the larger *arts* curriculum, studied in the universities before the 'higher' degrees of *medicine*, *law*, and *theology*, the last acknowledged as the authoritative discipline. *Experimental philosophy* was a new phrase to describe *natural philosophy* transacted with particular emphasis on experiments undertaken, witnessed, or described. *Experimental philosophers* or *experimentalists* are the forerunners of today's scientists, but 'scientist' was not a term used until long after this period. An eclectic colloquial term for a scholar with interests in natural philosophy, but also in some or any of the disciplines of antiquarianism, philology, numismatics, chorography, botany, and indeed other activities, was a *virtuoso*, a term that could also be used mockingly. A more useful distinction used by practitioners was of the *geometer* or *mathematician* (a student of algebra, geometry, or astronomy) versus the *naturalist* (zoology, botany, medicine), fast becoming two temperamentally opposed groups, at least in England. Finally, *alchymy*, *alchemy*, *chymistry*, and *chemistry* were all terms used in the period more or less interchangeably, and in these murky waters I understand an alchemist to be interested in the exegesis of the traditional corpus of alchemical texts, whereas someone with chemical interests need not be interested in such literary recuperation. All the terms discussed above were themselves unstable at the time, and further precision would be misleading.

The last contemporary term requiring some unpacking is that borrowed for the title of this book itself – the 'World Makers'. This phrase, as we shall see again later, was coined by a hostile but highly qualified reader, the mathematician John Keill (1671–1721). Unlike 'naturalist' or 'geometer', it was therefore in both origin and currency an insult. Keill was naming and shaming a small number of 'Theorists' – that was the other name this group attracted – who from the 1680s in England published works purporting to explain in terms intelligible to physicists events in biblical history, usually the Creation and the Flood, but also often stretching to the future Conflagration. Their master, so Keill not unreasonably claimed, was the French philosopher and physicist René Descartes (1596–1650). The World Makers' attempts to weld physics to biblical history in the name of defending the truth of the Bible were eagerly read, ubiquitously and hotly debated, but in the end judged largely unsatisfactory. Each succeeding World Maker truly thought that he was fixing the problems of his predecessor, and hence should really be classified as a different kind of philosopher altogether. But, as we shall see, the polemic identification of the 'Theorists' as alike dangerous to piety was probably the better judgment. How often the hostile, reactionary observer sees more clearly than the doting parent the true danger of a novel theory!

1

The Physics of Creation

And really it is much more unlikely, that so many admirable Creatures that constitute this one exquisite and stupendous Fabrick of the World should be made by the casual confluence of falling Atoms, justling or knocking one another in the immense vacuity, then that in a Printers Working-house a multitude of small Letters, being thrown upon the Ground, should fall dispos'd into such an order, as clearly to exhibit the History of the Creation of the World, describ'd in the 3 or 4 first Chapters of *Genesis* ...

— ROBERT BOYLE (1663)

God's Creation of the universe out of nothing at some date between 3928 BC and 4103 BC was a fact to almost every educated Westerner in the later seventeenth century. The early chapters of Genesis described a literal, datable process, and although increasingly difficult questions were being asked about the state and genre of the received biblical text, 'Creationism' in this basic sense had been and would remain the default position for centuries. We therefore commence by considering contemporary theories of the Creation itself under three broad headings: the biblical inheritance; the academic Aristotelian tradition; and the receipt of the new philosophies of first the Swiss medical reformer and prophet Paracelsus, and then later of the French philosophers Descartes and Gassendi. All of these models could be mobilised to explain how Creation happened. In particular, the corpuscular, non-biblical model of Creation published by Descartes in 1644 sparked off the English dynasty of 'World Makers', and the violence that this innovation did to traditional biblical scholarship can only be appreciated if we establish this latter tradition first. As we shall also see, powerful continental voices were also destabilising traditional claims for the biblical text at exactly the point that the English naturalists were developing their own challenging theories of geomorphology.

The Biblical Inheritance

Although this book will discuss biblical events recorded mainly in Genesis and in Revelation, it is important to grasp at the outset the overwhelming presumption in this period of the unfailing truth of the entire Bible, and the way in which its text impinged upon all types of intellectual enquiry. Belief in the textual inerrancy of the Bible is itself biblically persuaded: 2 Timothy claims that 'All Scripture is given by the inspiration of God' (2 Tim 3:16), and Revelation concludes on a threat to all those who would tamper with biblical text: 'If any man shall add unto these things, God shall add unto him the plagues that are written in this book. And if any man shall take away from the words of the prophecy of this book, God shall take away his part out of the book of life' (Rev 22:18–19). If the claim of the first text is true and the threat of the second successful, then biblical inerrancy ensues. This internal argument was accompanied by a strong external theory of the divine inspiration of the first penmen of Scripture, particularly in Reformed contexts. English Elizabethan Protestant theology tended to follow Calvin's comments on the matter of inspiration, where the writers of Scripture are little more than amanuenses of the Spirit: the Scriptures 'came to us, by the instrumentality of men, from the very mouth of God'; they must be 'believed to have come from heaven, as directly as if God had been heard giving utterance to them'. The English Calvinist William Ames distinguished between inspiration that revealed to the biblical writers things they cannot previously have known (the Creation, for instance), and inspiration that made their accounts of known history inerrant (the Gospels, for instance). But he insisted that supernatural inspiration 'did dictate and suggest all the words' of Scripture to the writers, thereby identifying the actual verbal text of the Bible as revelation itself, not a secondary report of it.

When pondering the fortunes of the Bible as it was handed across continents and down the centuries, only the most dogmatic claimed absolute and continual textual purity. But the purity of its origins, and our ability to ascribe whole books of the Bible to named individuals writing in one inspired sitting, went unchallenged by almost all. Important for our purposes was the assumed authorship of the Pentateuch or first five books of the Bible by Moses himself. This was inferred from Deuteronomy 31:24–6: Moses 'made an end of writing the words of this law in a book' subsequently placed in the Ark of the Covenant, a verse often interpreted as referring not just to Deuteronomy but to the whole 'autograph volume of the Law' from the beginning of Genesis to the end of Deuteronomy. That Moses' death is also recounted in these books was a problem that could be solved by allowing Moses prophetic foresight of his own death or, in a few quarters (with surprisingly rich medieval genealogies), quiet admission that a later inspired writer had tied up the loose ends in Moses' manuscript. Even in devotional sources we can find now and then examples of open-mindedness on this issue. As one prominent Lutheran Reformer, in a work intended for instruction and translated into English, lightly remarked: 'they [the books of the Pentateuch] are ascribed to Moses, either because Moses wrote them, or because they contain the story of Moses in them.'

If the original writers of the Bible were uniformly inspired, and if their text had passed down the centuries (virtually) intact, this still left open the correct manner of interpreting them. The strong presumption in the Christian West since the days of the Church Fathers had been that Scripture should be read literally, unless, as St Augustine taught, such a reading conflicts with 'good morals or true faith'. Such advice borders on circularity, but it was not a circularity St Augustine regarded as vicious, nor did medieval and early-modern biblical rhetoricians disagree. Yet from the later medieval period on, a greater interest in classifying the genres of the biblical books can be detected too. The great medieval scholar Nicholas of Lyra (c. 1270–1349) opened his exhaustive biblical commentary further subdividing the Old Testament into legal, historical, wisdom-teaching, and prophetic sections. These four subdivisions, he then explained, mapped exactly onto the four corresponding subdivisions of the New Testament. Turning to Genesis, Nicholas states that he will prefer a 'literal' interpretation of the opening of Genesis, and his commentary is steeped in the terminology of Aristotelian physics. Commonsensical astronomical explanations are furnished: 'And He divided the light from the darkness', for instance, refers to the daily movement of the Sun from one hemisphere to the next, for the opacity of the globe guarantees that when the Sun is in one hemisphere, it is dark in the opposing one. Care was also taken to respect the Hebraism of the original text: when Genesis says that the seas were gathered into one place, exposing dry land for the habitation of man and beast, we must understand by 'seas' all bodies of waters including freshwater lakes. This kind of attitude would dominate Christian exegesis after Nicholas of Lyra for centuries to come, and was in no sense a discovery or invention of the Protestant Reformers.

The narrative of the first three chapters of Genesis describes in two separable phases the creation of the heavens and the earth by one supreme God through divine utterance alone, and then the first actions of the two humans placed by God in paradise. In the first phase, in six days God creates in specific order the heavens, sublunary matter, light, the terraqueous globe, flora, the heavenly bodies, marine life, birds, all things that live on the land, and finally a man and a woman, before resting for a seventh day (Gen 1:1–2:3). In the second phase, the biblical text then seemingly turns back on itself in order to expatiate upon the final acts of the 'Hexameron' or Six Days' Work, now describing in detail a garden placed in the east of Eden, the creation of the first man outside Eden, the subsequent creation inside Eden of the first woman from a rib of the first man, and the brief drama of their Fall and Expulsion. After the Fall, Adam gives Eve her proper name for the first time, and the couple are driven out of Eden (Gen 2:4–3:24). Commentators had long noted the disparity in tone and content between these two opening phases of the Bible, but whereas modern textual critics recognise in this the splicing together of two distinct prior texts, their early-modern counterparts preferred to see in the redoubling of Genesis 1–3 a powerful rhetorical lesson delivered by the Holy Ghost working through the pen of one later author, Moses. His purpose was to insist upon the continuity of natural and human history. In the biblical economy, there is no easy separation of physical and theological modes: the creation of heaven and earth is presented in the same frame as the origin of sin and its punishment. Theology, physics, and ethics, are all here aspects of one historical process.[1]

This book is concerned almost exclusively with how natural philosophers related their work to the events of the first phase, the 'scientific' as opposed to the 'ethical' narrative, the time of Creation as opposed to the time of Fall. However, it is crucial to open our enquiry with the reminder that the biblical inheritance resisted any easy opposition of these categories. The vast theological commentaries on Genesis so typical of the sixteenth and seventeenth centuries functioned in their opening Hexameral sections as repositories for what we would consider today to be scientific hypotheses. Conversely, works that are now classified as primarily scientific in genre repeatedly, indeed obsessively, returned to the text of the Hexameron to gloss and to justify contemporary speculations in physics, astronomy, geography, and natural history. The early-modern natural philosopher styled his work as a form of pious meditation on the works of God in Creation, but in turn the terse brevity of the opening chapters of the Bible forced upon admirers of the works of God a contrasting sense of shame at the works of man, made in God's image, yet so soon neglecting it. These two complementary yet intertwined pressures inform the great epic of the early Restoration, John Milton's *Paradise Lost* (1667), which may stand as a symbol for this double inheritance. *Paradise Lost* was chiefly a theological poem, yet Milton interjected a long physical description of Creation itself, bringing his epic into line with the earlier, predominantly French tradition of scientific poetry on the Creation, witnessed in seventeenth-century England by the many translations of the Huguenot poet Guillaume de Salluste, Sieur Du Bartas, on the 'Week' of Creation. The desire to keep theological and scientific poetry combined and up to date can also be observed in the unrealised plans of the otherwise completely inactive FRS and poet Samuel Woodforde (1636–1700), who in the very year *Paradise Lost* was published threatened to revamp the genre of biblical Creation epic using the experimental discoveries of the Royal Society.[2]

Trust that the text of Genesis was both uncorrupted in itself and perennially relevant to the enquiries of natural philosophers survived the period, but was nevertheless felt to be under increasing attack after the Restoration from a number of different parties. Stillingfleet, for instance, devoted hundreds of pages to arguing that it was rational to believe both that Moses wrote the first five books of the Bible, and that his testimony was to be preferred before that of any other source. Theologians and natural philosophers alike continually protested that they faced an army of 'atheistical' or 'Deistical' persons who sought to undermine the truth of Scripture.

It is today difficult to assess this alarm for two different reasons. First, genuine atheists or Deists would have been very unwise to publicise in either print or manuscript such views; and secondly, the apologetic genre often invites the creation by the writer of a kind of inner sceptic, who can then be refuted all the more intimately. Nevertheless I will argue at several points in this book that we can in fact attach many of these threatening tendencies to identifiable writers, even – indeed especially – when such writers may not have intended such an interpretation. Then as now, it is often the reviewer rather than the originator who has a clearer sense of the wider ramifications of a new theory. Indeed, as we shall now survey, by the turn of the century many of the problems facing the text of the Bible in general and of Genesis in particular were internally rather than externally generated – that is, contrived by would-be apologists, who were themselves then identified as the real threat. This movement, whereby intended defence is subsequently 'exposed' as unwitting attack, was the defining strategy of the theological polemic of the age.

Most of these internal influences derived from continental controversies. Philologists violently disputed the antiquity of the Hebrew vowel-points, some now proposing that the vocalisation of the Old Testament was entirely of human origin. The Socinian heretics developed a reductive logico-philological method of exegesis that struck at many doctrinal fundamentals: how could God have created the universe out of nothing, they argued, if the Hebrew verb for 'create' nowhere else in the Old Testament bore that meaning? The Dutch jurist and theologian Hugo Grotius (1583–1645) proposed some controversial theoretical concessions in *On the Truth of the Christian Religion* (1629), translated from Dutch verse first into Latin, then into the vernaculars, and even into Arabic in 1660 by Oxford's first Laudian Professor of that language. Grotius admitted that no text remains uncorrupted over time, and that the Bible too must show signs of textual decay. He argued that Moses harmonised his writings with the received opinions of his age and the ancient writings on which such opinions were based. He defended the inconsistency of the Gospels by a legal analogy: only fraudsters 'by compact and agreement' produce exactly the same account of events under questioning; that the Gospels are not exact mutual corroborations paradoxically attests their authenticity. Grotius also argued, as we shall later see, that the Apocalypse of John described events in the early patristic period, not a future sequence leading into the Last Judgment, a direct attack on the Millenarianism so popular in the period.

Grotius' criticism influenced important figures among the younger generation of Anglican divines. Key among them was the Royalist biblical commentator and textual critic Henry Hammond (1605–60), who, like his colleagues, would subsequently write most of his theology in English, not Latin. The French biblical critic Jean Morin (1591–1659) was being read in England too, and he advanced the dangerous thesis that a good critical text of the Bible must be eclectic, based on a number of different prior texts. Morin therefore assumed that no one ancient manuscript of the biblical text is free from error. Such scepticism had political charge in revolutionary England. *The Liberty of Prophesying* (1647) by the maverick Anglican apologist Jeremy Taylor (1613–67), emerging out of the smoke of the first civil war, blasted

Presbyterian confidence by insisting that neither 'external' nor 'internal' approaches to Scripture produced absolute certainty. 'Externally', no Church Father or Kirk elder retailed infallibility; and 'internally' Scripture itself was so knotted with textual and rhetorical problems that we had best agree on the bare articles of the Creed, and leave everyone after that free to interpret Scripture as they think best.[3]

However, the major explosion in later seventeenth-century biblical criticism was the publication of the *Histoire Critique du Vieux Testament* (Critical History of the Old Testament; 1678) by the French Oratorian Richard Simon (1638–1712). Bossuet, the Gallican bishop of Meaux, was so appalled that he had the entire edition seized and burned, although a few copies slipped away, and some made it to England. A young London lawyer then translated the work in 1682 to please his father, but his publisher, when he learned of the Paris combustion, took financial fright, and complex printing manoeuvres ensued before the work finally appeared. Simon's thesis was that 'the Books of the Bible that are come into our hands, are but abridgments of the ancient Records, which were more full and copious, before the last abridgment was made for the public use of the people.' In other words, although Simon endorsed the principle of inspiration, it was now a question of inspired editing, and if that were the case, then no matter how 'inspired' the initial editor had been, how Moses knew so well about the past had ceased to become a solely supernatural matter. Moses' account of Creation might be based on other, fuller, but now lost books. The textual critic could now begin to detect signs of editorial sutures or even un-Mosaic passages in 'Moses'' work; and the scholar of ancient mythology might enquire whether other ancient Near Eastern cosmogonies preserved antediluvian learning not redacted by Moses.

News of Simon's disintegrationist theory travelled fast to London. Henri Justel (1620–93) in Paris wrote in early 1677 to the Royal Society that 'there is a Book in the Press now which will make some Noise intituled the History of the Text of the Bible which the Author holds to be Corrupted and altered.' Especially following its translation, the book was read widely in England for the next two decades, and although the natural philosophers did not have much cause to talk in session about the text, we know from their private manuscripts and library catalogues that it had some influence, particularly in the circle of Robert Hooke and Edmond Halley. Simultaneously, the radically historicist *Tractatus Theologico-Politicus* (1670; English translation 1689) of Benedict Spinoza (1632–77) argued that the Bible was merely a set of culturally

specific books aimed at local audiences. As its writers were prophets and not
philosophers, Moses' account of Creation was not a scientific text: 'those
Men therefore, who endeavor out of the Books of the *Prophets*, to find the
true knowledge of Natural and Spiritual things, are extremely mistaken.' As
a result of this publication, the Royal Society's Secretary Henry Oldenburg
felt obliged to break off correspondence with Spinoza for a few years. The
Society's Treasurer Abraham Hill (1635–1722), however, noted down in his
commonplace book from Spinoza that a 'very smal part of the Pentateuch
writ by Moses'. He also recorded various remarks on lost biblical books, the
incompleteness of the canon, and the relative novelty of the Hebrew vowel-
points.[4] His friend the FRS Francis Lodwick (1619–94) took down similar
notes from his reading, and we know that Lodwick for one certainly believed
such claims. The Spinozan thesis of cultural specificity was expounded in
Thomas Burnet's *Archæologiæ Philosophicæ* (1692), which we shall encounter
again. Burnet's real design in the *Archæologiæ*, however, was to excuse Moses
from the responsibility of scientific truth in order to clear the stage for Burnet's
own recuperation of other, non-biblical accounts of the Creation. This was
not at all the intention behind Spinoza's historicism, although Burnet was
exploiting exactly the possibility opened by Simon's criticism. Burnet's book
was reviewed by Robert Hooke for the *Philosophical Transactions* the next
year, but despite Hooke's appreciative mentions of the *Archæologiæ* in his
subsequent lectures on earthquakes, the more typical reaction was that of
Humphrey Prideaux (1648–1724) in Oxford in the same year: 'I find the
Republicarians in these parts openly sedulous to promote atheisme, to wch
end they spread themselfes in coffy houses and talk violently for it, and Dr
Burnets Archaiologia is much made use of by them to confute ye account ye
scriptures give us of ye creation of ye world.' That Moses was not a natural
philosopher was soon a Deist touch-stone: as a 1695 Deistical writer insisted,
Moses was a prophet concerned merely with explaining 'true Theocracy
and good Morals', not the physics of Creation.[5] Some sense of the knife-
edge walked by radicals here is provided by the admittedly extreme but
shockingly late case of Thomas Aikenhead (1676–97), a young Edinburgh
student. Aikenhead was apprehended in the Scottish capital late in 1696 for
claiming, amongst other blasphemies, that the Old Testament was a late
compilation of fables, and that the New Testament was the history of an
impostor. His terminology suggested that he had been reading Spinoza. He
was burnt at the stake.[6]

The Aristotelian Inheritance

Aristotelian science remained central to the integration of biblical and physical ideas in the period for two reasons: because the Aristotelian synthesis formed the starting-point of most educated people's experience of these questions; and because it was above all a highly organised philosophy. As Ralph Bohun (1639–1716), employed in the late 1660s by John Evelyn (1620–1706) as resident tutor to his son, insisted, studies must be structured according to the Aristotelian corpus, 'since Aristotle has so universally obtained in all the universitys of Christendome for so many ages [and] thus insensibly crept into all modern writers by the use of his terms'. Many sophomore manuscript cribs of the Aristotelian cursus survive from late in the seventeenth century, and it is not uncommon to find university tutors even in the eighteenth century advocating the Aristotelian curriculum as the bedrock of a good education because it possessed an established structure and literature. University-educated men therefore learnt their physics in an increasingly eclectic, inclusive environment, in which the old-fashioned physics was typically encountered first, and then supplemented by the new philosophies. Even after the publication of Newton's *Principia* the old physics was very much alive as an educational tradition, and the conservative Aristotelian textbook *Physicæ Scientiæ Compendium* of Robert Sanderson, for instance, was published for student use at Oxford as late as 1671 and again in 1690. Many copies of the 1690 edition survive in an interleaved form, heavily annotated by their users, and are in effect a combination of textbook and adversarial notebook. Sanderson's physics was thus commonly sold in a form designed to function as a structure to be supplemented or qualified by its users.[7]

The Aristotelian universe, working from the outermost to the innermost, consisted of the spherical heavens in motion around a spherical earth at rest. Sanderson described this system as 'eternal' because time and the universe begin and end together. Physically speaking, the universe has no proper beginning, because that is not a moment in time, and 'beginning' is a temporal word. Sanderson was here subtly baptising the most notorious of Aristotle's physical doctrines, that of the eternity of the world. Because the opening of Genesis appeared to record a divine miracle of Creation at a specific point in time, Aristotelian eternity had traditionally been regarded by Christians as atheist in implication. Yet as Sanderson had earlier stated in his 'theoremata' on time, time and motion are reciprocal measures of one another, and so he could later assume without apparent strain that before Creation – a doctrine explicitly rejected by Aristotle – time was not. In Christianised Aristotelianism, an 'eternal' universe might nevertheless have been created at a datable point in time.

The content of Aristotelian physics had been used to gloss the Creation of Genesis for many centuries. One example still being read well after the Restoration will stand for all: John Swan's conservative *Speculum Mundi* (1635; four editions to 1698), a work that functioned simultaneously as a course in traditional physics and an exhaustive gloss on the opening chapters of Genesis. Swan larded his work with extracts from the creation epic of Du Bartas in Sylvester's translation, and he also alluded to a host of modern astronomical authorities. Nevertheless Aristotelian physics, with its changeless heavens moving in eternal circles, and its sublunary realm of four elements moving in finite straight lines was unsatisfactory to specialists, even after Aristotle's eternal world had been replaced by one created in time. Particularly as a result of Platonist and Paracelsian cosmologies, many theorists increasingly demanded a universe that was, in Amos Funkenstein's definition, 'homogeneous, uniform, symmetrical'. As Isaac Newton stated in his *Principia Mathematica* (1687), the cause of respiration in man and in beast, of the fall of a stone in Europe and in America, of light in the Sun and in the cooking-fire, and of the reflection of light in the Earth and in the planets, must be the same. 'For nature is simple', he stipulated just before this observation, 'and does not luxuriate in superfluous causes.'[8]

If the content of Aristotelian physics was dating fast, its lasting impact was to be in geographical theory. Underpinning Aristotle's *Meteorologica* was the notion of perpetual vicissitude or the theory that the face of the earth changed gradually and continually. As Aristotle stated at the head of the final chapter of the first book of the *Meteorologica*:

> The same parts of the earth are not always moist or dry, but change their character according to the appearance or failure of rivers. So also mainland and sea change places and one area does not remain earth, another sea, for all time, but sea replaces what was once dry land, and where there is now sea there is at another time land. This process must, however, be supposed to take place in an orderly cycle.

This was a potentially explosive idea, as it gestured towards an older planet than was witnessed by purely textual sources. Standard commentators on the

Meteorologica such as the Jesuit magnetician Nicolaus Cabeus (1586–1650) hence rejected full vicissitude:

> By means of this doctrine of the vicissitude of seas and rivers, Aristotle aimed to establish his own dogma – or rather his terrible error – of the world's eternity, of the necessity of causes [i.e. fatalism], and to make light of the authority of the Mosaic history. For he saw that the eternity of the universe and the earth, as it now appears, was altogether refuted by the alluvial deposit of rivers. So he took refuge in time immemorial, by which these changes might come to pass.[9]

Vicissitude was present, too, in foundational Latin works of natural philosophy, notably Seneca's *Natural Questions*, where it is affirmed that 'Fate goes around in a circle, and that which once happened, is repeated.' These physical doctrines, originating in a pagan philosophy that denied Creation itself, might have been theologically inadmissible to most, but the geological possibilities they empowered were to prove attractive to the later seventeenth-century neoterics Bernard Varenius (1622–50), Nicolaus Steno (1638–86), and Robert Hooke, even as the Aristotelian physical gloss of Creation was itself retired.

The Paracelsian Inheritance

The first new physics of Genesis still influential in the later seventeenth century was the 'chemical philosophy' of Philippus Theophrastus Aureolus Bombastus von Hohenheim, called Paracelsus (1493–1541). Paracelsian philosophy was powered by backlash antagonism towards the pagan Aristotle, and by its advocacy of the two great analogies of macro- to microcosm, and of God the Creator to man the chemical artist. Such a philosophy was predisposed towards a chemical reading of Genesis. Paracelsus himself (possibly pseudo-Paracelsus) developed this exegesis in his *Philosophia ad Athenienses*, only published in 1564. This 'philosophy for the Athenians' taught that 'all things proceeded out of one *Matter*'; that God then separated the elements from this matter; and that individual things, including planets, terrestrial bodies, even spirits and dreams, were successively separated out from the basic elements. Creation itself was thus a chemical process, the true meaning of

God's 'separations' in the opening verses of Genesis. The Paracelsian Genesis stands apart from the other physical models of Creation developed in the period, because in making God into a chemist, the Paracelsian artist was thereby reciprocally identifying his own labours as deiform. In his own view he was also cutting out the impious middleman Aristotle, and reading Moses directly.[10]

The Paracelsian cosmological inheritance in England as elsewhere was conflicted. Thomas Tymme (d. 1620) presented the alchemical Genesis in his dedication to his translation of Quercetanus in 1605: God worked on the primal Chaos by 'Halchymicall Extraction, Separation, Sublimation, and Coniunction'. Conversely, Francis Bacon (1561–1626), echoing the earlier criticisms of Thomas Erastus on the continent, attacked in an influential passage all those who erected their natural philosophy on Genesis as builders of 'not only a fantastic philosophy but also a heretical religion'. Bacon was referring to the Paracelsians, yet ironically his own cosmogony has been shown to be 'semi-Paracelsian'. The *Apologie or Declaration of the Power and Providence of God* (1627, 1630, 1635) by George Hakewill (1578–1649) praised the clinical successes of the modern '*Chymiques*, *Hermetiques*, or *Paracelsians*', but accused them too of arrogance and exaggerated criticism of the Ancients. Despite this ambivalent heritage, in the revolutionary decades of the century there was a flood of interest in some of the more mystical aspects of Paracelsianism, often appearing in English translation for the first time. The Moravian bishop Jan Amos Comenius (1592–1670) was an indefatigable writer of illustrated textbooks, and many English editions of his pedagogical works appeared, insinuating through their illustrations a basically Aristotelian view of the structure and order of the universe. Yet Comenius was also a conduit for Paracelsian ideas on Creation. In 1651 an English translation of his work on Mosaic physics was produced, under the title of *Naturall Philosophie Reformed by Divine Light*. 'Is the light of Hierusalem so put out, that we must needs borrow lamps at Athens?' Comenius complained in his preface, an allusion to (pseudo-)Paracelsus' *Philosophia ad Atheniensis*, itself imitating the Church Father Tertullian's famous *quid Athenæ Hierosolymis?*, 'what has Athens to do with Jerusalem?' Comenius set out his textbook as *seriatim* quotations from the opening of Genesis accompanied by physical glosses. He then broadened out into more detailed discussion of motion, quality, and mutation, before ascending through the elements, plants, animals, and man, finally arriving at angels. Comenius affirmed that atomic processes lie at the heart of matter, adopting the alchemical, Paracelsian trinity of 'salt', 'sulphur', and 'mercury' as the three 'substantial qualities' of material being.[11]

Interest in Paracelsian cosmology is sometimes said to have petered out after the collapse of the interregnum government. This is not so, and certainly interest in chemical research increased to the point where a bibliography of 'chymical books' written or translated into English was required. This need was met by William Cooper's catalogue (1673, 1675), in which Cooper claimed for his topic original works by prominent FRSs Robert Boyle, Walter Charleton (1620–1707), Nehemiah Grew (1641–1712), Henry More (1614–87), Robert Sharrock (1630–84), and even John Wilkins (1614–72). Several major Paracelsian texts were published in English translation for the first time across the Restoration: Oswald Croll's *Philosophy Reformed and Improved* appeared in 1657, Jean-Baptiste Van Helmont's *Oriatrike* in 1662, and Michael Sendivogius's *New Light of Alchymy* in 1674. Appended to the translation of Croll was (pseudo-)Paracelsus' *Philosophia ad Athenienses* itself. Paracelsianism also generated its own Creation poetry: Samuel Pordage (1633–?91) published *Mundorum Explicatio* (1661), a very long, rhymed verse epic popular enough to be reprinted in 1663. Between these two years, Van Helmont's *Oriatrike* included a chemical reading of Creation in which he insisted that Genesis taught that all things arise out of the element of water. Van Helmont also offered a chemical interpretation of the Fall, in which the forbidden fruit is loaded with a chemical provoking sexual desire. It is now appreciated how persistently if covertly Robert Boyle engaged with Van Helmont and the alchemical tradition, and some of his remarks on the opening of Genesis should be read in this light. Although his *Sceptical Chymist* (1661) was critical of the three-element system of the chymists, Boyle's speaker Carneades there proposed too that in the Creation the universal first matter was plausibly corpuscular ('corpuscularian' was a term coined by Henry Power (c. 1626–66), but popularised by Boyle), and that Moses' account in Genesis, interposing the separation of water and earth before the creation of the plants, beasts, and birds, may be read as supportive of this hypothesis. The next year Stillingfleet appreciatively cited Boyle's book to support the notion that the physics of Creation was founded on the motions of fluid matter. Later, in the 1690s, the biblical commentator Simon Patrick, himself an early apologist for the new experimental philosophy, thought that God worked chaos into matter in Genesis 1:2 'by long fermentations perhaps'.[12]

The most influential student of alchemy was, however, Isaac Newton, although this obsessive interest was all but invisible to his contemporaries. In the late 1660s, Newton began to study the alchemist 'Eirenaeus Philalethes', whose *Secrets Reveal'd* was printed in 1669. (In reality, Eirenaeus was the *alter ego* of the notorious Scoto-American alchemist George Starkey (1628–65), an only recently uncovered piece of pseudonomy.) Eirenaeus once more explicitly paralleled the work of the alchemical adept with the work of biblical Creation, quoting the opening of Genesis at length. When Newton came to correspond with Thomas Burnet in 1680–1 on the latter's *Sacred Theory*, he spoke of Creation in obviously chemical terms, offering as analogies for the irregularities of mountains the coagulation of dissolved saltpetre into irregular bars, of tin into irregular lumps, and of curdling milk. Only a little later, in around 1684, Newton took notes on the alchemical *tabula smaragdina* or Emerald Tablet of Hermes Trismegistus, and 'unselfconsciously poured much of the Genesis story into the empty mould provided by Hermes's "Thus was the world created"':

> And just as the world was created from dark Chaos through the bringing forth of the light and through the separation of the aery firmament and of the waters of the earth, so our work brings forth the beginning out of black Chaos and its first matter through the separation of the elements and the illumination of matter.

Hence although Newton did not address the issue directly in his major printed works, scattered remarks in letters and manuscripts strongly suggest that he too supported the chemical Genesis.[13] In 1692–3 Newton was drawn into a correspondence with the philologist and academician Richard Bentley (1662–1742) while the latter was delivering the first series of Boyle Lectures. Newton attacked Cartesian cosmology, affirming that the organisation of the universe shows unmistakable signs of intelligent design, and that gravity is not inherent to matter, but is a separate, rule-bound phenomenon; 'but whether this agent be material or immaterial, is a question I have left to the consideration of my readers.' Newton himself appears to have believed in private in an alchemical micro-material realm, guiding and impelling the larger phenomena his public mathematics modelled.[14]

The most important legacy of Paracelsian ideas, however, as with their Aristotelian counterparts, was the enduring contribution they made to the physics of the geocosm. Paracelsians were particularly interested in earthquakes and subterranean fires, and the notion of the Earth as a giant chemical alembic or furnace fitted with similar Paracelsian models for the universe at large and for man himself. This inheritance is obviously present in works such as

John Webster's *Metallographia* (1671), and the more eccentric *Anatomy of the Earth* (1694) and *New Observations on the Natural History of this World of Matter and this World of Life* (1696) by cleric and mining speculator Thomas Robinson (d. 1719). Robinson insisted that his own chemical, animist Earth was more aligned to Moses' philosophy than the unbiblical earths of Thomas Burnet and John Woodward. His Earth, in contrast, was created as a living being, 'a great *Animal*; having Skin, Flesh, Blood, Bones, Nerves, &c.', and which revolved on its own axis once a day due to the 'hot and fiery Particles' in its belly, moving in a perpetual circle and dragging the Earth around with them. Mediated Paracelsian influence is also present, less obviously, in the geological speculations of Robert Hooke. Although Hooke was unimpressed by the obscurity of alchemical terminology, his theories of a dynamic Earth, wracked by internal fires and earthquakes, has obvious affinities with the chemical philosophy.[15]

The Cartesian and Gassendist Inheritances

The Aristotelian and Paracelsian inheritances offered a physics of Creation, but the Paracelsian attack on Aristotelianism was in this area outgunned by the arrival of the entire alternative cosmogony and physics of René Descartes (1596–1650). Descartes took the learned world by storm. The English scientific publicist Joseph Glanvill (1636–80) deliberately awarded the French philosopher the title previously given by Izaak Walton to Francis Bacon when he dubbed him 'the grand secretary of nature, the miraculous Descartes.' After Descartes' *Principia Philosophiæ* of 1644, discussions of method and matter were permanently altered, even if most people came to reject and often despise the actual physics Descartes espoused. In a famed passage from which the title of this book derives, the mathematician and Newtonian John Keill looked back in 1698 over the previous half-century of theorising, and commented bitterly on Descartes:

> who, as his followers pretended, could solve all the phenomena in nature, by his principles of matter, and motion, without the help of attraction and occult qualities. He was the first world-maker this Century produced, for he supposes that God at the beginning created only a certain quantity of matter, and motion,

and from thence he endeavours to show, how, by the necessary laws of Mechanism, without any extraordinary concurrence of the Divine Power, the world and all that therein is might have been produced.

In the initial years of Descartes' reception, the most influential aspect of Cartesianism was the system of physics he erected upon his freshly wiped mental slate, the *cogito*. Descartes carefully prefaced his model with the caveat that he was not describing things as they really were when the universe came into being, but conjectured by the light of philosophy as they *might have been*: 'I may even retrace their causes here to a stage earlier than any I think they ever passed through', Descartes added. God, we know from revelation, created the world in full perfection, with Adam and Eve and their surrounding vegetation in corresponding maturity. Nevertheless, Descartes maintained, if we can explain how things 'could have sprung forth as if from certain seeds (even though we know that things did not happen this way)', then we will understand them better.[16]

One of Descartes' earliest stated conclusions in his *Principia* was that God exists, and so Descartes' universe, like his mind, was subtended by theistic presence. But Descartes banished biblical exegesis from his ensuing exploration, and there is no mention in the *Principia* how or if Descartes' system squares with revealed text other than the claim rehearsed above: that philosophical might-have-beens can be unbiblical and yet serve a beneficial intellectual purpose. Nevertheless Descartes too appears to have fantasised that his hypothetical cosmogony was compatible with the biblical Genesis. In around 1640, Descartes found the Dutch scholar Anna Maria van Schurman (1607–78) reading Genesis in Hebrew, and apparently asked her why she was bothering with 'a thing of so little importance'. She vowed to avoid Descartes thereafter. But in 1646, two years after the publication of the *Principia*, we find Descartes writing to the diplomat Sir William Boswell (d. 1650) in these terms:

I am now at the description of the birth of the world, in which I hope to include the greatest part of physics. Moreover, I will say that, in rereading the first chapter of Genesis, not unlike a miracle, I discovered that it could be explained according to my thoughts much better, it seems to me, than in all the ways in which the exegetes have explained it, something I had never hoped for until now.

For a few years after this point Descartes toyed in his correspondence with the idea of glossing Genesis with his physics, but ultimately nothing came of it. Although the printed *Principia* made no such overtures, as we shall later see the trend of English Cartesian reception was to follow unawares these private letters. In England, as often on the Continent, the Cartesian system was interpreted as a bid to describe what had actually happened in the beginning, regardless of the careful protests of its author.[17]

Descartes, breaking the traditional ordering of the Aristotelian textbook, offered in the first book of the *Principia* a 'metaphysics' in which he deduced the necessary existence of God and the impertinence of introducing 'final causes' into philosophy. We should not ask for what end God created man and the universe; 'we ought not to presume so much of ourselves as to think that we are the confidants of His intentions.' This provocative truncation disallowed discussion of providence as a cause in a world supposedly providentially governed, and was to prove particularly offensive to the English philosophers. In the remaining three books of the *Principia* Descartes established his new physics, which, like its Aristotelian predecessor, rested on the notion of the *plenum*, or the view that all space is filled – there is, properly speaking, no 'space'. Particles are packed together in such a way that any one movement results in adjacent movements, which are likewise communicated through direct contact, and so the universe works as a closed system in fluid dynamics. At Creation, God imparted a certain fixed quantity of motion to the universe, and that motion is always conserved, as is the general stock of matter undergoing such motion. Descartes insisted too that the universe contained countless planetary systems revolving around countless suns, the first appearance in a major textbook of the thesis of 'the plurality of worlds'. At the end of the century, developing on Keill's snub, Thomas Baker (1656–1740) in his *Reflections upon Learning* (1699) accused the astronomer Huygens and his ilk as 'world-mongers' on this score.[18]

According to Descartes, God first created matter and divided it into small corpuscles. These corpuscles he endowed with two types of circular motion: spin, and motion around a given point. One system of spinning particles arranged around one centre is termed a *vortex*, and the universe comprises an infinite or indefinite number of contiguous vortices in dynamic equilibrium. The first corpuscles cannot have been created spheres, as the initial distinction of the first matter into components, if the *plenum* is to be maintained, must have been into solids with plane faces. The spin of the first particles caused these sharp objects to grind each other down into spheres. The interstices between the spheres were filled with the resultant scrapings, and indeed such scrapings must be indefinitely divisible in order to maintain the *plenum*. Descartes termed these types of matter First Matter (the scrapings) and Second Matter (the spheres). A Third Matter was in turn generated, bulkier and less prone to movement. First Matter, swift in motion and light-emitting, forms the Sun and fixed stars. Second matter comprises the fabric of the heavens, opaque and permeable. Third Matter forms the planets and comets. Vortices were first generated when superfluous First Matter collected into a fluid ball (our Sun). Other fluid balls also formed (now the planets), each accompanied by its own vortex. Now and then spots of matter (sunspots) formed on the surface of these spheres, and in extreme cases such spots might completely smother their globe. In such cases, the vortex destabilises and is absorbed by an adjacent vortex. Hence the planets were once suns which at length became buried in their own sunspots, and, converted into Third Matter, ended up orbiting the Sun. The current diurnal spin of the Earth, for instance, is a remnant of its ancient rotation as a sun. Occasionally such planets are not caught entirely in one vortex, but drift from one to the next, and these are comets. Thus the whole universe works as a system of numberless rough ellipses, all bodies acting on all other bodies. Quite unlike the deathless harmony of the Aristotelian heavens, this was a universe in which suns were just as mortal as people; suns that eventually became enveloped in their own dark contagion, and ceased to be suns.

Descartes' work travelled fast. From the late 1630s he was being digested by a select few in England, and in the 1640s he received an enthusiastic welcome from the influential and widely read philosopher and Cambridge don Henry More. More was subsequently encouraged to enter into a correspondence with Descartes by the foremost 'intelligencer' of the time, Samuel Hartlib (1600–62), and from 1648 the two men exchanged a number of letters. More's first reaction to the cosmogony of this 'sublime and subtil Mechanick' was positive: if anyone suspected that Descartes and Genesis might accord, then More 'dare[d] confidently pronounce … that if they be so, those truths were ever lodged in the Text of Moses'. In Oxford, after Robert Hooke's arrival in the 1650s, he came under the patronage of Robert Boyle, 'and made him understand Descartes' philosophy', as John Aubrey recalled. The *Principia* itself received a London printing in 1664. More translated parts of the crucial third book, in which the system of creation was expounded, and as late as 1674 he was teaching parts of the *Principia* to his Cambridge undergraduates. The tendency to gloss Genesis with Descartes had a certain life after More in both continental and insular traditions: Joannes Amerpoel wrote *Cartesius Mosaizans* (Leeuwarden, 1669) and Géraud de Cordemoy (1626–84) a *Discourse … shewing that the Systeme of M. Des Cartes, and particularly his Opinion concerning Bruets, does contain nothing dangerous; and that all he hath written of both, seems to have been taken out of the First Chapter of Genesis* (the title as translated into English in 1670). Amerpoel organised his work into sections in which 'Moses' quotes and then explains his own text, and then 'Cartesius' glosses Moses' physics with explanations helpfully keyed to the relevant sections of the *Principia*. De Cordemoy's shorter text correspondingly works through the six 'days' of Genesis.

One initial problem was to excuse Descartes himself from more extreme interpretations of Cartesianism. Stillingfleet's long chapter 'Of the Origine of the Universe' in the *Origines Sacræ* affirmed the Mosaic Creation against two enemy propositions: the eternity of Aristotle, and the atomism of Epicurus, the latter of which being 'that which makes most noise in the world'. Stillingfleet was at pains to demonstrate that Descartes himself had envisaged not only a Creator who made the initial matter of the universe, but also one who was required to 'conserve' the motions of matter, an attempt to insist that the Cartesian God did not retire after his one initial fillip at Creation. Stillingfleet was a corpuscularian, but one typically anxious to defend a strongly theistic reading of Cartesian cosmogony, 'because it is apt to be *abused* to that end by persons *Atheistically* disposed'. However, Stillingfleet became uneasy over time, and set about rewriting his famous book. The ensuing transformation of his work is an excellent barometer of the philosophical fears of the age. Stillingfleet soon laid aside the manuscript of the new *Origines*, but he completed some of it and planned the chapter structure of the whole. The revamped *Origines*, probably undertaken in the mid-1690s, now opened on a defence of natural religion against the 'modern atheistical hypotheses' of fear as the root of religion (Hobbes), of the irrelevance of final causes (Descartes), and of the merely political origin of religions (Spinoza). Stillingfleet appealed to many works of the new experimental philosophy that had appeared since his first edition, expanding his earlier passing mentions of Harvey and Boyle, and enlisting over a dozen other modern English and European naturalists. Conversely, Descartes was now the explicit villain of the piece, no longer the interesting new force in European physics, but the enemy of pious science. Only after this analysis of natural religion and its enemies did Stillingfleet plan to address revealed religion, which conversely had been the priority of his first book. The *Origines* therefore metamorphosed from a text that commenced with the most ancient historical records into a text that opened on 'The Atheistical Pretences of this Age'. Stillingfleet abandoned his new *Origines* at the very point where he cited for the first time Isaac Newton's recent *Principia Mathematica* against Descartes, a serendipitous signpost to the path English physics was swiftly taking.[19]

Descartes' physics was exciting but defective, and satirical popularisations, such as the *Voyage to the World of Cartesius*, translated by a Magdalen College demy in 1692 from the work of a French Jesuit, functioned at once to advertise and lampoon. The problems that Descartes' *plenum* faced are illuminated in one early encounter: the annotations made by the mathematician and first President of the Royal Society, William Brouncker (1620–84), to his presentation copy of Walter Charleton's Gassendist treatise *Physiologia Epicuro-Gassendo-Charletoniana* (1654). Brouncker's carefully recorded objections are primarily logical or mathematical, although he was by no means entirely hostile to corpuscularianism, as his frequent references to atoms surrounded by 'aether' demonstrates. Yet Brouncker objected that not even circumambient 'aether', if all matter is truly corpuscular, can resist the vacuum. He provided the following geometric proof: if we suppose that there are smaller particles than the standard atoms, and that these particles fill up the spaces between atoms, in order for the filling particles to be most effective, their forms must tend to that of the sphere. But this of course means that a supply of aetherial particles can only fill the spaces between atoms in so far as spheres can pack. Now the least wastage of space when stacking spherical particles is equal to the ratio of the volume of a sphere to its circumscribing cube, or $4/3 \, \pi r : (2r)$, which reduces to $4/3 \, \pi : 8$ or $\sim 0.5236 : 1$, the ratio Brouncker produces: 'For a Sphaere is to its circumscribed Cube 5236 to 10000 fere [Lat. approximately]'. Descartes himself had refined his model to allow the spheres subsequently to move closer to one another than in cubic lattice, from the interstices of which were squeezed out grooved screw-shaped bars, the particles responsible for magnetism. Nonetheless, Brouncker's basic objection, hinging on the assumption that corpuscular matter cannot both pack with no wastage and still possess local motion, hits home. This points to the growing English distrust of the notion of 'indefinitely' divisible matter, and preference for the purer atomism of the Epicurean revivalist Pierre Gassendi (1592–1655), in which fixed-shape discrete particles collided in a void. Versions of the geometrical argument would later be employed by Henry More and Pierre-Daniel Huet (1630–1721), the most prominent English and

French critics of Descartes respectively, often recommended in tandem to new readers of Descartes as safe guides.[20]

Behind such physical objections lay more powerful metaphysical ones. Henry More as a Platonist found Descartes' general anti-Aristotelianism and his use of reason rather than the senses as the arbiter of philosophy highly congenial. However, from the inception of the two men's correspondence it was obvious that as it stood Descartes' system required pious modification. Central to More's view of the world was that it was filled with not only matter but 'spirit', a category that encompassed souls, ghosts, and eventually a general 'Spirit of Nature' that shaped unseen the course and behaviour of matter. 'Spirit' was also a component of More's physics for more local reasons. England was home soil to Thomas Hobbes (1588–1679), and Hobbesian materialism was the single most lambasted and feared terminus of the new corpuscularian philosophy. Gassendi and Descartes had in their different ways preserved the spirit world: for both philosophers, souls exist, even if they cannot be modelled in material terms. (Rational souls, Descartes notoriously proposed, had not been granted to animals, who became, in Huygens' striking phrase, 'nothing but Clocks and Engines of Flesh'.) Hobbes disagreed with both men, judging the phrase 'incorporeal substance' incoherent, and after Hobbes' 1651 *Leviathan*, almost all other English philosophers nervously distanced themselves from his extreme materialist extrapolation.[21]

More therefore insisted that there are motions in matter that cannot be explained by materialism alone. He collected examples where Cartesian physical prediction was at odds with what actually happened, and then bridged the gap by positing a non-material 'plastic spirit' or 'virtue' that subtended matter. Such a spirit testified to a theistic presence in the universe unexplained by materialism. This two-tier model, whereby atomic interaction was endorsed but only alongside non-material forces, was the hallmark of mainstream English corpuscularianism. More became the spokesman for the non-material realm of reality, and eventually declared that *no* physical action could be explained by matter alone. The idea that matter could of itself do the things it did became the standard whipping-block of English scientific theology or 'Physico-Theology' as it was henceforth known, a term that had first appeared in the title of Walter Charleton's *The Darkness of Atheism, Dispelled by the Light of Nature: A Physico-Theologicall Treatise* (1652). The notion of 'plastic nature' was further developed by Ralph Cudworth in his *True Intellectual System of the Universe* (1678), and endorsed by John Ray. As it was beneath the dignity of God, both argued, to 'set his own hand as it were to every work', and as it was impious to hold that matter was self-moving, God, although directly responsible for the original Creation, delegates the normal oversight of natural affairs to the 'plastic nature', much as he delegates to his angels the transactions of providence. The hypothesis of a plastic nature also provided an explanation for monsters and freaks: because it was not itself omnipotent, the plastic nature might occasionally make mistakes. Cudworth is notable in this context for his proposal in the same book (retired by his early eighteenth-century abridger) that an ancient Phoenician atomist known from Greek sources as Moschus or Mochus, and the Biblical Moses, were one and the same man, thereby providing a string of earlier similar conjectures on the Mosaic origin of atomism with direct biblical anchorage.[22]

By the end of the century, Cartesian physics was widely taught and widely contested in England. Manuscript cribs started to appear alongside the sophomore Aristotelian notebooks we mentioned earlier, notably the 'Principia Cartesiana' of John Felton (d. 1667) of Gonville and Caius, a digest that must have been exceedingly popular to judge from the number of surviving manuscripts. Nevertheless the Newtonians would soon triumph in the textbook tradition, and meanwhile Gassendi and his atoms were rapidly eclipsing Descartes and his *plenum*. William Whiston recalled worked through Newton's more difficult treatise on his own in 1690s Cambridge, having heard that the Scottish academic mathematician and astronomer David Gregory (1659–1708) was making his students in Edinburgh dispute on Newton, 'while we at Cambridge, poor wretches, were ignominiously studying the fictitious hypotheses of the Cartesian'. In broad terms, English philosophy therefore had only a brief flirtation with Cartesianism: the insular Aristotle–Descartes–Newton sandwich had only the thinnest Cartesian inner layer, whereas on the Continent modified Cartesianism reigned in especially Catholic locales late into the eighteenth century. Despite its relatively brief hey-day in England, Cartesianism was nevertheless vital for the development specifically of the earth sciences. Descartes was the first major theorist to treat the whole of the Earth from the top of the atmosphere to the centre of the core as an integral subject for study, and as we shall see, he cast a long shadow down the dynasty of English cosmogonists.[23]

Nevertheless, as has been hinted, Gassendi and his atoms ultimately fared better in England than Descartes and his vortices. Gassendi's atomic Creation physics weathered the objections to the Cartesian model not least because Gassendi was independently popular in England as a logician, astronomer, and hammer of judicial astrology. Gassendi was personally respected too. Sir William Petty knew him, and his physics converted Walter Charleton from Helmontian allegiance in the early 1650s; Charleton's 1654 *Physiologia Epicuro-Gassendo-Charletoniana*, the text Brouncker annotated, was to be the major vernacular transmitter of Gassendist ideas for decades, read with care by the young Isaac Newton. Most importantly, Gassendi was epistemologically modest in his physics, often proposing two hypotheses for one phenomenon. His system therefore proved particularly congenial, and was available in textbook form long before that of Descartes. Gassendi's books could be obtained from abroad, but the English market soon demanded four insular printings of his *Syntagma*, as opposed to only one of Descartes' *Principia*. As early as 1663 the French visitor Samuel Sorbière had identified the followers of the *Principia* and of the *Syntagma* as opposed schools: the English 'mathematicians' were behind Descartes; the 'literati' (*literateurs*) were for Gassendi. The Cambridge academician John Eachard (1637–97) joked in 1671 about the 'young pert sophister with his atoms and globuli', with his 'Cartes's *Principles*' and 'Gassendus's *Syntagma* lying upon the table', again recognising the two different corpuscular systems available in England. The previous year however he had described the academe as 'under the Reign of *Atoms*', a Gassendist term. The conservative scholar Meric Casaubon (1599–1671) attacked the philosophies of both Frenchmen, but regarded the humanistic, modest Gassendi as by far the lesser evil.[24]

The ascendancy of Gassendi and his atoms was nevertheless a theologically sensitive issue, because Gassendi was reviving a system of physics with strong atheist associations. The Greek of Epicurus survived only in fragments in later authors, but everyone knew the long Latin scientific epic of Lucretius, in which the entire Epicurean system of physics, politics, ethics, and theology, was detailed. And as the Epicurean system explicitly rejected providence, replacing God's creative interest in the universe with a random conglomeration of atoms, atomism and atheism were conceptually twinned. The religious dubiety of the poem prevented it from achieving an English translation until late in the period. A French prose translation appeared only in 1650, and the English were even more cautious. In this decade, Lucy Hutchinson (1620–81) commenced a manuscript translation of the poem, but was later so appalled to learn that a copy had been circulating without her knowledge that she turned to versifying Genesis itself in penance. The aristocratic gardener and future FRS John Evelyn was pressed by his friends again in the 1650s to commence a verse translation, which he did; but when he finally published Lucretius' first book alone with a commentary in 1656 he was so anxious to dissociate himself from Lucretius that he even annotated the commendatory poems written by his friends with nervous protestations distancing himself from his translated text. Evelyn later repented of the whole venture. The first full translation was only achieved in print in 1682, by the Oxonian classical scholar Thomas Creech (1659–1700), again draped with comments protesting Lucretius' 'errors'. This was an extremely popular book, and prompted what has to be the most openly atheistical piece of poetry in English from the period: the commendatory poem by Aphra Behn (1640?–89) attacking 'poor feeble faith's dull oracles'. At least, that is how the line reads in Behn's own collected *Poems* of 1684; but when it was printed before the 1683 edition of Creech's translation, the horrified editor bowdlerised the line to 'As strong as faith's resistless oracles'. Creech himself committed suicide in 1700, and of course some sneered that he had done this in imitation of Lucretius, his true master. The popular association of Lucretius with the new experimental scientists was sealed by the playwright Thomas Shadwell (1642?–92), whose satire on the Royal Society's activities, *The Virtuoso*, opens with a wit in a gown reading aloud in Latin from Lucretius, whom he praises as the philosopher who 'dost, almost alone, demonstrate that Poetry and Good Sence may go together'. It is as well that he quotes in Latin, for the verses Shadwell makes his actor speak aloud comprise the section in which Lucretius stated that the gods were entirely unmoved by human existence, a sentiment incompatible with Christian providentialism.[25]

English support for Gassendi, therefore, had to lean heavily on the fact that he was far more cautious than Descartes about how his revived Epicureanism might interact with biblical revelation. Classical Epicureanism insisted on the plurality of universes, rejecting the notion of a temporal creation of matter. Gassendi responded that Scripture teaches that there is one universe alone, even if it is a finite object located in infinite space. As Charleton summarised,

> … in *Moses* inæstimable Diary or Narrative of the Creation can be found no mention at all of a Multitude of Worlds, but on the contrary a positive assertion of *one* world; and the express declarement of the manner how the *Fiat* of *Omnipotence* educed the several Parts thereof successively out of the Chaos, disposed them into subordinate Piles, and endowed them with exquisite configurations respective to their distinct destinations, motions and uses.

Again, Genesis teaches that this one world was created at a given point in time, in a six-day process, and therefore has not existed from eternity. It will end too. In response to Epicurus' random congeries of particles, Gassendi proposed that God orchestrated the original configurations of atoms, and that the *semina* or moulds out of which living things were first formed were themselves either constructed by atoms predisposed to such configurations, or directly formed and scattered about on the earth by God at Creation, placed in sunken wombs or *matrices*. Unlike Lucretius, who had proposed the generation of humans themselves from such *semina*, Gassendi carefully discussed the *semina* in the context solely of plant and animal life; mankind was still implicitly something special, created directly by divine miracle, and not an indirect, autochthonous production, something sprung from the ground. Gassendi was thus a theological 'voluntarist', one who stresses the primacy of God's will over His intellect: although God normally works through secondary causes (what we would term 'scientific laws'), there is nothing preventing him from dispensing with such causes, and acting directly, as in miracles. The ordinary phenomena of the universe run on Epicurean physics; the extraordinary betoken miraculous intervention. Creation itself is an example of this latter category.[26]

Gassendi therefore baptised his atoms by arguing for their divine arrangement at Creation, so that their orderly combinations were no longer the processes of random impacts, as in classical Epicureanism. Robert Boyle used a pertinent metaphor when in 1663 he complained that Epicurus' creation was as likely as a printer dropping his tray of type on his shop floor, and finding that he had managed to spell out the opening three or four chapters of Genesis (see page 1 of this book). For Boyle, Gassendist voluntarism provided his atomic type with a Creator who composed perfect copy. Boyle was always polite about Gassendi, taking pains to distinguish him from the heretic Epicurus, and when Boyle in 1666 identified his own position on corpuscularianism as distinct from the views of both Epicurus and Descartes, he articulated it using vocabulary drawn directly from Gassendist texts:

And therefore [in distinction to both Epicurus and Descartes] I think, that the wise Author of Nature did not onely *put Matter into Motion*, but, when he resolv'd to make the World, did so regulate and *guide the Motions* of the small parts of the Universal Matter, as to reduce the greater Systems of them into the Order they were to continue in; and did more particularly contrive some portions of that

Matter into Seminal Rudiments or Principles, lodg'd in convenient Receptacles, (and, as it were Wombs,) and others into the Bodies of Plants and Animals.[27]

This would be the conclusion of Newton, too, in his *Optickes*:

God in the Beginning form'd Matter in solid, massy, hard, impenetrable, moveable Particles, of such Sizes and Figures, and with such other Properties, and in such Proportion to Space, as most conduced to the End for which he formed them.

Finally, then, we can see that many prominent English natural philosophers were content to treat their contemporary physical theories as implicit in the text of Genesis, even if enthusiastic Cartesian eisegesis or the reading into Scripture of one's own ideas soon gave way to a more circumspect Gassendist rapprochement. The Platonic and Paracelsian desire for homogeneity in physical explanation also played a persistent role, as the older two-realm physics of Aristotle was retired from advanced if not sophomore speculation. Developments in biblical criticism, however, offered some more subversive possibilities, notably that Genesis was not textually reliable or the work of one inspired man; or, more radically, that it had nothing whatsoever to say to modern natural philosophers. Boyle and Newton could never take up these offers. Some other natural philosophers did.

2

The Preadamite Hypothesis

Among all the Hypotheses of those who would destroy our most holy Faith, none is so plausible as that of the *Eternity of the World*.

— WILLIAM WOTTON (1694)

Perhaps the most scandalous of the ideas targeted by Stillingfleet in the first edition of the *Origines Sacræ* was the new hypothesis of the '*Præadamitæ*', the notion that Adam and Eve had not been the first people. Consequently natural, human, and biblical histories were not necessarily coextensive, the date and perhaps the manner of Creation remain hidden, and attempts to track humankind's path from Eden to Babel and thence to the modern nation states were based upon a false premise. Furthermore, 'it is hard to conceive how the effects of mans fall should extend to all mankinde, unless all mankind were propagated from *Adam*', Stillingfleet complained. The Preadamite hypothesis therefore disconnected questions about the ultimate origin of the universe and the prehistory of man from biblical theology and chronology, and the originator of the heresy even dared to restrict the Flood to the regions around Palestine alone. The hypothesis assumed that a chasm of indefinite duration stood between Creation itself, and the events recorded from Adam and Eve, and accordingly we now turn to the fortunes of the Preadamite hypothesis.[1]

In 1643 a French lawyer and secretary named Isaac La Peyrère (1596–1676) published anonymously a Messianic tract *Du Rappel des Juifs* (On the Recall of the Jews). In it, he proposed the recall and reintegration of the scattered Jewish peoples into a new pan-European state, presided over by the French king. The various correspondents of the intelligencer Marin Mersenne

(1588–1648) discussed the work, and some even afforded it moderate support. Mersenne, however, was also circulating a manuscript version of La Peyrère's companion work that would later earn its author international notoriety for over a century. At this time too, Mersenne's correspondent, the jurist Claude Sarrau (1600–51), wrote to the philologist Claude Saumaise (1588–1653) with the news that La Peyrère had come to visit him, bearing a manuscript which he called *Somnium Nobilis Aquitani de Prae-Adamitis*, or 'The Dream of a Noble Aquitaine concerning the Preadamites'. This was the tract Mersenne held too. What, worried Sarrau, should he say?[2]

La Peyrère's *Somnium* was explosive: not of very sophisticated construction perhaps, but violent and effective. The *Somnium* – here we must reconstruct a manuscript that cannot with certainty be identified today – argued a theological point on theological grounds, offering a new interpretation of a few verses from Paul's letter to the Romans. When Paul wrote that 'For until the law sin was not in the world: but sin is not imputed where there is no law' (Rom 5:13), La Peyrère explained that the law there referred to was not as always assumed the Law given to Moses (the Ten Commandments), but that given to Adam (the Forbidden Fruit). But, if so, then the phrase '*until the law*' must mean that there was a world before Adam, and that it had been inhabited, by a humanity bereft of law. (The actual emendation 'is not imputed' to 'was not imputed' was made on textual grounds, the Greek, La Peyrère claimed, having been corrupted 'by the carelessness of the Transcribers'.)

This was a single pebble cast into one of the more difficult ponds of the New Testament, but its repercussions agitated the entire Bible. La Peyrère claimed that this new exegesis allowed him to make sense of something that had troubled him as a child – why did Cain fear being assaulted in his exile if nobody other than his parents existed? Who did he get married to? La Peyrère could now propose that Cain simply went to the next city. But if all do not descend from Adam and Eve, then how can everyone partake in their original sin? And, as Stillingfleet's complaint assumed, if some people are not tainted by original sin, then they might not need saving, an absurd conclusion for a Christian.

La Peyrère claimed that biblical silence on the Preadamite nations did not hinder his theory, as the Mosaic books were written for a Mosaic audience alone, with no aspirations to universal history. The Bible, as Spinoza too would soon argue, comprised a set of culturally specific books aimed at local audiences, and could not be treated as a seamless, transhistorical object. For La Peyrère, the Preadamite nations had been around for time literally immemorial, something so obvious that the original writers of the Bible had not thought to point it out. To explain his idea of immemorial time, La Peyrère later invoked the (ultimately Greek) three-age schema of time, which he derived from a quotation from the scholar Varro preserved in the work of the Latin chronologer Censorinus: *uncertain* (from the creation to the (Ogygian) flood); *mythic* (from the flood to first Olympiad (776 BC, an Olympiad being a period of four years)), and *historical* (from the first Olympiad on). Technical chronology typically limited the pre-historical era by mapping it onto just over three thousand years of biblical time. La Peyrère reinstated the truly uncertain time of the Greeks, the sense that chronologically precise history is merely the brightly lit end of a long, gradually darkening corridor, the beginning of which we can no longer discern. In those lost times civilisations now unknown may have risen and fallen, and, as Robert Hooke was later to muse, may even have known everything we consider new, their knowledge disappearing with the collapse of their nameless empires. This was simply too much for La Peyrère's readers, but this Greek scheme of time became a commonplace in chronological and cosmogonical works. Both Thomas Burnet and Robert Hooke repeated the division, for instance, as did the popular vernacular manuals of current scholarship on Creation and chronology by Stillingfleet himself and Matthew Hale (1609–76).

La Peyrère's initial work circulated in the middle decades of the century on the Continent; there are a few manuscripts in Paris of what must be versions of this initial tract, argued almost solely on exegetical grounds, with just a few references in passing to the long chronologies of the Chaldeans, the Egyptians, and the Chinese. Meanwhile, La Peyrère was collecting up scraps of support, especially in recent travel publications. In 1653 he visited England, but was apparently very ill, and left no traces. At length, he was persuaded to publish his revision, apparently with financial aid from Queen Kristina of Sweden, and in 1655 the work Cardinal Richelieu had banned over a decade previously was on sale in Amsterdam, and almost immediately elsewhere, printed surreptitiously by the famous Elzevier firm (a financial move merely, as they also published a refutation). Titled *Præ-Adamitæ* (The Preadamites), the short theological core was now followed by a long *Systema*, in which La Peyrère organised his confirmatory material and expounded his larger system. The work, though theological in origin, was now no longer just a piece of biblical exegesis, but borrowed freely from the literatures of geography, travel, and technical chronology.

Over a dozen smugly outraged Latin refutations appeared within a year, and La Peyrère himself later improbably claimed that the Pope and the General of the Jesuits had cried with appreciative laughter together over his pages. The Catholic authorities arrested La Peyrère, imprisoned him, and forced him to recant and convert, which he did, rather unconvincingly, and published his apology. But La Peyrère's later manuscripts show that he never sincerely abandoned his men before Adam.

What was La Peyrère trying to achieve? How serious was he? We have seen that he called his first draft a *Somnium*, or 'dream', a title which suggests outlandishness and perhaps fictional status. Nevertheless the actual content, of the earliest manuscripts as much as of the final printed version, does not resemble a joke. 'Somnium' as a title might also token serious but difficult new claims – we might compare Johannes Kepler's posthumous *Somnium* of 1634, for instance, in which he argued that the moon was inhabited by a strange, serpentine form of life. Again, La Peyrère's philosemitism, cogged carefully into his Preadamism, is obviously sincere if impractical, and it has been speculated, though not proven, whether La Peyrère were not himself from ultimately Jewish stock. A more tangible indication of intent comes from the term that La Peyrère himself applied to the *Præ-Adamitæ* in the manuscript of the unpublished segment of his philosemitic manifesto, now preserved in the Condé Library at Chantilly. There he looked back on the *Præ-Adamitæ*, remarking that everyone had been so annoyed by his 'paradox' ('irité de ce Paradoxe'), that he had been forced to break off publishing his system. This system he described as comprising three works, one concerning the Jews Elected ('Juîs elus'), (which he equated with the *Præ-Adamitæ*), one on the Jew Rejected ('Juîs reietez') (the current manuscript), and one on the Jews Recalled ('Juîs rapelez') (covered by the printed *Du Rappel des Juifs*).[3] 'Paradox', moreover, denotes perhaps the most fascinating of all renaissance genres: the form of writing in which a branch of received wisdom was questioned, sometimes playfully, but more often seriously; people commonly referred to 'the Copernican paradox', for instance. In other words, La Peyrère's Preadamism was not prompted by some brand of scepticism, anti-scripturalism, or any other '-ism' that we care to associate with 'subversive' thinking in the period. Instead, he was obsessed by the plight of Jewry, and when considered as a whole his system thus has a coherence of vision. However, La Peyrère's philosemitism was of secondary importance to his readers, who rightly saw in the *Præ-Adamitæ* more arresting and immediate problems, and for our study the reception of La Peyrère is more significant than how La Peyrère himself understood his work. We will concentrate on what the English made of him.

La Peyrère wrote as a secular theologian, and his 'paradox' caused an immense stir within theology. Despite the fact that most of the initial replies to La Peyrère jeered at his exegesis, it was the critical impact of the *Præ-Adamitæ* which was to have lasting consequence, because La Peyrère was tampering with the very text of the Bible and hence the foundations of biblical interpretation itself. The *Præ-Adamitæ* travelled far and fast and was eagerly read; banning and burning only boosted its desirability. A mere few months after its publication, two London stationers complained to the government that an English translation had been prepared, and although they may have held up the work's dissemination, they did not stop it, as a very faithful English translation duly appeared early in 1656. A Dutch version followed in 1661. The work was acquired by scores of private and institutional libraries throughout Europe. Pierre Bayle commented almost half a century after the book's publication that it still fetched high prices at book auctions. Today, many copies can still be found bound with one or more of the refutations: it seems that one's heresy was frequently taken with its antidote.[4]

Did the *Præ-Adamitæ* have an extra-theological effect? It did, and this demonstrates that interventions in theological discussions could have wider repercussions. Theologians would continue to worry about the critical implications of the hypothesis long after they had dismissed its actual content, which was after all a precarious reading of Paul projected back onto Genesis. Seth Ward (1617–89), the astronomer and opponent of Hobbes, summarised and dispatched the *Præ-Adamitæ*'s 'paradox' in the context of an attack on Hobbes as early as 1656. Hobbes had himself been alerted to the book's arrival in Paris in early October 1655, where it had been 'immediately banned, but for all that it has not failed to find several admirers.'[5] Meanwhile the average educated man with an ear for new theories had a sensationalist claim to feast upon – what if there had indeed been men before Adam? Of course few were likely to assent to the idea, but all could secretly enjoy it, and see that it offered a seductive solution to some classic knots in chronology and geography: it simply cut them. If people had sprung up from the ground, all over the earth, time out of mind, as the Epicureans of antiquity had maintained, then the newly discovered chronologies of the Aztecs and the Chinese – let alone the well-known claims of cultural longevity made by the Egyptians and Chaldeans – suddenly made sense. Hugo Grotius on the Continent had been concerned enough by this implication to launch a pre-emptive strike against La Peyrère in print as early as 1643 in a work, significantly, on the origin of the Native Americans. Admittedly the almost universally assumed fabulousness of non-Hebraic history weakened the impact here, but as applied to the problem of population dispersal, it could have sinister application. For if, say, Africans or Native Americans were not from the seed of Adam then they could be classed as existing outside the economy of salvation. Opposition to such conclusions had been elaborated in the early sixteenth century, especially in Spain in the university of Salamanca, where academic theologians had struggled to develop a model whereby savages who could never conceivably have heard of Christ were not therefore to be abused at will.[6] Despite these academic cautions, the notion that the Gospel was never for the blacks or the reds remained strong among some colonials, and it could take Preadamite form. One late seventeenth-century missionary, Morgan Godwyn (1640–85/1709), published an anguished plea in 1680 for the proselytising of black slaves in Virginia, among whom he had lived. He perceived as his adversaries slavers who invoked 'the Pre-Adamites whimsey' to justify their lack of interest in the spiritual welfare of their goods. The slavers were scarcely scholars, but their purported recycling of La Peyrère's hypothesis illustrates neatly the consequences a recondite Latin theological work could have, and in future centuries, polygeneticism would regularly be invoked to buttress racist arguments. This would have horrified La Peyrère, who thought that his system would reunite rather than divide the nations. Such an outcome had however been predicted by the celebrated sixteenth-century French jurist and philosopher Jean Bodin (1530–96) at the end of his popular *Methodus ad facilem historiarum cognitionem* (Method for the Easy Comprehension of History) (1566). He had insisted on the common origin of man, and on the importance of comparative etymology as a tool for establishing confraternity and affiliation. Belief in autochthony, he warned, bred inhumanity:

> I know of no conviction more powerful than that of consanguinity for developing and maintaining the good will and friendship of mankind. … On the other hand, do not men who boast that they are indigenous and born of the earth violate the very bond of human society?[7]

Late seventeenth-century fiction saw this boast put into practice. The French renegade monk Gabriel de Foigny (c. 1630–92) wrote *La Terre Australe Connue* (1676; English translation 1693) featuring a shipwrecked hermaphrodite narrator Jacques Sadeur, who encounters for the first time the xenophobic nation of the Australians. The Australians, also hermaphrodites, are proud Preadamites, racially distinct from Europeans, deriving from three male protoplasts created directly by God. Their nation is twelve thousand years old, and their written records extend back eight thousand, preserved in 48 venerated codices. In a section amusing to those with an ear for patristic heresy, Foigny's huge Australians claim that the 'Adamite' nations arose around a mere three thousand years ago, from the sexual union of a serpent of 'unmeasurable bigness, and of an amphibious nature, which they call *Ams*', and a woman (actually just a man in the French text, but turned into a woman by the contemporary English translator). The two resultant children proved exceptionally wicked, and from them do we all derive. This distortion of the Edenic narrative, as Pierre Bayle snorted, was lifted straight from ancient tales told of the Christian Gnostic heretics: 'Would one not think this a wretched allusion to the fabulous story of some Heretics, who said that Eve had two children by the serpent which tempted her?' Foigny thus welded an old heresy of the Gnostics onto the new heresy of La Peyrère.[8]

At the time Foigny was writing his outrageous fiction in France, a more skeletal, but similarly Preadamite utopia was being composed in secret in London by Francis Lodwick (1619–94), FRS, friend of Robert Hooke and a pioneer deviser of artificial languages. In his manuscript 'Description of a Country Not Named', his ghostly, anonymous utopians commence their chronology 11,700 years earlier than the point from which 'we reckon the beginning of Time'. If we assume 'the beginning of Time' to be c. 4000 BC, then that puts Lodwick's utopian record-keeping back to 15,700 BC. Behind that, Lodwick's utopians 'have a Tradition of a far elder date by thousands of years, which they call the uncertain account'. The utopians insist that their chronology is nonetheless biblical: 'Moses or the Author of the book of Genesis having mentioned the beginning of all things and of mankind slips over that large track of Time and immediately falleth on the relation of the immediate Creation of Adam and his Wife Eve.' Their justification is the one offered by La Peyrère: how could Cain, having slain Abel, have feared revenge if there was no one else alive other than Adam and Eve? Albeit in fictional form, Lodwick's 'A Country Not Named' is a systematic homage to La Peyrère's theology.[9]

As an FRS, Lodwick was also part of the eclectic subgroup gathered around Robert Hooke. Within this milieu there were further reactions to the Preadamite hypothesis, reactions that again spill out of the category of

the simply theological. Francis Willughby (1635–72), pioneer taxonomer of
fish, birds, and English games, wrote a summary of the *Præ-Adamitæ* in his
commonplace book. Samuel Pepys (1633–1703), who presided over the Royal
Society from 1684 to 1686, commissioned an aspiring young cleric to write
him a book review. In a 1681 letter to his Royal Society colleague Sir Robert
Southwell (1635–1702), the pioneer economist and statistician Sir William
Petty (1623–87) essayed to prove that at the Resurrection there would be ample
leg-room for everyone who had ever lived. He saw his pious arithmetic as a
blow for the Preadamites:

> I find that the World being 5630 years old, and Adam & Eve doubling but every
> 200 years … there must be now 316 Millions of People upon the Earth; Which
> answers admirably, and is a brave Argument against Scripture-Scoffers & Prae-
> Adamites.

When Petty published his calculations, he further commented that, in terms
of mass, just two Irish mountains, or alternatively a one-foot deep slice of
a fifth of the surface of Ireland equated to the bulk and weight of 'all the
Bodies that had ever been from the beginning of the World'; and as for space,
standing-room or grave plots for the cumulative population of the world
could be furnished by just half the surface area of Ireland. Thus did Petty
silence the '*Scepticks*'. Yet elsewhere he listed as one of his 'Fundamentall
Questions' 'Whether many species of Man were made at or about the same
time, and when and where each was made?'

La Peyrère's comments on the Flood also attracted attention. Isaac Vossius
(1618–89), who was elected an FRS in 1664, is today remembered more for
his philological scholarship than his natural philosophy, but these interests
could be mutually informing. In a 1659 work in defence of the Septuagint
chronology, Vossius in passing took a fashionable swipe at La Peyrère. Critics
were quick to note that Vossius had surreptitiously carried off one piece of La
Peyrère intact: the hypothesis that the Flood was only a local phenomenon.
'Though he reprehend the *Præadamitæ*', commented Lord Chief Justice
Matthew Hale, 'yet he seems to mince the Universality of the Flood.' It was
a dangerous concession, and one that also made a surprising appearance in
Stillingfleet's *Origines Sacræ* itself. Stillingfleet maintained that as long as
we can agree that the Flood destroyed all people outside the Ark, then it is
indifferent whether it left uncovered some land, complete with its native flora
and fauna. He proposed that animals had spread much further than men by

the time of the Flood, and that only flora and fauna within the area of human expansion perished. Yet Stillingfleet too claimed that he wrote his book so that 'we may hope to hear no more of men before *Adam*'. It was a presupposition of almost all chronological work too that human and cosmic chronologies were coextensive. As Robert Cary (1615–88), clergyman and supporter of the Septuagint chronology, protested in 1677, '*Aborigines*' and '*Pre-Adamites*' 'have taken occasion to infer their Proposition from such Principles which our Chronology doth not only not own, but professedly refute'. On the other hand, Cary openly proposed that the Septuagint chronology permitted, amongst other advantages, the recuperation of Chinese history; and in the 'Canon' appended to his chronology he listed in parallel columns synchronisations of Hebrew, Chinese, Chaldean, and Arabian patriarchs and kings from the origin of the world to the destruction of the Temple/Han Dynasty.

In theory the Preadamite hypothesis also offered the seductive possibility that the basic task of biblical chronology might continue unimpeded. All that needed to be recognised was that the Greek 'uncertain' time, the 'long' pagan chronologies, Aristotle's eternity and geographical vicissitude, and the rise and fall of nations through famine, flood, war, and pestilence, are all aspects of the same truth. After these uncertain ages, biblical chronology could commence. It was this potential union between the wildly unorthodox La Peyrère and the curricular Aristotle that was the real threat. John Wilkins (1614–72) tried to counter the successive flood hypothesis by arguing rather weakly that random successive catastrophes would result over time in not enough or too many deaths, and a very old world would be either unpopulated or overcrowded, neither of which was true of the world in the 1670s. The same danger animated William Wotton (1666–1727) in 1694:

> Among all the Hypotheses of those who would destroy our most holy Faith, none is so plausible as that of the *Eternity of the World*. The fabulous Histories of the *Egyptians*, *Chaldeans* and *Chineses* seem to countenance that Assertion. The seeming Easiness of solving all Difficulties that occurr, by pretending that all sweeping Floods, or general and successive Invasions of Barbarous Enemies, may have, by Turns, destroyed all the Records of the World, till within these last Five or Six Thousand Years, makes it amiable to those whose Interest it is, that the *Christian Religion* should be but an empty Form of Words.

As we shall later see, these men were not arguing against fictitious targets: the geological theories of Robert Hooke, for one, were powered by a version of Aristotelian vicissitude, and Edmond Halley was to propose replacing biblical chronology with dating established on the scientific measurement of the salinity of the oceans.[10]

We have little evidence of how people talked about La Peyrère. But Hooke's journal provides one glimpse. In a typically terse entry for late 1675, Hooke recorded the evening's talk in the coffee house: 'Discoursed about Universal Character, about preadamites and of Creation.' This was in the company of John Aubrey (1626–97), FRS and antiquary, and Francis Lodwick, who as we have seen was a man much concerned with such topics. The 'Universal Character' refers to plans for an artificial language, and Lodwick had been the first man to print a workable scheme for one, back in 1647, when Hooke was still walking the fossil-laden beaches of his childhood Isle of Wight. But in the 1670s Lodwick was in the process of creating his utopian community, and it is plausible that his utopia arose from or prompted this very conversation.[11]

We do not know what Lodwick told Hooke about his own views. We do know from his manuscripts that Lodwick agreed with his fictional creations. His utopia is accompanied in the same manuscript by a series of short theological discussions in Lodwick's own voice. The first of these, on the 'Originall of Mankind', provides confirmatory arguments for the utopian Preadamism. Lodwick first noted the irreconcilable difference in complexion between blacks and whites, and the unlikelihood that blacks born in a hot climate, or whites in a cold, would ever consider migration. Lodwick the language theorist next presented an argument based on comparative linguistics: monogenesis, if true, would have left clear linguistic tracks radiating from an originary point, presumably located between the Tigris and the Euphrates. No such tracks are obvious – Lodwick claimed fundamental incompatibility between languages such as Irish, Dutch, Welsh, and Slavonic – and therefore mankind did not arise monogenetically.[12]

Lodwick opened his essay with a few biblical 'proofs' of his position, drawn directly from La Peyrère. Nevertheless he soon moved on, and at greater length, to what he termed his 'natural' reasons, based on climate and language, and here is where he left La Peyrère behind. La Peyrère was not involved in natural philosophy and presented his work as a piece of biblical exegesis. His non-biblical chronologies were wheeled on and off as cameos upon a stage that was primarily biblical in subject and theological in method. But once the theologians had stopped writing and the natural philosophers started reading, the Preadamite hypothesis expanded in significance. Regardless of where specific readers stood on the hypothesis itself, we witness a mutation in what people perceived the hypothesis to entail – in short, what kind of discussion was being had when the Preadamite hypothesis was debated. Petty on head-counts, Vossius on flooding, Lodwick on climate and on language-change, the worries of Wilkins and Wotton over periodic catastrophism – we are no longer breathing solely the air of academic theology. La Peyrère was also enlisted very early on for the Deist cause: Charles Blount's *The Oracles of Reason* (1693) contained explicit support for the Preadamite hypothesis: 'It plainly appears out of the Bible, that there were two Creations both of Man and Woman, and that *Adam* was not the first Man, nor *Eve* the first Woman, only the first of the Holy Race.' The most violent example of this mutation is a 1695 work entitled *Two Essays sent in a Letter from Oxford to a Nobleman in London*. It was signed 'L. P.', whose exact identity has eluded scholars, but who was said to be John Toland (1670–1722), the early Deist. L. P. reviewed and commented upon contemporary theories on fossils, the Creation, the Flood, and the origin of nations. What emerges is that L. P. was a committed Spinozan and Preadamist, who brusquely rejected any need to index this hypothesis to the Bible. Invoking a provocatively strong version of the principle of accommodation, he placed an absolute barrier between scientific investigation and biblical exegesis – the Old Testament was written for an ancient, scientifically unsophisticated audience, and must be banished from all modern investigations into the natural world. For L. P., then, Preadamism was true because it explained problems in physical and human history better than other hypotheses. The Bible had nothing to do with it. This was nevertheless a violent intervention, was received as such, and we should remember that Lodwick restricted his Preadamism to manuscript and that L. P. hid behind his spurious initials. 'L. P.' – a nod to 'La Peyrère', perhaps?[13]

3
Chronology

I encline to this opinion, that from the evening ushering in the first day of
the World, to that midnight which began the first day of the Christian aera,
there was 4003 years, seventy dayes, and six temporarie howers; and that the
true Nativity of our Saviour was full four years before the beginning of the
vulgar Christian aera, as is demonstrable by the time of *Herods* death.

— JAMES USSHER (1650/8)

In order to move from Creation to Flood, Babel, and beyond, scholars next
required a chronological framework for such events, and this was again
supplied largely by the Bible. As this framework was assumed by most to be
coextensive with geological time too, we shall address it before considering
the Flood itself. In the words of Thomas Burnet, 'The Scripture sets down the
precise age of a series of antediluvian Patriarchs, and by that measures the
time from the beginning of the World to the Deluge; so as all Chronology
stands upon that bottom.' Burnet is referring to Genesis 5:1–7:6, from which
was extracted a simple list of fathers and sons from Creation to Flood:

					Anno Mundi:
Adam	begat	Seth	in his	130th year;	130
Seth	begat	Enosh	in his	105th year;	235
Enosh	begat	Kenan	in his	90th year;	325
Kenan	begat	Mahalalel	in his	70th year;	395
Mahalalel	begat	Jared	in his	65th year;	460
Jared	begat	Enoch	in his	162nd year;	622
Enoch	begat	Methuselah	in his	65th year;	687

Methuselah	begat	Lamech	in his	187th year;	874
Lamech	begat	Noah	in his	182nd year;	1056
Noah	begat	Shem, Ham, and Japhet	in his	500th year.	1556

Noah is stated to have been 600 (Genesis 7:6) at the time of the Flood, therefore the Flood itself can be fixed at 1656 years after Creation itself. Some preachers in the mid-seventeenth century had speculated that 1656 AD would see some apocalyptic event: the conversion of the Jews, perhaps even 'the Flood of God's wrath', the Conflagration itself. Such preachers took their cue from the arithmetic above: from the first Creation to the first destruction took 1656 years; so from the coming of the Redeemer to the second and final destruction would also take 1656 years. This arithmetic also showed that the patriarchs lived much longer than modern man, and the similar figures provided for the postdiluvian generations demonstrate that longevity plummeted immediately after the Flood. Postdiluvian sons were born when their fathers were usually in their thirties, and so human biology was settling down into a recognisably modern state. These statistics fed into environmental discussions about the effects of soil and atmosphere on human longevity.[1]

The Bible also specified the years of the deaths of the patriarchs; hence too readers could calculate how many antediluvian generations coexisted. If Adam, for instance, was 930 when he died, then from the table above we can see that he was still alive in the days of Methuselah, his great-great-great-great-great-grandson. Methuselah himself lived for 969 years, and thus died 1656 years after Creation, at the time of the Flood itself. Such generational persistence would play an important part in later speculation on the filiation of human knowledge. For if postdiluvian man could boast contact right back to Adam through Methuselah or Lamech, then the accurate transmission of patriarchal, perhaps Adamic wisdom was unproblematic, even in the face of the one-and-a-half-millennium gap between the creation of Adam and the repopulation of the Earth by the eight people who survived in the Ark – Noah, his three sons, and the wives of the four men. After that, knowledge could be transmitted to Moses himself, supposed author of the Pentateuch, by a very few steps. As the Bishop of Ely Simon Patrick explained in his long-surviving 1695 commentary on Genesis:

> For from *Adam* to *Noah*, there was one Man (*Methuselah*) who lived so long as to see them both. And so it was from *Noah* to *Abraham*: *Shem* conversed with both. And *Isaac* did with *Abraham* and *Joseph*: From whom these things might easily be conveyed to *Moses*, by *Amram*; who lived long enough with *Joseph*.[2]

Yet these confident first steps in chronology could soon falter. The AM (*anno mundi*) figures above agree with the famous *Annales* (1650) of James Ussher (1581–1656), the Archbishop of Armagh. If, however, we reflect that Adam was made on the sixth day of Creation, then his 130th birthday should really fall very early in 131 AM. This form of reckoning adds one onto all AM figures above, and it was followed by the earlier Oxonian chronologist Thomas Lydiat (1572–1646). (Hence 1657 as the date of the Apocalypse also had its adherents.) Because Methuselah, who is stated to have lived 969 years, would therefore have died a year into the deluge – a theological difficulty for a virtuous patriarch – Lydiat judged that the reference to Noah's six centuries really meant 'about to have his 600 birthday', and accordingly dated the Flood itself to 1656. Again, immediately after the Flood, Shem is stated to have fathered his son Arpachshad when he was 100, two years after the Flood. The problem is that Noah fathered his three sons one hundred years before the Flood, and so surely Shem would have been 102 when he sired Arpachshad, not 100. This discrepancy could be solved by assuming that Noah only began to sire his children 1556 years after Creation, producing three in two years rather than triplets in 1556 AM. Ham was actually born first, with Shem coming two years later, but Shem is the one named as the primogeniture passed from Ham to Shem in this case, because Ham wickedly looked upon his father's nakedness after the Flood (so Lydiat).[3]

Such problems could be patched up on an ad hoc basis, but specialists soon faced greater difficulties. The two testaments, Old and New, do not specify their point of chronological interface; unsurprisingly, the Old Testament must be reckoned in AM terms, not from a BC/AD divide, and the New Testament failed to cog into the older system of reckoning. Chronological aid was therefore required from extra-biblical sources. According to 'Chaldean' tradition, derived from the Chaldean priest-scholar Berosus, the death of Nebuchadnezzar took place in the year from which Greek and Roman history can be dated, 563 BC. As the Bible too dates this event, sacred history could be grafted onto pagan history, which was then used to extrapolate the sacred. Thus a complex reciprocity resulted, with the proviso that sacred history was assumed to be infallible.

This infallibility soon encountered a second, enduring problem with the arrival in England in 1628 of the Codex Alexandrinus, a gift from Cyril Lucaris (1572–1637), Patriarch of Alexandria, to King Charles I. The Codex Alexandrinus, one of the oldest manuscripts of the Greek Old Testament (the Septuagint) in existence, provided very different figures for the ages of the patriarchs both at the time when their sons were born, and when they died.

These figures were uniformly greater than those preserved in the Hebrew text, and when added together, they pushed back the date of Creation by roughly 1300 years, a huge discrepancy when one considers that the total age of the universe on a Vulgate understanding fell well short of six thousand years in the seventeenth century. As the younger Vossius provocatively maintained in his 1659 essay on the true age of the world, the Greek text allows us 2256 years between the Creation and the Flood, over a third again the time-span that the Vulgate dictated.[4] Vossius always supported the more outlandish of any two positions, but he actually had strong support from among the more orthodox too. Last chapter we encountered Robert Cary, who hoped to gather all world chronologies under the canopy of the Septuagint. Most influentially of all, Brian Walton (1600–61), the general editor of that pinnacle of mid-century scholarship, the London Polyglot Bible (1654–7), had vigorously supported the authority and antiquity of the Septuagint in one of the dissertations that accompanied the Polyglot Bible. In the Restoration, the great biblical scholar John Pearson (1613–86) concurred, publishing a text of the Septuagint in Cambridge in 1665 with a preface in which he affirmed Septuagint antiquity while freely admitting that all copies of it even since the time of Jerome were to varying degrees corrupted, and in need of proper editing, a task for which he proposed Vossius himself. Stillingfleet, too, in the *Origines Sacræ*, lent his support to the Greek text, citing as his authorities Walton and Vossius, as well as the venerable Sir Walter Ralegh. So while advocacy of the short Hebrew chronology remained *an* orthodox position, it was no longer true that advocacy of the Septuagint was therefore simply to be regarded as heterodox. By the Restoration, too many eminent voices had been raised in its support, and between the two choices lay a vast tract of potential time.

Nevertheless, although specialist chronologists would be active throughout the eighteenth century, by the middle of the seventeenth century many had grown sceptical that the discipline could ever produce consensus. As the Norwich doctor Sir Thomas Browne (1605–82) in his encyclopedia of common errors, the *Pseudodoxia Epidemica* (1646), complained, 'for the doubts concerning the time of the Judges are inexplicable, that of the Reigns and succession of Kings is as perplexed, it being uncertain whether the years both of their lives and reigns ought to bee taken as complete, or in their beginning and but current accounts'. Only rarely did the major chronologists agree, and despite the famous Ussherian '4004 BC' date for the beginning of the world, in the time of Ussher himself that was only one of the many conjectures. Helvicus, to take only the most common chronological tabulator, adopted 3947 BC as a better date; Scaliger preferred 3949 BC; John Lightfoot 3929 BC. One modern scholar has collected 108 figures proposed in the early-modern period for the date of Creation as being between 3928 BC and 4103 BC, and these exclude supporters of the Septuagint. But early-modern estimates of the same sum leapt from 24 in 1561 to two hundred in 1728. It was only in 1701 upon the publication of Bishop William Lloyd's edition of the Bible that Ussher's 4004 BC became properly ubiquitous, a number seen in the page margins of Genesis and retained by millions who had no reason or ability to challenge it. The irony is that it was after the hey-day of biblical chronology that this famous number solidified in popular consciousness, and in a way that would have been impossible in the days of its originator. (If, for instance, we turn back to Sir William Petty's statement in the previous chapter that the world was 5630 years old in 1681, we can see that Petty adopted Scaliger's, not Ussher's, date for Creation (3949 BC).) Chronologists after Scaliger and Kepler appreciated the value of astronomical observations as absolute dating agents, but frustration at the whole enterprise was growing. Hence men including Thomas Browne, Nicolaus Steno, John Aubrey, Robert Plot, and Robert Hooke increasingly turned to methods for investigating the past that relied on field work and geological analysis. As Browne rhapsodised in 1658,

> The treasures of time lie high, in Urnes, Coynes, and Monuments, scarce below the roots of some vegetables. Time hath endlesse rarities, and shows of all varieties; which reveals old things in heaven, makes new discoveries in earth, and even earth it self a discovery. That great Antiquity *America* lay buried for a thousand years; and a large part of the earth is still in the Urne unto us.[5]

Although the naturalists initially presented their findings as confirming the traditional textual disciplines, their *modus operandi* at length undermined purely philological approaches. Some even talked of issues of chronology as dependent on issues of geomorphology or hydrology. This can be seen in a conversation in the 'Rhenish wine house' in 1661 recalled by Samuel Pepys:

> … there came Jonas Moore the Mathematician to us. And there he did by discourse make us fully believe that England and France were once the same continent, by very good arguments. And spoke many things, not so much to prove the Scripture false, as that the time therein is not so well computed nor understood.

Later, Edmond Halley argued in his paper on the salinity of the oceans (based on experiments carried out in the 1690s, but only published much later) that the true age of the world could be calculated by back-extrapolation: if we establish the rate of increase of salt in the ocean, we could calculate the exact time at which there was no salt. Halley thought that this date would be the same as that of Creation itself, or would at least put chronology on a scientific footing. (When this back-extrapolation was finally carried out in 1898, the figure obtained was 80–90 million years.) Halley claimed that his experiments were designed chiefly to confute the hypothesis of the eternity of the world, but the danger to traditional scholarship posed by his approach is obvious in his conclusion: '… the foregoing Argument … is chiefly intended to refute the ancient Notion, some have of late entertained, of the Eternity of all Things; though perhaps by it the World may be found much older than many have hitherto imagined.'

Halley may have had in mind here not a paper target but his colleague the natural philosopher and FRS John Beaumont (1640–1731), who commented in a 1693 discussion of Thomas Burnet's physics of Creation that the earth was either eternal, or created at a point so remote in time that it is 'indefinite, and wholly inscrutable' to modern man. Yet Halley too, as we shall later see, suggested that the 'days' of Creation in Genesis may well have been of immense duration, and even the orthodox biblical commentator Simon Patrick affirmed that the Chaos of the second verse of the Bible might have endured 'a great while' before God said 'Let there be light' in the next verse. We are a century and a half short of William Buckland's *Reliquiæ Diluvianæ, or the Connexion of Geology with Religion Explained* (1820) in which Buckland would argue that fossil remains demonstrate a Flood, though one many thousands of years earlier than where traditional biblical chronology had placed it.

However, thoughts about chronology and thoughts about natural evidence were for an important few already becoming disconnected in the late seventeenth century. We perhaps should not overemphasise this: most had an implicit faith in the general gist of biblical chronology, although endorsement of the longer Septuagint figures was increasingly common among some biblical critics and natural philosophers. Nevertheless, for almost all commentators, the world was still some small number of thousands of years old. As Browne said, 'and earth it self [is] an Infant; and without Ægyptian account makes but small noise in thousands.'[6]

4

Flood and Ark

... some hereticks of old, and some Atheistical scoffers in these later times, having taken the advantage of raising objections ... against the truth and authority of Scripture, particularly as to the description which is given by *Moses*, concerning *Noah's* Ark ... it seemed to them ... utterly impossible for this Ark to hold so vast a multitude of Animals, with a whole years provision of food for each of them.

— JOHN WILKINS (1668)

In an age increasingly interested in the quantification of physical phenomena, some scholars were starting to ask just how much water had been required to drown the world. The Elizabethan mathematician Thomas Harriot (c. 1560–1621) appears to have written on the subject, as did the later Caroline inventor Sir Samuel Morland (1625–95), both in papers now lost. Marin Mersenne in his *Cogitata Physico-Mathematica* (1644) described an experiment in which open bronze vessels were left out in heavy rain, and the time which it took for them to fill up to the brim was measured. It could then be extrapolated how long it should take for the highest mountains to be completely covered by such a rainfall, given a roughly agreed maximum height. That (very large) number could then be compared with the biblical figure of forty solar days to work out the strength of the Flood rains: they must have been, so the experiment suggested, 'thrice ninety' times that of the rain that filled his bronze vessels. This was a very rough experiment, of course, and disregarded the role of the fountains of the deep and the porous nature of the earth, but it sufficed to give an impression of the stupendous force of the deluge. Indeed, it underscored its miraculous nature, as Mersenne commented: 'this could not have been without a miracle, so that the Judge might avenge unbelievable crimes with an unbelievable flood.'

This passage in Mersenne is one indicator that the attempt to quantify biblical events often led commentators to reassert rather than reject miracle. As Sir William Petty wrote to Sir Robert Southwell in 1677, 'I shall now thank you for your Theory of the Deluge, but do candidly say that I know not what to say in the point; but take it to be a Scripture Mystery, which to explain is to destroy.' In 1688 Robert Boyle too listed the Flood, the parting of the Red Sea, the eclipse at the Crucifixion, and the stopping of the Sun at Joshua's command, as suspensions or overrulings of natural law by miracle. Later still, the Newtonian mathematician John Keill would trounce Thomas Burnet's *Sacred Theory* by recalculating the liquid volumes needed for the Flood in order to reassert that only miracle could accomplish such things. Ironically, Burnet had cited the very experiment in Mersenne to underscore the quantity of (non-miraculous) liquid required; hence Herbert Croft's dismay that Burnet weighed his 'trivial experiments' with a 'Cubical Pot' more than the testimony of Scripture.

Nevertheless, for many thinkers the Flood could be miraculous without entirely eluding the grasp of physics. The Bible specified that the fountains of the deep contributed, as well as the rains from above. If the vast inner bodies of water were forced out 'by the falling down of the Earth, or some other Cause unknown to us' to meet entire clouds crashing down from above, then the Flood was a miracle that was nevertheless physically imaginable, unlike some of the New Testament's more challenging examples. Simon Patrick rehearsed at length Seneca's discussion of how the world will end in a flood, reversed his chronology, and complimented Seneca's accidental pertinence, 'as if he had been directed to make a Commentary on *Moses*'. Yet the tendency to tamper with the apparent, simple meaning of the biblical texts on the Flood had already been witnessed by Stillingfleet who, as we earlier saw, had been willing to render the Flood 'rational' by restricting its extent. Stillingfleet, however, immediately pacified his more sensitive readers by supplying the conventional argument that a concurrence of causes at the Flood might indeed have caused the mountains to be topped by the waters in the manner of the familiar understanding of the passage.[1]

We will deal with the more radical theories of the Flood in the next chapter, but now we turn to the Ark itself. For the logistics of the Ark, in contrast to those of the Flood, might exercise the ingenious because these, although divinely dictated to Noah, were nonetheless executed in wood and pitch by Noah and his family without any further divine assistance. Contemporary illustrations such as those of Wenceslaus Hollar (1607–77) of the Ark resemble more of a bitumen-sealed garden shed than a boat. But they look so for scrupulously biblical reasons. God himself had specified to Noah a 300 × 50 × 30 cubit construction, of three storeys, with a window, a door in the side, 'and in a cubit shalt thou finish it above', usually interpreted as an extra elevation required to produce a gabled upper surface for the rains to run off (Gen 6:15–16).

This was enough information for early-modern geometers. Most later seventeenth-century depictions depend on an earlier essay that set the tone, the 'On the Ark of Noah, its Shape, and its Capacity' (1554) by the sixteenth-century French geometer Johannes Buteo or Borrel. As Buteo explained, all commentators agreed that the Ark was rectangular in plan, in sextuple proportion. But there were at least four different theories of what its superstructure was. The Church Father Origen had imagined it as a kind of pyramid with its top cut off, though a pyramid with one pair of parallel sides six times longer than the other pair. The next theory was that of the medieval theologian Hugh of St Victor, who combined a cuboidal base with the cut-off pyramid superstructure. Others varied this model by increasing the height of the cuboid base. A new model by Cardinal Cajetan resembled what to the modern viewer looks like a flat-topped Toblerone bar. Buteo, reading literally, constructed the garden-shed model adopted by Hollar's literalistic Ark and most other English versions. 'We do not find it had any Rudder,' added Simon Patrick helpfully, 'being steered by Angels'; and in the frontispiece to Thomas Burnet's *Sacred Theory*, there are indeed visible angels guiding the Ark over the torrents.[2]

Buteo also provided a discussion of the space available in the Ark reckoned against the various twos and sevens of animals that Noah was required to fit into it. He reduced all the creatures to three types: larger, smaller, and carnivorous. He then adopted comparative unit standards suitable to his divisions, so that space taken can be measured in terms of multiples of oxen, sheep, and wolves. He next listed the various animals, and the food they would require. Finally, he reckoned this all up in geometrical terms as comfortably short of the total volume available. Against the common grain of the theologians, Buteo also suggested that although the carnivores obviously did not eat each other in the Ark, there was nothing preventing Noah from stocking the Ark with non-essential animals for the lions, wolves, leopards, and tigers to feed on. Even with this extra volume, there was still room for everyone. Biblical commentators had more or less ignored how precisely all the animals and birds could fit into the Ark; Buteo was demonstrating that when a geometer set himself the task, the results easily supported a literal reading of the Bible. As in chronology, so in geometry: when the Old Testament specified exact figures, these figures could be mathematically extrapolated.

Buteo's short dissertation quickly became part of mainstream commentary, and in England its influence was sealed for the later seventeenth and eighteenth centuries when Matthew Poole included a detailed abstract of the work in his confection of biblical commentary, the massive *Synopsis Criticorum Aliorumque S. Scripturae Interpretum* (Synopsis of the Critics and Other Interpreters of Holy Scripture) of 1669. (Buteo, indeed, has recently been rediscovered by modern Creationists: in 2008, an American Creationist 'research' outfit advertised a new translation of 'The Shape and Capacity of Noah's Ark'.) In genre, Buteo was not a 'critic' but one of the 'others' that Poole's title recognised might have something useful to say about Scripture. Poole also reprinted Buteo's tract in full in an appendix volume, along with Matthew Host's similar essay. Both had also been used by Stillingfleet. Another of Poole's 'others' was John Wilkins, who had published the year before a revised Butean account of the Ark, complete with fold-out illustrations of exactly where the animals of the lower deck were penned. Poole must have been compiling his work long before Wilkins published, and hence Poole notes that Wilkins himself had kindly sent Poole his 'more accurate dissertation' separately, which Poole then redacts. Poole's Latin abstract of Wilkins' English ensured that what had been a digression for Wilkins in one genre entered into the mainstream of another.

Wilkins' digression came from his *Essay towards a Real Character, and a Philosophical Language* (1668), his celebrated model of an artificial language. Wilkins' language was based on a taxonomy keyed to a script that could also be spoken, and governed by a 'philosophical grammar'. But when he came to taxonomise animals and birds, Wilkins treated the reader to 'A Digression concerning Noah's Ark'. His thesis was that 'the measure and capacity of the Ark, which some Atheistical irreligious men make use of, as an argument against the Scripture, ought rather to be esteemed a most rational confirmation of the truth and divine authority of it'. Wilkins, abstracting from Buteo, noted that there had been several wrong-headed attempts to rationalise the Ark in the past. The Church fathers Origen and Augustine had appealed to the 'Egyptian geometrical cubit', three times the length of the standard cubit, in order to upsize what seemed to them an improbably cramped vessel. But, countered Wilkins, there appears never to have been such a measure. Perhaps, then, people were larger in those days, and so were their measures? Wilkins replied that larger people suggested larger animals too, and so the geometrical problem persisted, just on a larger scale. A final attempt had been to appeal to the 'sacred' cubit, a hand's breadth longer than the 'civil' cubit. Wilkins likewise dismissed this option, as the Ark was not a sacred structure such as a temple. Rather, concluded Wilkins, we should follow Buteo, adopt the standard foot-and-a-half cubit, read the Bible literally, and puzzle out the geometry from there. Wilkins, like all his contemporaries, regarded this as the best method, but he did take issue with Buteo's actual execution. Buteo's taxonomy of the animals in the Ark excluded certain known species, and included fabulous beings as well as beasts not actually of distinct species. Wilkins, then, updated Buteo by confirming his geometry and correcting his zoology.

Wilkins' Ark was divided into three storeys of ten cubits each, as we might expect, 'besides one cubit allowed for the declivity of the roof in the upper storey'. The bottom storey in the now typical arrangement was inhabited by the beasts, the middle their food stores, and the top was given over to the birds, their food, and the humans. Wilkins excluded amphibious creatures from the Ark, but he was otherwise generous in his provisions: even though he doubted that present-day carnivorous animals were so before the Flood, and even though he suspected that several of his distinct animals were really of the same species, he allowed for the sake of argument both meat-eating aboard the Ark and places for the potentially supernumerary beasts. He then tabulated the contents of the ground floor of the Ark, with animals separated by diet, and with the relative proportions and the breadth of stall supplied in columns (see Figure 1). On Wilkins' arithmetic, the carnivores present amount to only twenty pairs, requiring five sheep to eat per day among them, which will amount to 1825 sheep in one year. So the bottom floor has to have room for all the above-mentioned saved animals plus 1825 doomed sheep. All of these can easily be accommodated in a 300 × 50 × 10 cubit (450 × 75 × 15 foot) space, and Wilkins supplies a fold-out chart to show this, with all the stalls divided into three tiers running the length of the Ark, packed with the animals in their twos or sevens, the sheep, and some empty bays and walkways. As for the second storey, Wilkins, following Buteo's lead, calculates that 109,500 cubits of hay will be needed for the animals below, which falls well short of the volume available (506,250 cubits, as the first storey). The

Number.	Beasts feeding on Hay. Name.	Proportion to Beeves.	Breadth of Stalls feet	Number.	Beasts feeding on Fruits, Roots and Insects. Name	Proportion to Sheep.	Breadth of the Stalls. feet	Number.	Carnivorous Beasts Name	Proportion to Wolves.	Breadth of their Stalls. feet
2	Horfe	3	20	2	Hog	4		2	Lion	4	10
2	Affe	2	12	2	Baboon	2		2	Beare	4	10
2	Camel	4	20	2	Ape	2		2	Tigre	3	8
2	Elephant	8	36	2	Monky			2	Pard	3	8
7	Bull	7	40	2	Sloth			2	Ounce	2	6
7	Urus	7	40	2	Porcupine	7	20	2	Cat	2	6
7	Bifons	7	40	2	Hedghog			2	Civet-cat		
7	Bonafus	7	40	2	Squirril			2	Ferret		
7	Buffalo	7	40	2	Ginny pig			2	Polecat		
7	Sheep	1		2	Ant-bear	2		2	Martin		
7	Stepciferos	1	30	2	Armadilla	2		2	Stoat	3	6
7	Broad-tail	1		2	Tortoife	2		2	Weefle		
7	Goat	1						2	Caftor		
7	Stone-buck	1	30			21	20	2	Otter		
7	Shamois	1						2	Dog	2	6
7	Antilope	1						2	Wolf	2	6
7	Elke	7	30					2	Fox		
7	Hart	4	30					2	Badger	2	6
7	Buck	3	20					2	Jackall		
7	Rein-deer	3	20					2	Caraguya		
7	Roe	2	36								
2	Rhinocerot	8									
2	Camelopard	6	30								
2	Hare										
2	Rabbet	2 Sheep.									
2	Marmotto										
		92	514							27	72

Figure 1. John Wilkins, *An Essay concerning a Real Character, and a Philosophical Language* (London, 1668), p. 164: quantification of the animals in the Ark. Courtesy of the Warden and Fellows of New College, Oxford.

space can be used for other foodstuffs, as well as for the beams needed to support the structure, and spaces for trapdoors for dropping hay to the lower deck. As for the top deck, birds take up very little room, and could at any rate be caged one on top of the other. Indeed, the wonder is that the Ark was so big rather than so small. Perhaps, remarked Wilkins, we may apportion this extra room to the beasts and birds yet unknown to us.

Discussion of the Flood and the Ark, in other words, by taking a quantitative turn did not therefore take an 'Atheistical irreligious' turn too. Quantification of the Flood was leading to a reassertion of miracle in some quarters, a sign that reason can be used to point to things that reason itself cannot grasp. This was the message, too, of Robert Boyle's apologetic tract *A Discourse of Things Above Reason* (1681), a work written in defence of the piety of natural philosophy by listing the matters that reason itself perceives to be above reason, such as the infinity implied by the infinite divisibility of a line. In terms of the Ark, quantification led to the realisation that the Ark was more than capable of carrying out the task assigned to it, always assuming that its contents were not killed in transit by the violence of the surrounding waters. Nevertheless, the confidence of commentators from Buteo to Wilkins was itself grounded in confidence that their zoological taxonomy was stable; early-modern zoological thought informed biblical exegesis, and vice versa. This indeed was a major problem with Wilkins' artificial language as a whole: it could only be as accurate as its underlying taxonomy and its presuppositions about the non-variation of species. Wilkins' collaborator John Ray, for instance, quantifying the number of species, estimated 150 species of beasts, around 500 of birds, 500 of fish, over 500 of shellfish, and 10,000 of insects. Compare the modern zoological estimate that the earth has produced around thirty billion species so far, albeit most of them very tiny indeed, and most of them now extinct.[3]

One consequence of the receipt of many travellers' reports as the seventeenth century progressed was that the pagan nations were revealed to possess their own creation narratives and usually the recollection of some primal deluge. These garbled accounts could therefore be added or compared to the cosmogonies related by classical writers, and all used to buttress the ultimate historical truth of the biblical Flood. As these ancillary testimonies were addressed by all scholars in the period, we should not neglect them either. In 1630, for instance, a chaplain to the East India Company, Henry Lord (b. 1563), wrote in a work still being discussed by Robert Hooke and his friends fifty years later of the far eastern 'Banian' religion (that is, the religion of the Hindu Banias), which taught that God had at first created the world by blowing through a cane upon the primal waters, making an egg-shaped bubble that expanded to form the firmament. The first man ('Pourous') was created by God from the earth, and given as a consort the first woman ('Parcutee'). They had four sons, who were each then paired with separately created wives.

The Japanese, in a variation on the egg theme, thought that before the creation the world was enclosed in an egg whose shell was made of brass. At length, the divine Ox butting against the shell broke it, releasing the world within. Snorting with his labour, the Ox breathed out upon a calabash or gourd ('pou'), which grew into the first man ('pourang'). This story of the worldly egg was traced by the compiler of the *Atlas Japannensis* (English translation 1670) to Zoroastrian influence.

As for the Chinese, in the beginning, according to one Western version of their views, 'one resident in heaven', named 'Tayn', separated 'heaven and earth'. He then created out of nothing a man and a woman named 'Pauson' and 'Pausona'; 'Pauson' subsequently created a further man out of nothing, 'Tanhom', who was wise and gave names to things; he and his siblings begat the subsequent generations. This race lasted for ninety thousand years, until Tayn destroyed them in their wickedness by collapsing the heavens upon them. Tayn, in a moment reminiscent of La Peyrère's Old Testament God, then created a new race, which poured out of the twin horns of the new protoplast, and this is the current race of men. Several of the patriarchs of this race are named along with their talents – the inventors of fire, musical instruments, and so forth.

Moving a global quarter-turn still further east, the Jesuit José de Acosta (1540–1600), who travelled widely throughout the Americas from 1573 onwards, reported in his classic *Natural and Moral History of the Indias* (English translation 1604) on analogous tales among the Mexica. The Mexica, Acosta recounted, 'make great mention of a deluge [that] happened in their country', although he was inclined to interpret this as a recent and partial inundation rather than the ancient and universal Flood. However the Mexica do claim that all men drowned in this deluge, until out of Lake 'Titicaca' came the man 'Viracocha', from whom mankind then redeveloped. Others report that in the beginning six men emerged 'out of a certain cave by a window', and from these men the original race sprang.[4]

These and similar tales were widely cited by seventeenth-century scholars as proof that heathen mythology tended to witness unawares to its own

Hebraic origins. In doing so, they adapted the traditional approach to Graeco-Roman origin myths to those of the more recondite nations slowly coming into view in the seventeenth century. Most of these new creation stories (of course recorded by Christian observers) contain biblical footprints: most, for instance, recount the idea of the creation of a race from a fixed number of protoplasts at a point in time, who are recalled by name and for their actions and abilities. The Chinese 'Pauson' and 'Pausona', for instance, will have reminded educated Westerners of the Hebrew words for the initial man and woman, 'Ish' and 'Isha', a suggestive link preserved in the English terms too; and the other oriental names for protoplasts appear similarly echoic. Importantly, most also contain an account of a primal disaster in which the creator wipes out all of his human creation bar a limited number who must re-establish the race. Inevitably these and many other such narratives were therefore understood as dim recollections of original Israelite origins, and subsequent almost total destruction in a deluge. These pagan creation narratives were, in other words, ever-dimming, post-Flood stories told by the disparate branches of Noah's family as they strayed ever further from their original territories. Having lost contact with the Pentateuch-reading nations altogether, their creation-and-cataclysm history decayed into these fables.

One advantage of this rigorously historicist interpretation of pagan fable and philosophy was that it was free from reliance on the notion of the universal consent of mankind in a few basic philosophical truths, such as theism and Creation. Earlier latitudinarian thinkers such as John Wilkins had argued for the truth of theism and the non-eternal universe on the grounds that the human mind, regardless of time or place, is in possession of certain truths, even if such truths find cultural expression in fable or poetry. The rising popularity of the philosophy of John Locke (1632–1704) after the publication of his *Essay concerning Human Understanding* (1690) rendered this assumption problematic. Locke argued that we have no innate ideas, not even of God, and he cited over half a dozen recent travel accounts to show that many pagan nations were strictly speaking atheist, emphasising that this was true of both uncultivated and cultivated peoples. This had the effect of rendering the traces of deep historical memory in the pagan nations especially important. As William Nicholls (1655–1716), Canon of Chichester, in his popular *Conference with a Theist* (1697) insisted, now the notion of innate ideas has been exploded, we can see that there never was a naked natural religion: what people call 'natural religion' was at first in fact divinely revealed to Adam and Eve. Later Nicholls therefore stressed how important it was that the Babylonians, Assyrians, and Phoenicians recorded by Josephus and Eusebius, and the Chinese and Americans encountered by modern travellers, all preserved some testimony of an ancient flood that had almost destroyed mankind. If the consent of nations was not philosophical, it was at least historical. The fast-multiplying accounts of seventeenth-century traders and missionaries of remote and strange cultures are usually regarded by historians as the first steps towards a pluralistic or relativistic understanding of human society. But the reception of these early accounts shows equally that they were co-opted for a historiography that reasserted rather than contested biblical origins.[5]

5

The World Makers:
Burnet, Woodward, Whiston

But we have been taught to distinguish betwixt *Hypotheses* and *Theories*, the latter of which are shrewd things, as being built upon Observations in Nature, whereas Hypotheses may be only Chymæras: I should be glad to see that *Theory*, that is built upon such Observations.

— THOMAS BAKER (1699)

The quantification of the Flood and the Ark discussed in the previous chapter was modest in intent. For Protestant Wilkins, no less for his Roman Catholic predecessors Buteo and Mersenne, the contribution of mixed mathematics to scriptural exegesis was to show that the literal truth of the Bible was confirmed by specialist enquiry, and that there was consequently no need for it to be superseded by allegorical or mystical interpretation. Such interventions proposed no new theory of Scripture, merely a broadening of the range of tools that might be applied to its exegesis. The theorists examined in this chapter proposed far more radical readings of the Flood, and indeed usually extended their attentions to the Creation and Conflagration too. Descartes' physics provided the inspiration for these World Makers, who sought not merely to assist traditional exegesis with some new data supplied from experimental philosophy, but to effect a fusion of modern cosmogonical theories with biblical exegesis, and this was indeed to intervene in areas traditionally reserved for biblical criticism. The first and most dangerous of the English World Makers was Thomas Burnet (1638–1715).

Thomas Burnet was the author of the most controversial set of books in English natural philosophy in the 1680s: he published his *Telluris Theoria Sacra / Theory of the Earth* in Latin and then in slightly abridged English (dropping at first the 'Sacred' appellation), in two sets in each language, and then as a complete run. Burnet's *Sacred Theory* prompted decades of extensive debate within academic, scientific, and theological communities concerning the proper relation between physical hypothesis and biblical exegesis. He proposed an apparently biblical solution to the unbiblical physics of Descartes that for many left matters in an even worse plight than that caused by the original Cartesian problem.

Burnet's first two books came into the field in 1681 in Latin, and then in 1684 in English. At this point Burnet was known to members of the scientific and ecclesiastical communities because of his academic record. He had been at Christ's College, Cambridge, the incunabulum of latitudinarianism, under its master Ralph Cudworth (1617–88) the Platonist, and had likewise been influenced there by Henry More, who at that point was spreading Cartesianism with initial applause. Over three decades later, in 1685, John Tillotson (1630–94) helped Burnet to the Mastership of the Charterhouse, a wealthy London almshouse and school. In 1686–7 Burnet achieved prominence by standing up to the Popish machinations of James II, and after the Revolution he was appointed chaplain in ordinary and clerk of the closet to William III. His period of ascendancy corresponds roughly, then, to the decade in which he published his major work, and there was a political thrill too at the release of his final two books on the apocalyptic physics of the Last Judgment in that time of great revolution, the final expulsion of the Stuart line. Certainly, Burnet's later books chimed with a renewed English interest in apocalypticism, and Burnet tinkered considerably with the text of his final books, as we shall see in the last chapter. By the mid-1690s, however, Burnet had sunk into eclipse, because the heterodox implications of his published work had caught up with him, and the only people now publicly defending his theories were such as by whom he would have done better to be attacked.[1]

Burnet wrote fine prose in both Latin and English. The mathematician and Newtonian acolyte John Keill, who execrated Burnet and his work, admitted of his English that 'there was never any book of Philosophy written with a more lofty and plausible stile than it is.' 'His language is Latin, his style eloquent,' commented the *mathematicus regius* John Flamsteed of the first instalment, 'but [he] has more of the orator in him than a philosopher would admit of.' This would be the ostinato of Burnet's detractors: he wrote 'fables'; he was merely 'romantick'; he was even likened to Domingo Gonzales, the fictitious Spanish astronaut of Francis Godwin's science-fictional *Man in the Moone* (1638). Again, Burnet wrote both as a theologian and as a natural philosopher, but he was primarily a prominent churchman, and unlike other churchmen never became a leading experimentalist. He was therefore viewed with suspicion by more applied researchers, both naturalists and mathematicians alike. On the other hand, as the Church supplied what was in effect the only career option for the unmoneyed scholar in the period, the hostility shown to Burnet was in another sense an only half-articulated manifestation of the anxiety experienced as scientific achievement failed to create matching structures of scientific employment.[2]

For all its popularity, Burnet's *Sacred Theory* was in many respects a backwards text even when it appeared. Although Burnet sensibly understated his debt to Descartes' *Principia Philosophiæ*, his *Theory* was immediately recognised as an attempted reconnection of Cartesian cosmogony with a biblical understanding of history, specifically of the Creation, Flood, and (after a long gap in publication) final Conflagration, as described in the Bible. Burnet also remained largely silent about his intellectual debt to his old Cambridge masters Cudworth and More, and he likewise failed to mention the last tenth of Joseph Glanvill's *Lux Orientalis* (1662), which had preceded him by two decades into the English field of Mosaic Cartesianism, describing not only the formation of the earth but also its apocalyptic fate. Glanvill compacted into less than thirty pages what Burnet would later spend four lengthy books and almost a decade traversing. Glanvill was likewise heavily influenced by Henry More, whom he cited repeatedly. But Glanvill's main purpose in *Lux Orientalis* had been to support the doctrine of the transmigration of souls, and in the 1680s Burnet was again wise not to enlist such antecedents.[3]

In Burnet's Creation, a confused Chaos of matter slowly settled out into layers of relative densities. The region of Chaos that would become Earth formed into a smooth, egg-shaped body, rotating on its longer axis, paradise throughout all its territories, and the home to antediluvian mankind. It was also egg-like in its structure: a shell of mantle enclosed an inner ocean, and the 'yolk' consisted of a central fire. (Strictly speaking, the central fire was not entailed by Burnet's physics, not was the Earth's spheroid as opposed to spherical form; the former was borrowed from Descartes, and the latter from Burnet's interpretation of ancient classical, Persian, and Egyptian wisdom.) In its paradisal form, this Earth possessed no seas and no axial tilt. There was therefore nothing to vary or diminish the impact of the Sun's heat on the equatorial plane, which in length of time dried out and cracked, releasing the waters within. This cataclysm caused the restructuring of the Earth's surface as well as its reorientation in space: a terraqueous, irregular surface now covered a sphere tilted with respect to the plane of the ecliptic, and hence seasons, mountains, and oceans were of an age and an origin. Burnet compared this to the forms of Jupiter and Saturn as they appeared through the telescope: Jupiter, Burnet claimed, was still in its pre-deluge form, whereas Saturn's rings were thrown up when its polar regions collapsed inwards. Burnet then connected his Earth history to sacred history by arguing that the cracking of the initial Earth, which he identified as the biblical deluge, was providentially coordinated to occur at the point of man's maximal sinfulness. Burnet referred to God's 'due harmony or Synchronism' between these moral and physical events (see Figure 2).

Burnet undoubtedly exerted a lasting aesthetic influence. In literary history he is recalled as the pioneer of 'the sublime' and the earliest English exponent of Romanticism. Joseph Addison wrote a Latin ode on the work, and much later Samuel Taylor Coleridge threatened to turn it into English verse. Burnet assumed that the ruined Earth that we see around us cannot have been designed thus by God, and must therefore be the result of some primal disaster. He had walked with awe over the Alps himself, and wrote eloquently and ambiguously about this complex of tragedy and grandeur. The immediate effect he had on English prose can be seen in the literary critic John Dennis's 1688 letter from Turin, describing his own crossing of the Alps. 'Surely … the best opinion', he thought, was that these mountains were 'form'd by universal Destruction, when the Arch with a mighty flaw dissolv'd and fell into the vast Abyss'. This was of course Burnet's theory, but Dennis also shared Burnet's emotional reaction: 'The sense of all this produc'd different motions in me, *viz.* a delightful Horrour, a terrible Joy, and at the same time, that I was infinitely pleas'd, I trembled.' Burnet's literary appeal however was strictly ancillary, and was viewed by many of his immediate contemporaries with suspicion. His book generated dozens of responses, and his *Theory* is the prominent example in the period of the importance of the dangerous flop, especially when it was felt to worry standards of rhetorical, theological, even institutional decorum. Burnet was speaking primarily to natural philosophers and to theologians, and he must first be listened to with natural philosophical and theological ears. This approach reveals three dangerous consequences for Burnet's theory, all recognised at the time.[4]

The first concerns the role of providence. Burnet was promoting a model of God's general providence ('the laws of nature') that would limit the need for the philosopher to appeal to special providence ('miracles'). This was a Cartesian move, as Descartes too had insisted on the necessity for God's general providence as the caretaker and conserver of Creation's regular movements. The coincidence of the point of man's maximal sinfulness with the point at which the Earth's shell was ready by natural means to crack open, releasing the waters within, was for Burnet therefore not a piece of non-providential rationalism, but rather an expression of a rational or natural providence governing sacred history. But this could easily be interpreted as indistinguishable from restricting God's role in the universe to setting the mechanism running, and then ceasing to intervene supernaturally at all after this one initial fillip. This was exactly what Blaise Pascal (1623–62) had accused Descartes of doing, and it was this that later led the Bishop of Hereford, Herbert Croft (1603–91), to brand Burnet 'a kind of Deist'.[5]

The second danger concerns Burnet's attempted reconnection of natural and sacred history. Concerning his reading of Genesis alone, it is obvious that if Burnet were reconnecting natural history to sacred history, then he was bolting the wrong bits together. The theologically significant moment in the history of sin is not the Flood but the Fall. In *Paradise Lost* (1667), for instance, John Milton – no natural philosopher but a man with a sci-fi imagination – likewise has the planet knocked from polar perpendicularity to polar tilt following the entrance of sin, but the sin of Adam and Eve, not of the giants and the younger antediluvians. This problem in the fabric of Burnet was swiftly exposed by contemporaries. As Archibald Lovell (fl. 1677–96), himself of the Charterhouse, commented, if Adam did not lose Paradise, then the Fall did not take place. If this were so, then Burnet had also erased the need for Christ the Redeemer, and hence the *Theory* was in reality a destruction of Christianity, a 'rotten Egg thrown by a Left-handed Philosopher in Holy Orders'. John Keill, the Hammer of Burnet, remarked that even the ogre Descartes was to be preferred in this matter to Burnet, as the Frenchman had cracked his crust before the creation of man, thus avoiding any such theological confrontations.[6]

The third danger is connected to the relation between natural and sacred history in Burnet, and is concerned with the critical presuppositions of Burnet's exegetical model. Burnet had started his work by discussing not the Creation but the Flood, and he presented his entire labour as a way of solving a *physical* problem arising from a *literal* reading of Genesis. Burnet

Figure 2. Thomas Burnet, *Telluris theoria sacra* (London, 1681),
illustrated title-page: Christ surmounts the sacred transformations of the Earth.
Courtesy of the Warden and Fellows of New College, Oxford.

calculated that neither the oceans nor the rains nor any other atmospheric phenomena could provide the requisite volume of water in the requisite biblical time. In order to preserve this literalism, therefore, Burnet looked inside the Earth, and there he found his missing water and an excuse to launch his theory of the antediluvian egg. In this he was moved by Descartes, and also by the Cambridge tradition of the *prisca theologia*, or 'ancient theology', a tradition swayed by the pagan *cosmopoeia* and the possibility that such accounts might unlock the physics of Creation, so briefly and so mysteriously canvassed by the Bible.

It was here that Burnet made his major mistake. His eloquent chapters on the search for the waters of the Flood were buttressed by some arguments in the quantitative and dynamic sciences that did not convince his more expert readers, but which naturally gave the impression that Burnet's *Theory* had been prompted by a problem in the exegesis of the *literal* sense of a part of Genesis that was to result in a solution that preserved that *literal* sense. But his antediluvian Earth was demonstrably unbiblical. In concentrating on the Flood of Genesis 7, Burnet had abandoned the Creation of Genesis 1. Aware of the problem, Burnet proposed at the end of his second book that the opening chapters of Genesis were to be understood allegorically, or as written to be accommodated to a primitive Israelite audience, and he promised to defend his critical theory in a separate, later work. This appeared in Latin as the *Archæologiæ Philosophicæ, sive doctrina antiqua de rebus originibus* (On Philosophical Ancient History, or the ancient teaching concerning the original events) of 1692, which Burnet prudently did not translate. Unfortunately, pertinent sections of the *Archæologiæ* soon appeared in English, both in manuscript form and published at the front of Charles Blount's notorious Deist collection *The Oracles of Reason* (1693); and in the two Dutch Latin reprints of the *Telluris theoria sacra* (1694, 1699), the *Archæologiæ* was simply appended, with continuous pagination. This is another source for the 'Deist' Burnet, and it was in this guise that parts of his work entered into the eighteenth-century French clandestine manuscript tradition.[7]

Burnet's attempt to present Moses as what he called a 'Lawgiver' rather than a 'Philosopher' is what was most significant about his work. Burnet was offering an extreme view of biblical accommodation, one in which Moses did not accommodate difficult truths to human understanding, but replaced them entirely with placebos. Now it could be argued in Burnet's defence that he was merely bracketing off the opening of Genesis from the rest of the Bible, and in the 1680s at least Burnet would probably have thanked us for it. The Hexameron, indeed, is much harder to imagine in terms of physical truth than the Flood: we know nothing else like the former in nature, but restricted versions of the latter are common. Nevertheless the irony of Burnet's situation is apparent. Burnet had opened the first instalment of his *Theory* with a physical defence of the literal truth of certain biblical texts; and he had closed it with an attack on the physical truth of other biblical texts *from the same biblical book*. Burnet's own replacement physics was so unfamiliar that it begged the question why Moses had not provided an at least not incompatible account of events.

And who is to decide what is and what is not literally meant in the Bible? Burnet's critical theory, therefore, was unstable. As his critic Erasmus Warren (1644/5–1718) wrote, 'For if it [the Bible] fails in some instances, it may do so in many: and that which renders it suspected in part, will impeach the credit of the whole.' Herbert Croft pointed out that Burnet's statement that not all the survivors of the Flood need derive from Noah was in flagrant contradiction to the Bible – 'And every living substance was destroyed which was upon the face of the ground ... and Noah only remained alive, and they that were with him in the ark' (Gen 7:23) – in a place that Burnet had otherwise striven to explain literally! By the end of his life, as well as embracing various other heresies, Burnet had also written against the notion of hell, and therefore had finally mobilised his biblical criticism for action in the New Testament too. Burnet, once tipped as a future Archbishop of Canterbury, had indeed trod just the primrose path his critics had sketched out for him.[8]

The appearance of Burnet's slightly compressed English translation of 1684 was a spur to readers, and also shows the rising dominance of the vernacular as the indispensable language of English philosophy. John Locke read the book in translation in early 1685, commenting later to his friend the political theorist James Tyrell (1642–1718) that 'The *New Theory of the Earth* I have read in English, and cannot but like the style and way of writing upon thoughts wholly a man's own.' Yet Locke was not convinced by Burnet's physics, let alone his claims for scriptural reconciliation, and he thought that he could do better: 'I imagine, if I should trouble you with my fancies, I could give you an hypothesis would explain the deluge without half the difficulties, which seem to me to cumber this.' Tyrell promptly forwarded the letter to Robert Boyle. More sympathetic was John Evelyn, who wrote to Samuel Pepys in early June 1684, singling out the tenth and eleventh chapters of the second book for especial praise, precisely the chapters announcing Burnet's contentious interpretation of providence. Pepys himself drily opened a set of manuscript 'Notes from Discourses touching Religion' that 'The Bishop of Carlisle [actually Hereford, i.e. Croft] in his answer to Mr Burnet's book of the Earth, does himself question, the authority of the second Epistle of St Peter', a reference to the fact that Burnet had leant very heavily on a New Testament Petrine text on the 'fountains of the deep' to gloss the physics of the Flood. Pepys' remark, situated in an interesting set of sceptical musings, shows that he considered that at least one 'orthodox' response to Burnet had ended up duplicating the problems it set out to solve.[9]

The most interesting early response to the English Burnet is a manuscript dialogue on Burnet's *Theory* written by the diplomat Sir Robert Southwell, a current fellow and future president of the Royal Society. This dialogue Southwell drafted in May 1684, the very month Burnet's translation appeared. Southwell, who is not usually suspected of original thought, valued this manuscript enough to enter it by title into his own manuscript library, for which he maintained a classified catalogue. Through its adoption of the form of dialogue – it is titled 'C & S discourse of Mr Burnet's Theory of the Earth' – this short text captures that mixture of enthusiasm and unease with which Burnet's work was initially greeted in learned circles. Its structure also affords a clue towards how Burnet was read: it is divided into two halves, one concerned with Burnet's view of Moses ('how Moses wrote in this matter'), the other with specific physical objections to the *Theory* (from 'the way of Philosophy and free reasoning'). A short conclusion keenly anticipates Burnet's sequel. While Burnet had concluded his first two books with a discussion of his critical theory, Southwell's interlocutors now commence upon this topic, signalling how central and how problematic Burnet's biblical criticism was. The suspicion was that, as 'C' says, 'if it be permitted to take and leave in Holy Writ' whatever we like, then Burnet's critical principles could be radicalised and even used to disconnect physical enquiries from biblical exegesis altogether. Southwell's 'C' was proven right in 1695 when 'L. P.', earlier encountered as a Preadamist, published his *Two Essays*. 'L. P.' opened by praising Burnet explicitly for both his *Sacred Theory* and his *Archæologiæ*, 'Pieces of admirable Workmanship'. But by the conclusion of his first essay 'L. P.' had restricted Moses entirely to the role of lawgiver, dismissed him from 'philosophical' discussions, and solved the problem of species dispersal by invoking the forbidden doctrine of polygenism, a trajectory that Burnet had emphatically resisted.[10]

Burnet's *Theory*, it is now apparent, was for most just not *Sacred* enough, and required major revision. This was achieved in his own opinion by the colourful John Woodward (1665/8–1728), Gresham Professor of Physic from 1692, FRS from 1693, created MD 1695, and the most self-publicising naturalist and antiquary of his time. Woodward duelled outside Gresham College in 1719 with his fellow medic and FRS Richard Mead (1673–1754) after a medical disagreement over how to treat smallpox; vanquished by Mead, so one account claimed, and required to beg for his life, Woodward riposted with 'Anything but your medicine, sir!' Woodward brought to the Burnet affair an expertise in fossils, a topic that Burnet had not mentioned at all. By the 1690s, especially as a result of all the debates on 'figured stones' set in motion by Hooke on the one hand and the Oxonian naturalists on the other, the question of fossils had become paramount, and it will be addressed in a later chapter. Woodward was to become the most famous fossil-collector of the age, and bequeathed his collection to Cambridge University, now in the Sedgwick Museum. In the 1690s, however, he was only just starting out as a collector, but was confident enough to start lecturing on a biblical theory of fossils, and then to publish in 1695 his *Essay toward a Natural History of the Earth and Terrestrial Bodies*, a prodromus or forerunner of a larger treatise in preparation. It was dedicated to Sir Robert Southwell, and Southwell, and subsequently his son, would correspond for many years with Woodward about the *Essay*, as problems were identified and fixes supplied.[11]

Woodward's system sought to recognise that fossils were organic in origin while avoiding the kinds of providentialist problem that usually dogged the organic model. Hence Woodward proposed that the Earth was created in a fertile state, and maintained this state right up to the Flood. At that point, God then temporarily suspended or at least greatly reduced the strength of gravity by miraculous means. This had the effect of briefly cancelling the cohesion of most bodies, and the planet therefore turned into a kind of pudding. Organic matter, however, escaped liquefaction; as Woodward later elaborated in a letter to one of the Southwells, as organic matter is fibrous, whereas inorganic matter is granular, if the force of gravity were to be suddenly slackened, then the former would maintain its current structure, whereas the latter would fall apart. In the gravitic conditions obtaining at the Flood, therefore, matter such as stone liquefied, whereas perishing sea- and land-animals did not. The organic components within the general hodgepodge subsequently sank gradually to a level appropriate to their specific gravity. When gravity was reasserted, they were set in newly hardened stone in the positions in which they are now found. This is how once living things found their way inside rocks.

Woodward had a great deal to offer. John Ray's opinions on fossils were to be found buried in rambling, deliberately digressive works, and Ray was too intellectually scrupulous to present an over-positive theory of a phenomenon that genuinely puzzled him. Hooke on the other hand delivered his rather repetitive lectures orally, and apart from the material published in the *Micrographia* we do not know if they circulated at all in textual form. Burnet was a churchman and a headmaster, wrote well, but betrayed too little field experience and too much heterodoxy. Woodward, in contrast, possessed all the requisite strengths. He had the professional knowledge of Ray, the focus of Hooke, and the confidence of Burnet, all bodied forth in terse prose. His theory might also soothe tender consciences. He defended Moses strongly as an accurate historian, and in confining himself explicitly to Moses as a historian he managed to trounce Burnet without having to engage in controversies concerning inspiration. (This had become a delicate topic in the 1690s as a result not just of Burnet's writings, but also of those of the Swiss Remonstrant theologian Jean Le Clerc; one of Le Clerc's English translators likened Le Clerc to Burnet.[12]) Woodward also preserved the miraculism of the Flood and supported a traditional chronology. He was vocal in his belief that the surface of the world had barely changed at all since the Flood, and that notions of perpetual or even just significant vicissitude were entirely without evidential support. Where Burnet saw ruin, Woodward saw providential order. As a package, then, Woodward's *Essay* was attractive. Non-theologians were happy to trust a man who said that he proved Moses' historicity; and non-naturalists were happy to trust the word of a Gresham Professor on how to interpret fossils and earths. It is for this reason that what appears today a rather unconvincing performance was probably the most successful of all the 'theories' of the period: for many readers, Woodward was a tonic. When he was attacked – as he was – there were disciples ready to spring into the lists for him, and his work remained intellectually live for decades.

Nevertheless, expert readers once again right from the start were not convinced. Natural philosophers were quick to point out that, ironically, Woodward's theory fell down on the simplest of natural grounds: fossils were not found in layers that followed specific gravity. The great field expert was so keen on his own theory that he had blinded himself to what far less experienced naturalists could see at once. As William Nicolson of Carlisle (1655–1727) whimsically observed of his local fossils to Edward Lhuyd (1659/60?–1709) in Oxford, 'Here seems to be a mighty jumble of sea bodies, without the ceremony of taking their places according to the rules of specific gravity.' Lhuyd himself wrote to Martin Lister (1639–1712) with angry wit that unbiblical Woodward at least performed two services for proper naturalists such as themselves. The first was to make good philosophers pay more attention to fossils. The second was that:

> … the invalidity of this Hypothesis, as well as that of Dr Burnet; will make men
> preferre Natural History, to these romantic theories, which serve to no other
> use, but to give us some shew of ingenuity in ye inventors; who are yet in my
> opinion to be lesse valued than the authors of ingenious romances, for whereas
> those deliver their writeings as fables; these doe not onely fully believe what they
> write themselves, but endeavour to possesse others with the same perswasions,
> and have indeed too often succeeded therein in all ages.

Theologians too perceived that the difficulties Woodward faced were not so different from those facing Burnet, merely better disguised, or rather unacknowledged. There were providentialist criticisms, such as where fish come from if they had all perished in the Flood. Was a new miracle of Creation required? This was a problem that had faced Burnet too. Likewise, Woodward too appeared to date the completion of punishment of sin to the Flood and not the Fall. One theologian, the non-juring Thomas Baker (1656–1740), tried his hand at some physical objections: compared to Burnet and Whiston, Woodward's theory was 'very natural and so pious as to incline a good man to wish it true', but what kind of a solvent could melt through all matter other than organic? (Woodward's point, however, was that lessening the force of gravity was all that was required, not the presence of a new liquid.) Baker was also worried about Woodward's ideas on the relation between sacred and secular sources. In response, Woodward smashed Baker down, taking offence at any criticism. Next, John Edwards (1637–1716), a Cambridge cleric and academic of strong Calvinist convictions, tried to help out by tidying up Woodward's theology: the Earth was cursed at the Fall, not the Flood, he reminded Woodward, and so at least the section of the *Essay* arguing the contrary would have to go. Woodward suspended gravity once again, hit the roof, and alienated Edwards as he had Baker. Edwards stood firm, though, and Woodward turned another initial well-wisher into a sceptic.[13]

The final problem, it will be becoming apparent, was that Woodward was a braggart. His style was confident to the point of overconfidence. Even the mild John Ray found Woodward 'arrogant and usurping'.[14] The mathematician, medic, and satirist John Arbuthnot (1667–1735) exposed Woodward's virtual plagiarism of Steno in his killer *Examination of Dr. Woodward's Account of the Deluge* (1697). Steno had argued for gradual change in the Earth's surface structure, whereas the Doctor (as Arbuthnot mockingly insisted on addressing Woodward throughout) tried to do everything at once with a diluvial miracle. Steno offered his theories as at best probable conjectures; Woodward presented absolute and demonstrative certainty. Steno dealt in particulars, offering local analyses, not a grand theory of everything; Woodward had crudely universalised Steno's theory, 'extending it to the whole Mass of Solids that constitute the Globe; this I must needs say is the Parent of the numerous Difficulties which press the Doctor's Hypothesis'.

Exactly twenty years after this initial clash between Arbuthnot and Woodward, Arbuthnot's friend John Gay's satirical play *Three Hours After Marriage* enjoyed a brief but blazing success. Alexander Pope and Arbuthnot himself collaborated with Gay on the text. The play concerned one Dr Fossile, a silly old medic and collector just married to a flighty girl of 'almost' 23. Fossile's niece is writing a terrible play on the Deluge. As the critic Sir Tremendous comments on her churches disappearing under the waves, 'I believe it can be proved, that Weather-cocks are of a modern Invention. Besides, if Stones were dissolved, as a late Philosopher hath proved, how could Steeples stand?' Fossile himself is gulled by two young men after his wife, who gain access to his house by disguising themselves as accessions to Fossile's museum: an alligator and a mummy. Arbuthnot was surely the man behind these public swipes at Woodward and his diluvian fantasies, and this indicates too that Woodward and his theories must have still been easily recognisable to an audience of 1719.[15]

Woodward was supplying a naturalist's solution to Burnet. The mathematicians too had an attempt. The doubts voiced by the more conservative of Robert Southwell's two interlocutors and the cautionary tale provided by L. P. above also provide some context for what is probably the earliest extended reaction to Burnet's hypothesis, the brief correspondence Burnet held with Isaac Newton in December 1680 and January 1681. Burnet had evidently sent Newton a copy of his book, and, in a letter that is now lost, Newton had raised some polite objections. Burnet's response earned a further detailed letter from Newton in which the latter made clear that although he found 'the main part of your Hypothesis as probable as what I have here written, if not in some respects more probable', he was still unsatisfied with Burnet's attitude to Moses. Indeed, for all his sympathetic noises, Newton could not have found Burnet's *Sacred Theory* acceptable as a package, as

Burnet and Newton differed crucially at the level of criticism. As Newton revealingly wrote: 'As to Moses I do not think his description of the creation either Philosophical or feigned, but that he described realities in a language artificially adapted to the sense of the vulgar [i.e. the common people].' This shrewd remark in many ways set the tone for most subsequent discussions. Burnet's criticism, Newton was suggesting, relied on a false opposition – Burnet supposed that *either* Moses was writing as a philosopher, that is a physicist, *or* he was merely feigning physical description. Newton attempted to steer the middle, more orthodox course in which the non-philosophical genre and audience of Scripture are recognised without this sliding into a doctrine of the absolute independence of or even incompatibility between the languages of the philosopher and of the common man.[16]

Newton's critical insight was used by one of his disciples to rewrite Burnet entirely. In his *New Theory of the Earth from its Original to the Consummation of Things* (1696), William Whiston (1667–1752) retracked Earth history from creation to destruction. (Whiston, as we will see in a later chapter, took the hint for his own theory from Edmond Halley.) Whiston's central critical claim is that Burnet's under-theorised *Theory* had not provided any guide about how to distinguish lawgiving text from philosophical text. Whiston, in response, reaffirmed the old Augustinian canon – the 'SACRED RULE' – for reading Scripture: 'That we never forsake the plain, obvious, easy and natural sense, unless where the nature of the thing it self, parallel places, or evident reason, afford a solid and sufficient ground for so doing.' He argued that his version of accommodation was controlled by the criterion of reading adapted to the standards of human perception, but for all that only very rarely requiring departure from pure literalism. Nevertheless Whiston's own physical system at first sight is scarcely less bizarre than Burnet's, and plausibly more so. He drew on Newton's work on comets in the *Principia*, proposing that the planetary system had solidified from comets first drawn together by the Sun's gravitation. Later in sacred history, the near approach of a comet had initiated the diurnal rotation of the Earth, transforming its orbit from circular to elliptical. Later still, impact between the tail of a comet and the atmosphere of the Earth caused the Flood through the condensation of vapours from the comet's tail (see Figure 3).[17]

In many ways Whiston continued Burnet's work. He politely agreed with Burnet that pagan cosmogony had its part to play in glossing the biblical account. He also proposed that the poles were initially untilted, and he improved on Burnet by extending these adjustments to the question of

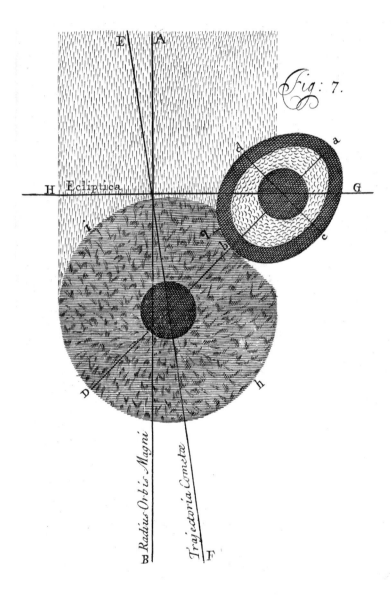

Figure 3. William Whiston, *A New Theory of the Earth* (London, 1696),
figure 7: a comet collides with the primeval Earth.
Courtesy of the Warden and Fellows of New College, Oxford.

diurnal motion and the initial curvature of the Earth's annual orbit. He even
agreed that the Earth was egg-like in structure if not in shape, with a central
fire, a watery abyss, and a shell-like crust. Despite such similarities, however,
the two men differed crucially in their manner of expression. Whiston's
work was structured *more geometrico* as a series of *postulata, lemmata,
hypotheses, phænomena,* and *solutions*; gone is Burnet's accessible prose.
Whiston's tract is very much the work of a mathematician and not a naturalist,
conducted with a rigour that makes Burnet seem all smoke and mirrors in
retrospect. Despite the outlandishness of his cometography, Whiston was at
the critical level reversing the drift of Burnet, reasserting a conservative view
of accommodation that corresponded to that of Newton. His introduction
of cometary influence at the point of the Fall of Man as well as at Creation
and Flood also shows commitment to full reconnection with sacred history.
The physical component of Whiston's *New Theory* could be and was attacked
on physical grounds; but his long opening 'Discourse concerning the nature,
style, and extent of the Mosaic History of Creation' should be recognised as
a text most at home in the tradition of English rational theology. Despite
Nicolson of Carlisle's splendid 1698 summary to Lhuyd of the physics of
the three major theorists – 'Dr. Burnet's roasted egg, Dr. Woodward's hasty
pudding, or Mr. Whiston's snuff of a comet' – we can now appreciate each
theorist was in fact offering a distinct model of how to combine physical and
biblical-critical theories.[18]

Can we therefore simply say of Whiston that, surprisingly, from a
theological point of view his *New Theory* is a reactionary document? Not
quite. For Whiston's comets brushing the earth at theologically convenient
moments are, once again, ultimately subject to most of the criticisms levelled
at Burnet: *special* theological events are again merely synchronised with the
actions of a *general* providence. As before, this arrangement appears to leave
little or no room for human volition. Burnet had been criticised because
geomorphological cataclysm on his model would have taken place no matter
how man had chosen to behave. This is no less true of Whiston. When William
Nicholls came in 1697 to review the three theorists in one of the instalments
of his *Conference with a Theist*, he acknowledged Whiston's superiority to
Burnet and Woodward, but judged ultimately that 'The chief fault I find in
him is, that he has stuck more to Mr. *Newton*'s than *Moses* his Philosophy,
and seems too too fond and credulous of his Ingenious Hypothesis of the
Comet.' Nicholls also noted that Whiston had again turned a punishment
for wickedness into mathematical fatalism. Nevertheless, this did not stop

Nicholls proposing his own astronomically influenced model. He suggested that an acceleration of the Earth's annual motion threw the planet from its initially circular orbit, pushing it nearer to the Moon for a time. The Moon's gravitic force then sucked out the subterraneal waters. Hence the forty days' rain was merely to bear up the Ark; the real deluge commenced when the abyss was unlocked by the Moon. We might return Nicholls' own objection to him: where is the divine punishment for man's freely committed sin in his model? – to which he flippantly replied that the deity would be 'in it either first or last', a solution just as unsatisfactory as any of those he had attacked. It is interesting to note, too, that by this date Nicholls could argue for the historicity of the Flood on the grounds not just of the consent of nations, but the assumed organic origin of fossils.[19]

A second problem with Whiston's solution is his view of inspiration. Whiston resisted the hard thesis that science and the Bible have nothing to do with one another, instead (re)asserting a model of accommodation in which from the human perspective the Bible voices both theological and physical truth. Yet rather than adopting the commonplace that Moses condescended to the capacities of his audience, Whiston in one place suggested that '... the Prophets and Holy Penmen themselves, unless over-ruled by that Spirit which spake by them, being seldom or never Philosophers, were not capable of representing things otherwise than they, with the Vulgar, understood them.' Despite Whiston's cautionary 'unless' sub-clause, his dominant thought is clear: divine inspiration may not have extended to matters of physical truth at all. Although such moments are fleeting in Whiston, their presence witnesses to the kind of dangerous drift inherent in all such projects. For all his superiority to Burnet, Whiston had not managed to find a model for providentialism that was free of the Deistic tinges detected in Burnet.[20]

This tendency was precisely what troubled another card-carrying Newtonian, the pugnacious Scotsman John Keill. Keill's devastating *Examination of Dr. Burnet's Theory of the Earth* (1698) took on more than just Burnet. For Keill, Burnet was one in a long line of free-thinking renegades with Descartes as their master, and behind him, the original world-maker, Epicurus. Burnet is thus ranked alongside Spinoza, More, Hobbes, Richard Burthogge, Malebranche, and others. Keill was a vocal supporter of the consideration of final causes in natural philosophy, a tradition most prominently represented by the many publications of John Ray, notably his *Wisdom of God Manifested in the Works of the Creation* (1691). He defended providentialism, but insisted that sin and catastrophe in the Bible must trigger recourse to special providence, and hence to miracle. Keill rehearsed the demonstration of the impossibility of finding adequate water for the Flood to affirm not some new physical model for supplying it, but the miraculous nature of the deluge.

Turning to Whiston, whom he treated with a far greater degree of respect and toleration than he did Burnet – they were of course both mathematicians – Keill found much to praise. He thought that the mathematics of Whiston's cometary hypotheses was convincing, and was willing to confess that one such comet may indeed have passed the earth at the point of Creation. Again, he found Whiston's comments on fossils persuasive, and not encumbered with the difficulties of John Woodward's alternative hypothesis of the sudden slackening of gravity at the point of the Flood. But these were sops. Keill once again stated that there can be no 'True and Mechanical account' of the Deluge as it was accomplished by divine power and not by ordinary mechanical causes: 'no secondary causes without the interposition of Omnipotence could have brought such an effect to pass.' Whiston had argued from an explicitly, even militantly Newtonian position that mechanical causes could be found for pivotal moments in sacred history. Keill argued from an explicitly, even militantly Newtonian position that mechanical causes could not be found for pivotal moments in sacred history. In doing so, Keill was contributing towards an interpretation of Newtonianism in which the place of special providence and miracle was to be jealously guarded. We have encountered William Petty's letter to Southwell on the 'Scripture Mistery, which to explain is to destroy'. Later, Newton's friend the FRS and antiquary William Stukeley (1686–1765) would write to Sir Hans Sloane in an explicitly pro-Newtonian, anti-World Makers vein that despite 'many natural causes' in operation, 'Yet in the mean it [the Flood] was purely miraculous: and to pretend to solve it by Philosophical or Astronomical Principles is no less an impotent than an impious attempt and among other things has given a handle to the late Sceptics, who doubt of the Divine Authority of the Scriptures.'[21]

Burnet and the World Makers left a long tail stretching about two-thirds of the way through the eighteenth century. Republication statistics alone suggest this. Ray's *Three Physico-Theological Discourses* were translated into Dutch and German by the end of the seventeenth century, reprinted in those languages again in the new century, as well as three times in English by 1732; his related *Wisdom of God* went through at least eleven editions in the eighteenth century alone. Burnet himself achieved six further appearances between 1701 and 1759. Keill's objections were reprinted in 1734. Likewise

Whiston, who went through six editions in five decades, was translated into German and abstracted in French. John Woodward had a particularly strong eighteenth-century record, and his own manuscripts fed into the 'Hutchinsonian' movement, the followers of the naturalist and theologian John Hutchinson (1674–1737), whose *Moses's Principia* (1724, 1727) enjoyed a brief but widespread reputation. By 1725, Johannes Albertus Fabricius, the Atlas of eighteenth-century bibliographers, could list around fifty European authors arguing the 'Mundi Origines Mosaicæ', many of them explicitly exercised by Burnet and his English successors, whom he also classified under that heading. In the English universities, the whole Burnet–Woodward–Whiston canon 'with the answers to them &c.' was being recommended to students for impartial comparison in the early decades of the eighteenth century. The eighteenth century itself had its own continuation of the tradition of physico-theology, written and rewritten, published and republished by men like Nehemiah Grew and William Derham (1657–1735), especially as a result of the late seventeenth-century establishment of the Boyle Lectures.[22]

Nevertheless, from the point of view of a theory of interpretation, almost everything significant in the debate had happened by around 1700, also the time that the Burnet–Woodward–Whiston cursus had solidified in the eyes of commentators as a canon. Burnet and his reception had shown clearly the dangers that lay around the corner for a theory of exegesis that sought to detach the business of proving physical hypothesis from the business of exegesis itself. Woodward, in response, had kept his own theory much closer to the text of Genesis, but it was up to Whiston, a greater figure, to articulate fully a theory of exegesis that had reaccommodated itself to physical discussion, even if his comets died the death of all such particular physical fixes. On the other hand, the opening of the eighteenth century also witnessed retrenchment in some quarters concerning the whole business of telling God how He created the world, how He managed the Flood, and how He will engineer the Conflagration. Despite Whiston's Newtonian credentials, the path of Keill was the one more followed, as it chimed with the epistemological modesty of Newtonianism. Newton himself, as we saw in the first chapter, made no great public statement on the physics of Creation. Although we know from his correspondence with Burnet how he thought the difficult business of biblical accommodation should be handled, Newton did not handle it himself in any major way to which his disciples could readily point.

Keill blamed modern cosmogonical troubles on Descartes. If Descartes' severance of cosmogony from sacred history was controversial, ironically

Burnet's reconnection fared even worse, because he found himself forced to adopt explicitly a biblical-critical model, merely implicit in Descartes, that ran riot with the literal meaning of Genesis. His 'accommodation' in other words proved ultimately not all that different from the accommodation of Descartes: no accommodation at all. This was what was recognised as wrong with this trajectory by its detractors, and as exciting by those who pushed it further than its initial exponents wanted it to travel. To varying extents, intentionally or unintentionally, all the World Makers after Burnet sailed this sea too. In rethinking an adequate mechanical model for the physics of Creation and Flood, investigators increasingly found themselves either retreating to the safe haven of miracle or adrift in heterodoxy.

6

Babel and the Rise of Nations

... without the miracle of Confusion at first, in so long a tract of time, there
had probably been a Babel.

— THOMAS BROWNE (1683)

In conventional chronology, there was over one and half thousand years of
extra-biblical world history unaccounted for between the biblical Confusion at
Babel and the commencement of Greek historical records, and within this lost
period the nations dispersed at Babel had somehow transformed themselves
into the nations of the modern world. Given that this gap spanned about a
quarter of all recorded time, it clamoured to be filled, and the demand was
met by the most notorious of all late medieval literary forgers, the Dominican
monk Annius of Viterbo (1432–1502). In 1498 Annius published thirteen
subtly interconnected *historiæ*, usually known simply as the *Antiquities*.
Some of these were written by figures known from other, reliable sources to
have been genuine, though lost or fragmentary, historians. Prominent in this
category were the Greek 'Metasthenes' (an error for the real Megasthenes, who
described India), the Egyptian Manetho, and especially the Chaldean Berosus
in five books, the core of Annius' deceit. The most important contribution
Annius made in terms of his later English readers was his establishment of a
filiation for the Western European nations leading back to Noah. According
to pseudo-Berosus, abstracting from 'our Chaldean and Scythian books', after
the Flood Europe was colonised by Noah's son Japheth and his progeny. Noah
himself even travelled with this favoured branch. From the line of Japheth
sprang Samothes, and it was he whose own extended line stretched across the
Channel into what are now the British Isles. Some of the names of his progeny

left an obvious anthropological mark: for instance, 'Magus', whence the Magi; 'Dryiudes', whence the druids; 'Bardus', whence the bards; and 'Celte', whence the Celts. Annius' commentary supplied helpful diagrams of the family trees of the 'Posteritas Iapeti', 'Posteritas Itali', 'Posteritas Samothis', and so forth, which of course more or less mapped onto the migratory paths of the fragmented Noachic tribes, like ladders laid across the board of Europe.[1]

This type of historiography, based as it is on a flexible and opportunistic alliance between personal names and toponyms, was destined to have a brief but important history in English antiquarian studies in the sixteenth and early seventeenth centuries. The militant Protestant bibliographer John Bale (1495–1563), for instance, opened the text proper of his catalogue of 'Famous Writers of Great Britain' (1548) by citing 'Berosus in his books on Chaldean antiquities' on the Samothean origins of the British peoples. A longer-lasting work, however, was Richard Verstegan's *A Restitution of Decayed Intelligence in Antiquities* (1605; six editions to 1673), one of the founding texts of Anglo-Saxon studies. Verstegan argued that the British were Germanic rather than Trojan in origin. Like Bale, he accepted Brutus or 'Brute' as a historical figure whose name gave rise to 'Britain', but Verstegan's Brute had nothing to do with Troy, and was instead a migrating king of Gaul. He had long been preceded into Britain by Samothes, who had travelled from Babel with his brother Gomer (indeed a biblical name: Genesis 10:2–3), and also Gomer's grandson Tuisco, the founder of the German nation (from 'Tuisco' comes 'Teutsch/ Deutsch' and 'Dutch') (see Figure 4). Tuisco, like the rest, was derived from pseudo-Berosus, smartly back-formed by Annius from the real 'Tuisco' named by the Roman historian Tacitus at the opening of his *Germania* as the god of the Germans: 'the god Tuisco, son of the earth, and his son Mannus, were their first founders and beginners'.[2]

Despite the popularity of Verstegan's *Restitution*, by the seventeenth century Annius' *Antiquities* itself had long been exploded. The greatest of the English chorographers William Camden (1551–1623) did not bother mentioning the Samothean hypothesis. The geographical encyclopedist Samuel Purchas (1577–1626) talked of the 'Berosus of fabling Annius'. In 1668 the younger Casaubon (1599–1671) execrated 'that wicked Monk, who did take such pains to cozen the world', and Stillingfleet himself debunked history 'covered over with the Cowl of the Monk of Viterbo'. Yet the thesis survived in the intellectual dragnet of the university textbook tradition. Nathanael Carpenter (1589–1628) accepted the veracity of pseudo-Berosus in his *Geographie Delineated* (1625, 1635). The very popular *An Easy and*

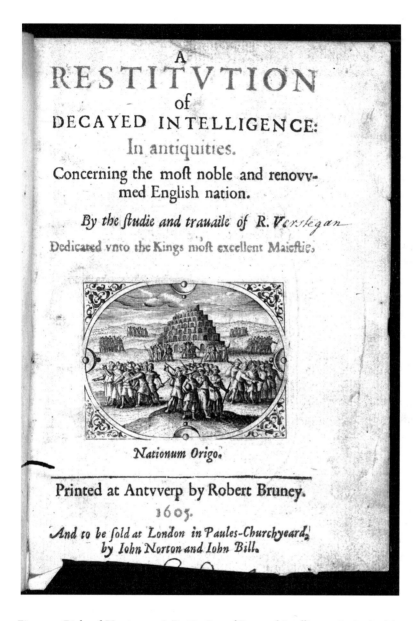

A
RESTITVTION
of
DECAYED INTELLIGENCE:
In antiquities.
Concerning the moſt noble and renovv-
med English nation.

By the ſtudie and trauaile of R. Verſtegan

Dedicated vnto the Kings moſt excellent Maieſtie,

Nationum Origo.

Printed at Antvverp by Robert Bruney.
1605.

And to be ſold at London in Paules-Churchyeard,
by Iohn Norton and Iohn Bill.

Figure 4. Richard Verstegan, *A Restitution of Decayed Intelligence in Antiquities*
(Antwerp, 1605), illustrated title-page: the dispersal after Babel.
Courtesy of the Warden and Fellows of New College, Oxford.

Compendious Introduction for Reading All Sorts of Histories (1648, nine editions
to 1682) by Mathias Prideaux (c. 1625–46?) still commenced English history
with the 'Samotheans', although now with the debating point for students
'[whether] those pieces of Berosus, and other Ancients, set forth by Annius
Viterbiensis, may be rejected as Fictions?'

The deeper importance of Annius, however, was that he set subsequent
scholarship the task of establishing each nation's precise biblical credentials,
and a project that in theory allowed one's own nation to claim precedence over
even Greek culture was obviously attractive. Pseudo-Berosus, for instance,
associated Celtic druidic practices with Noachic wisdom; later, Isaac Newton
too would interpret Stonehenge as evidence for the druidic preservation of
Noachic ritual. Stonehenge, Newton proposed, like its Danish equivalents,
would originally have contained a sacred fire at its centre. The need to
supply an ancient Near Eastern genealogy rapidly became not just a matter
of conjecture from proper names, but soon relied on comparison of customs
and philosophies. One of the monumental scholarly works of the Restoration,
The Court of the Gentiles (four volumes, with revisions 1669–82), by the
nonconformist minister Theophilus Gale (1628–79) argued precisely that all
pagan philosophy and mythology was derived from Adamic and Noachic
teaching, decayed and garbled by passage of time. This had been Stillingfleet's
basic hypothesis too. Another hypothesis that enjoyed a minor vogue was that
Britain had been settled by the Phoenicians, a thesis extrapolated from the
French scholar Samuel Bochart by the otherwise isolated English antiquary
Aylett Sammes (c. 1636–c. 1679) in his *Britannia Antiqua Illustrata* (1676).[3]

The major tool of all such enquiries was linguistic comparison, and the
legacy of the search for a Noachic genealogy was the indirect acceleration it
gave to linguistic scholarship. For any culture that believes itself to be both
monogenetic and to be part of a global economy only a handful of thousands
of years old, its historiography of foreign nations and their interrelations must
inevitably be based around narratives of migration and of cultural memory/
forgetfulness. In sharp distinction to most pagan models of language origin,
speech was usually considered in the Christian tradition as either a gift to or
a prelapsarian faculty of Adam, held more or less in stasis among his progeny
until the Flood, preserved by Noah and his family, and then later fragmented
at Babel. Indeed, Genesis 10, consisting entirely of the genealogy of the sons
of Noah, is followed immediately in Genesis 11 by the story of Babel – the
biblical contiguity of genealogy and language fragmentation ensured that
historical reconstructions of the Noachic dispersal were bound to discussions

of linguistic diversity. In some quarters, the purest recension of the pre-Babelic language was thought to have been preserved by Eber, great-grandson of Shem, and his branch; Eber (whence 'Hebrew') was conjectured without biblical backing to have refused to help in the building of Babel, and so was spared the Confusion. The history of the post-Babelic tribes could thus be excavated using the tools of comparative philology, and it was obvious to most that similarities between languages encoded geographical and historical data on the movements and interactions of the original Europeans, much as the emerging study of stratigraphy furnished a method for reading the history of a landscape from its present configuration.

Yet the sixteenth and seventeenth centuries witnessed an explosion of incompatible theories about how to sort the multiplicity of natural languages, swelled by new accounts of alien-sounding Near and Far Eastern and Native American, tongues. The monogenetic model encouraged most theorists to establish one language as a prime, and all subsequent ones as cladistic (branched) developments. But what was this original language? The majority of scholars naturally opted for Hebrew, and many earlier Renaissance authorities, such as Theodore Bibliander, would affirm that this first language was the most perfect of all, because its words explained the natures of things. How otherwise, asked the prominent Hebraist Hugh Broughton (1549–1612), could Adam's Hebrew-based puns work if they had not been spoken in Hebrew at first, and preserved exactly thus down to the time of Moses when they were written down? But there were many less conventional hypotheses. The English debated in particular the hypothesis of the Antwerp scholar Goropius Becanus (1519–72) that Flemish was the first language; much later, the Swedish scholar Georg Stiernhielm (1598–1672) claimed not only that all languages derived from Gothic, but that all nations therefore derived from the Nordic regions too. It was a claim repeated by Olaus Rudbeck (1630–1702), whose Swedish/ Latin *Atland eller Manheim/Atlantica, sive Manheim vera Japeti posterorum sedes ac patria* (Atlantica, or Manheim the true seat and fatherland of Japheth's line), published in Uppsala between 1675 and 1698, argued that the Scythians were the first race, that the northern lands are the most ancient settlements, that runes are consequently far older than Greek, and that Plato's Atlantis was really Sweden, named after Atlas the son of Japetus or Japheth. The work was favourably reviewed in Hooke's *Philosophical Collections* in 1682, probably by Thomas Gale or Detlev Cluverus, and as a result Rudbeck was proposed though not in the event elected to a fellowship of the Royal Society. The English polyglot scholar and FRS William Wotton later sharply criticised

Stiernhielm's thesis of the monolingual origin of all languages, noting that the Swede had had to exclude Native American and Far Eastern languages from his model, a concession that shifted him dangerously close to Preadamite waters. English interest in Scandinavian languages was at a high point at this time: the two imposing Swedish rune-stones standing in the Ashmolean Museum, Oxford, today, for instance, were acquired in Stockholm in 1687 by the diplomat and cleric John Robinson (1650–1723), who had studied Olaus Wormius' work on runes. There was also a corresponding English interest in Gothic. Robert Sheringham (c. 1604–78) of Caius College, Cambridge, in his *De Anglorum gentis origine* (On the origin of the English people) (1670), proposed that the English derived from the Goths, and the Goths not from Japheth, but from Shem. He also introduced the *Edda* to English scholarship, and spoke of Odin as the father of runes.[4] However, the most notorious English contribution to the search for an alternative first language was the 1669 thesis of the architect John Webb (1611–72) that Adam had spoken Chinese, and that Noah had landed in China, hence the eastern preservation of the Adamic tongue. Webb, a frustrated figure, was captivated by the high level of cultural stability and intellectual advancement that China was rumoured to enjoy – and which England and indeed Europe in his opinion did not. Isaac Vossius, too, grounded Chinese cultural achievement in the permanence that one enduring language gave to scholarship; and again Vossius was by implication fretting about Western scholarly decadence, and the encroaching of the vernaculars upon Latin.[5]

Within more conventional scholarship, a simple cladistic model of language was increasingly queried. Scaliger had declared in a short but widely read essay on the European tongues that there were four major and seven minor European 'matrix-' or mother-tongues, and that 'between matrices there is no kinship (*cognatio*), either in words, or by analogy'.[6] Scaliger, the most respected linguist of his age, was arguing *ex cathedra* against the possibility of a working cladistic model. His position was extreme, but the theory had an influence on even vernacular English discussions of language change. We may recall that Francis Lodwick rejected monolinguistic origins precisely because he could not detect ultimate linguistic *cognatio* between languages such as Slavonic, Dutch, Irish, and Welsh. These were in fact four of Scaliger's eleven *matrices*, and hence Lodwick appropriated Scaliger's linguistic argument to forward polygenesis, an issue Scaliger unsurprisingly did not mention at all.

A related and influential argument was presented by the antiquary and mathematician Edward Brerewood (c. 1565–1613) in his posthumous and often republished *Enquiries Touching the Diversity of Languages and Religions, through the Chief Parts of the World* (1614, 1622, 1635, twice in 1674). Brerewood, who supplied an English abstract of Scaliger's dissertation, did not himself deny the connection between languages as such. He did insist, however, that language was an inherently unstable thing, and that simple narratives of linguistic migration and conquest failed to acknowledge that even if one could seal off a given language, it would still become unrecognisable within a handful of centuries, solely as a result of internal mutations. As Brerewood stated, 'there is no language, which of ordinary course is not subject to change, although there were no foreign occasion at all'.[7] It is true that the general consensus backed monogenesis and hence monolinguistic models of language, but the questions raised by such influential and usually orthodox thinkers as Scaliger and Brerewood forced language theorists to meditate more deeply on the problem of the diversity of languages, particularly when one stepped out onto the global stage. By the late sixteenth century, the affinity between Persian and German had been spotted, and the seventeenth-century Dutch scholar Marcus Boxhorn (1612–53) posited that European languages sprang not from an extant yet historically prior language, but from a *lost* ur-European tongue which he termed 'Scythian'. (He published first in Dutch, but his theory was advertised by his fellow scholar Georg Horn in Latin after his death, and very widely cited.) Though Boxhorn was working over a century before Sir William Jones, his 'Scythian' is not conceptually far off the later notion of Indo-European, and his choice of the term 'Scythian' shows that Boxhorn was envisaging a cultural connection between the (northern) languages of the Near East and their Western European brethren, a perspicacious hypothesis that assumed some kind of ethnic drift between the two continents.[8]

William Wotton later developed Boxhorn's thesis of an underlying pan-continental language. In *A Discourse Concerning the Profusion of Languages at Babel* (written earlier but published in Latin only in 1715, and in English in 1730), Wotton upheld the 'essential difference' between modern language groups by insisting upon the miracle at Babel. For Wotton, the *confusio linguarum* was not merely a metaphor for a disagreement among the builders, as Le Clerc had recently argued, but a real miracle resulting in the simultaneous destruction of the original language and creation of the unrelated modern matrix-tongues. Wotton moved the whole debate on by dismissing coincidence in vocabulary as a reliable marker of common origins, cautioning that shared vocabulary was rather a sign of later borrowings. Instead he insisted that grammar was the key to language comparison, and that the 'Japhetic' languages, including Greek, Latin, and the Romance, Germanic, and Scandinavian vernaculars, were grammatically related and hence sprang from one origin. Grammar also proved that the Japhetic branch could never have derived from the Hebraic languages, as was usually assumed.[9]

Wotton's essay was not printed until the early eighteenth century, but Boxhorn's hypothesis was widely discussed by late seventeenth-century writers in England, including Sir Thomas Browne in his letter 'Of Languages', and John Wilkins in his *Essay towards a Real Character, and a Philosophical Language*. Browne speculated in a Brerewoodian fashion that time itself performed the office of Babel: even 'without the miracle of Confusion at first, in so long a tract of time, there had probably been a Babel'.[10] China, he commented, whose borders had been effectively closed for thousands of years, now echoed with different dialects, preserving only a written character in common; and the number of mutually unintelligible Native American languages far exceeded the number of different peoples who had originally settled the continent – they too now required a mediating script. Browne also recognised the conflicting political and geographical factors of conquering foreigners bearing new languages, and inaccessible terrain protecting indigenous speakers, and he distinguished those parts of speech that easily admit of foreign infiltration (nouns, adjectives, verbs) from those that do not (numbers, articles, pronouns, conjunctions). Wilkins likewise wrote of the gradual, inevitable change of all language and the resultant loss of ancient dialects. He also added an observation from the Dutch traveller Jan van Linschoten that the fishermen of Malay had invented by agreement a new language based on splicing the languages of 'Pegu' (i.e. Bago, part of modern Burma), Siam (modern Thailand), and Bengal. For Wilkins, therefore, language change could arise by design as well as by accident.[11]

The instability and multiplicity of natural languages therefore drove Wilkins and his associates to design an artificial language, one that would not only replace the tottering vernaculars, but would itself be founded on rational, philosophical principles. We have encountered this project in connection with the design of Noah's Ark. Wilkins' scheme, and a few others like it, inevitably failed, but it is a mark of how much certain people had intellectually invested in such proposals that when Hooke presented his conjectures on the Chinese language in 1686, he revived the claim that written Chinese had been the invention of ancient Chinese philosophers around 1400 years before the time of Moses. As Webb had argued, Chinese, not Hebrew, was hence the first human script, and Hooke now explicitly aligned it with the most recent human script, Wilkins' own artificial language. Ironically, Wilkins himself had rejected the notion that classical Chinese was a philosophical language.[12]

While most scholars continued to accept the monolingual origin of language, orthodox and heterodox alike were therefore increasingly pointing to the extreme difficulty of retracing the steps that languages had taken with their wandering speakers. A biblically circumscribed chronology and geography of migration inevitably hindered intellectual progress, but scholars were right to recognise that contamination and change were inevitable, and it was obvious that acceptance of a new, artificial language was a political and social impossibility. Great progress was made in the late seventeenth century in the understanding of both European and non-European historic and living scripts, notably in Oxford's Bodleian Library, where with Humfrey Wanley (1672–1726) English palaeography came of age, and where Bodley's Librarian Thomas Hyde (1636–1703), also the holder of the two oriental chairs, puzzled through Persian and Turkish and printed Malay. He even acquired some Chinese from a Latin-speaking Chinese Christian passing through England in 1687. Shen Fuzong's subsequent letters to England's most prominent orientalist broke the bad news that Chinese did not even possess conjugations or declensions.[13]

Inevitably, greater linguistic expertise was breeding greater appreciation of the difficulty of arriving at a secure global model for world languages and their historical interrelations. The origin and dispersal of humankind had doubtless left footprints in the history of human languages, but these footprints, it was increasingly admitted, were hard to follow unless languages were divided up into more manageable – and potentially irreconcilable – sub-groups. Here as elsewhere specialisation was prompting more modest scholarly parameters. Yet the biblical index had by no means disappeared: hence, as we saw, in order to undercut the conventional narrative of Hebraic dissemination, Wotton had to restore the miracle at Babel. Because Wotton was explicitly working within conventional biblical chronology, his 'Japhetic' language group, now correctly distinguished from the Semitic group, nonetheless needed a Semitic miracle to gain Indo-European independence.[14]

7

Archaeology and the Silent Past

And whereto serue that wondrous *trophei* now,
   That on the godly plaine neare *Wilton* stands
   That huge domb heap, that cannot tel vs how,
   Nor what, nor whence it is, nor with whose hands,
   Nor for whose glory, it was set to shew
   How much our pride mockes that of other lands?
Whereon when as the gazing passenger
   Hath greedy lookt with admiration,
   And faine would know his birth, and what he were,
   How there erected, and how long agone:
   Enquires and askes his fellow trauailer
   What he hath heard and his opinion:
And he knowes nothing.
                    — SAMUEL DANIEL on Stonehenge (1599)

Research into the earliest history of nations surveyed in the previous section was strongly linguistic in its assumptions, although William Wotton's essay, as we have seen, in effect turned comparative linguistics back on itself by deploying grammatical evidence to argue that such an approach could identify language groups, but little more. There were, however, other tools for investigating the remote past, and the development of these techniques connects pursuits that were antiquarian in origin to the new study of the Earth itself and the application of experimental methods to historical questions. Geography itself had traditionally comprehended not only mathematical and physical description but also chorography, or the study of locales, including their origins and history. Hence on the one hand we find that the English antiquarian tradition had always had a place for physical speculation; conversely, turning over the pages of the *Philosophical Transactions* from the 1680s right through the eighteenth century, the modern reader is struck by how many antiquarian articles rub shoulders with papers on mathematics and natural history. Indeed, by the late seventeenth century, experimentalism had transformed some branches of antiquarianism into archaeology. This transformation created a new discipline, one that by virtue of the constraints of biblical chronology, stepped into the gap between Babel and the opening of secular written history.

Elizabethan and Jacobean antiquaries had long suspected that the face of the Earth had changed significantly over time. Verstegan, for instance, meditating upon the similarities between the cliffs of Dover and Calais, posited that 'in time long past', there was 'a conjunction … between these two countries; whereby men did pass on dry land from the one unto the other, as it were over a bridge or Isthmus of land'. This bridge was twenty-four by six miles in dimension, and across it walked the progeny of Japheth. The Elizabethan antiquary John Twyne (c. 1505–81) had already mentioned such a bridge in his *De Rebus Albionicis* (1590), as had William Camden in his *Britannia* (1586, subsequently revised). Twyne supposed that the German and French waters wore away at the isthmus on either side until those seas joined. After that, the new island was named Britain from the Germanic word *Guit*, a separated place. On a global level, the positing of now-disappeared land bridges became especially important for explanations of how the Native Americans had arrived on their continent, and throughout the period scholars debated hotly whether there had once been such a path somewhere in the northwest extremes of Europe or the northeast extremes of Asia. Stillingfleet surveyed the controversy as it stood in 1662 in the *Origines Sacræ*, and decided that the problem was as yet unsolved, although he favoured several different phases of settlement from the north and from the east. This, the most popular option, stemmed from Acosta, who had proposed that the eastern branches of Noah's progeny had wandered across what is now the Bering Straits, and then worked their way down the unpopulated continent. This land bridge had since disappeared. Acosta too had proposed that this migration was unsystematic and piece-meal, and modern opinion accords with him. Fifteen years after Stillingfleet, Matthew Hale in *The Primitive Origination of Mankind* (1677) offered an eclectic model in which, over land and by boat, from different nations and in different ages, by design and by accident, the American continent had been settled by medieval British sailors, Norwegians passing from Greenland, 'Tartars' and 'Scythians' from the extremities of Asia, and Carthaginian and Phoenician traders.[1]

Such debates demonstrate the growing presence of non-textual evidence in historical enquiries into remote times or places, and this found its parallel in the institutional founding of repositories and museums for storing large quantities of such data. The Royal Society's Repository, described by Nehemiah Grew in his 1681 *Catalogue*, preserved in one locale 'animals' (including birds, fish, and insects), 'plants', 'minerals' (including fossils and metals), and 'artificial matters' (including chemical, mechanical, and antiquarian materials). The collection therefore contained not only devices and instruments invented by the fellows, but also the very metals, fossils, coins, and plants on which so many of their papers in the *Philosophical Transactions* were based. Earlier, in an attempt to align language reform with museum organisation, Robert Hooke commenced a catalogue of the Repository that was itself organised around the categories of John Wilkins' as yet unpublished artificial language; John Aubrey reported that he was continuing this task in 1674. In Oxford, the Ashmolean Museum, opened in 1683, functioned on its three different levels as a laboratory, a lecture hall and library, and, all rolled into one, a museum; correspondingly, its first curator, Robert Plot (1640–96), was appointed simultaneously professor of chemistry and curator of Ashmole's collections, residing on the premises. Plot, as we shall later see, was an important commentator on fossil origins as well as a major exponent of the new, chemically influenced approach to the writing of county histories, hitherto the preserve of antiquarians with their pedigrees and heraldic descriptions. Even the ultimate book collection, the Bodleian Library, itself started to maintain a collection of natural and artificial rarities, stored in the Anatomy School, and open to visitors for a small fee.[2]

An important figure in the transition between antiquarian study and archaeology was the Norwich physician Sir Thomas Browne (1605–82). We have encountered Browne on language decay, but his credentials as a natural philosopher were staked on his *Pseudodoxia Epidemica* (1646, seven revisions or reprintings to 1686), an eloquent catalogue of popular misconceptions, often cited appreciatively by subsequent naturalists. In 1658, however, he published *Hydriotaphia, Urn-Burial, or a Discourse of the Sepulchral Urns Lately Found in Norfolk*, a work sometimes claimed as the earliest English excavation report. *Urn-Burial* is impossible to classify absolutely, being part consolatory tract for a bereaved acquaintance, part religious meditation, and part archaeological monograph, complete with an illustration of dig finds (see Figure 5). Browne identified his urns as Roman, and the field in which they were dug up as a Roman *ustrina*, or place of burning. The urns contained bones, teeth, combs, and small metal objects. Browne cross-referenced his urns to many literary sources, and in the process he both mistook their origin (Browne's urns are in fact Saxon), and drifted away from the specificity of objects excavated from a field in Walsingham, turning instead to the eternal verities of death and burial as fit subjects for moral reflection. Yet Browne's essay was important because despite his continual use of literary sources, he compared his urns with other field discoveries, and his primary focus was on these non-textual, 'mute' objects, no longer featuring as passing anecdotes in primarily antiquarian discussions, but as objects worthy of separate consideration. This archaeological turn is also witnessed in Browne's correspondence with the antiquary Sir William Dugdale (1605–86), commencing in the year in which *Urn-Burial* was first published. Browne discussed fossil fish found inland, reviewing Aristotelian vicissitude and the operations of forgotten floods:

> And though wee hold noe Register of such deluges, & perhaps they may be too old for our records, yet since the same hath happened in other lower regions, the like is probably possible in this; wch might overturne woods & trees, alter the site & course of Rivers, wash, shave & pare away the upper grounds, raise & levell others, settle lakes & broades, & admitt of large sea fishes.[3]

Here we can see Browne making the crucial transition from the historical to the archaeological mentality – the recognition of a time preceding written records.

Nevertheless, Browne's work differed from subsequent archaeological reports in one major respect: his style. As mentioned at the outset of this book, the incorporation of the Royal Society brought with it the construction of new literary genres for scientific description, and Browne's justly celebrated prose was a casualty of the search for a purer, more 'naked' rhetoric. The effect this had on field reports can be seen clearly in works such as Robert Plot's *Natural History of Oxford-Shire* (1677), which deliberately eschewed traditional discussions of pedigrees and arms, or in Martin Lister's fine 1682 essay on Yorkshire pottery, published in Hooke's *Philosophical Collections*.

En sum quod digitis Quinque Levatur onus propert :

Figure 5. Thomas Browne, *Hydriotaphia*
(London, 1658; image taken from *Works*, 1686): illustration of urns.
Courtesy of the Warden and Fellows of New College, Oxford.

Lister, whom we shall later encounter as a fossilologist, identified the Yorkshire pottery as Roman in origin, subdivided it into three kinds, and discussed the technology of its production. His description, also accompanied by two plates of inscriptions, was entirely shorn of Browne's literary moralising, and set the trend for subsequent archaeological articles in the *Philosophical Transactions* by men such as Edward Lhuyd and Ralph Thoresby (1658–1725). As Lister said, his paper 'relate[s] to certain Antiquities ... But we shall here treat of them only in the relation they may have to the advancement of Natural Philosophy and Arts.'

The most wide-ranging of the early Royal Society archaeologists, however, was undoubtedly the FRS and polymath John Aubrey, and in Aubrey's fieldwork on megaliths we see for the first time the systematic use of archaeology to investigate what we would today term prehistoric time.[4]

John Aubrey published little, and his reputation as a county historian suffered from the posthumous edition by Richard Rawlinson of Aubrey's *History of Surrey* in five volumes (1718–19). Unfortunately this is a rather dull specimen of the genre, full of funerary inscriptions and pedigrees, and only incidentally marked by more progressive colours. Aubrey had only slightly better luck in the next century, when John Britton published his edition of Aubrey's *Natural History of Wiltshire* (1847), selected and mutilated, lest it offend the standards of nineteenth-century topography. Aubrey's real achievement is still only visible in its entirety in his own manuscript collections, which he deposited in the new Ashmolean Museum from 1689 to ensure their future preservation. The range of his achievement is as wide as its content is difficult to navigate. Aubrey set out to collect data on a vast scale: his manuscripts are an expression not just of antiquarian persistence but of a Baconian attitude to accumulation and documentation. He was a pioneer in biography, in the study of place- and proper names (onomastics), of folklore, of megaliths, and of the history of handwriting, clothing, shields, and architectural styles, as well as being a keen mathematician and hermetic philosopher. What unifies Aubrey's work is his sense of deep time, and his commitment to the full exploitation of neglected types of source. His manuscripts are filled with his own diagrams and illustrations, often in colour, and they comprehend not only his autograph accounts, but letters, printed texts, manuscript samples, and even pinned and pasted-in objects like fish-bones or leaves. This scrap-book complexity has until relatively recently obscured Aubrey's achievement, because his unique manuscript corpus presents almost insurmountable difficulties for would-be editors. The modern editors of his *Monumenta Britannica* manuscript, for instance, abandoned traditional editorial methods, opting instead for a partial facsimile of the manuscript in dialogue with marginal transcriptions and glosses. The result is hardly satisfactory, but Aubrey's materials are highly resistant to modernising, and the best way to absorb Aubrey is still to go straight to the manuscripts.[5]

Aubrey's sense of the deep past is well attested by his interpretation of British megaliths. Long before the flurry of publications spanning the decade 1655–65 on the origins of Stonehenge, Aubrey had stumbled across Avebury, one of the largest prehistoric stone circles in Europe, but not at the time recognised as such. Riding through the area on a hunting trip in January 1649, Aubrey found himself unexpectedly in Avebury, and among its vast stones. Returning to survey the stones, inside which a village had grown up, obscuring the interrelations of the megaliths, Aubrey was able not only to identify the stone circle for what it was, but also to reconstruct as best he could how it must originally have been organised. Aubrey subsequently surveyed Stonehenge, and investigated many other similar sites. And here it is accurate to use the technical verb 'survey', because Aubrey used a plane-table (an early surveying instrument) to measure the dimensions of his sites with mathematical accuracy, and as far as we know he was the first man to do so. The plane-table worked as a kind of mathematical map-generator: a sheet of paper was held in place on the table by a surrounding frame, and lines of sight were marked on the paper using an alidade or sighting rule.

Current theories of nearby and more famous Stonehenge were chronologically modest: the circle was either a Roman temple (so argued Inigo Jones and his disciple John Webb), or a ceremonial court erected by the Danes (so riposted Walter Charleton). Jones too had illustrated megaliths as displaying mathematical regularity, but he imposed an *a priori* and fanciful geometry onto the henge, without ever checking his assumptions against the stones themselves. Charleton's thesis, although dependent on a reading of Olaus Wormius's work on Danish megaliths, at least utilised Wormius to make connections between ancient monuments, and not just between one monument, a series of allusions in the Roman historical writers, and a presupposition of geometrical regularity. In this sense, Charleton's *Chorea Gigantum* (Dance of the Giants) (1663) was an example of the growth of the comparative method when dealing with otherwise silent relics of the past, and

Aubrey and Charleton were friends. Aubrey, however, in his vast manuscript *Monumenta Britannica*, of which the first draft was composed in the wake of Charleton's book, slowly developed the theory that *all* such megaliths were druidic in origin, and hence pre-Roman, to be located somewhere inside the long, dark bracket of time between the supposed biblical dispersal of mankind and the first historical records for northwestern Europe. All other contemporary theories of megaliths placed their origin within the world of 'textual time' – the advantage of a Roman or a Danish solution to the megaliths being that this could then be correlated with written sources. Aubrey dropped that crutch. His significance as an archaeologist therefore is not just that he carried out accurate surveys in the field or even that his hypothesis about British megaliths was nearer to what is now thought about the builders of the henges, but that his chronological framework for such investigations had transcended contemporary predispositions.

Aubrey's collection of data about the human past should be juxtaposed with his attitude to natural history, and his *Natural History of Wiltshire* (compiled 1656–91) shows well how Aubrey grounded his work as a county historian upon his activities as an experimental philosopher. Although the second part of this work does contain much conventional genealogical material, his first part is notable for its high chemical content. Aubrey discussed winds, springs, waters, soils, minerals, and fossils, as well as the expected flora and fauna. His accounts of springs and soils show that he conducted chemical experiments on samples taken in the field, and he records the results of the evaporation of spring waters into salts, of the colour of waters when mixed with galls, of the effect of some waters on milk, and so forth. Aubrey also commenced his *Wiltshire* in about 1656, well before the publication of either Joshua Childrey's *Britannia Baconica* (1660) or Plot's *Oxford-Shire* (1677), the works that Aubrey's contemporaries would most readily have associated with such an approach. Pre-empting the policy of the *Philosophical Transactions*, Aubrey's *Wiltshire* is notable too for its frequent inclusion of attributed contributions, or imitations of the methods of named innovators. Hence Aubrey's observations on parish registers are turned to demographical analysis, following the method of Sir William Petty, and Aubrey redacted Petty's list of 32 experiments to be carried out on mineral waters. Aubrey also cited Hooke in the *Monumenta Britannica*, as Hooke too had speculated on pre-Roman architecture. Aubrey copied out into that manuscript Hooke's diagram of 'Porsenna's Tomb', that is the (mythical) vast funerary monument of Lars Porsena, supposed late sixth-century BC king of Clusium, one of the twelve cities of the Etruscan federation. In like fashion, Aubrey's *Wiltshire* is peppered with Hookian comments, for instance on fossils 'the species whereof Mr. Hooke says is now lost', and especially on earthquakes, which are invoked on a number of occasions to explain current irregularities in the land. Aubrey also conjectured that land and sea have swapped places. With these observations, Aubrey coupled antiquarianism and archaeology to the larger issue of geomorphology, and it is to developments in this, the larger physical geocosm, that we now turn.[6]

8

Vicissitude and Geomorphology

... if the Mountains were not from the beginning, ... the World is a great deal older than is imagined or believed, there being an incredible space of time required to work such changes.

— JOHN RAY (1673)

The World Makers dealt with Creation, Flood, and, as we shall later see, Conflagration. What they did not deal with directly was the period between the Flood and the present day. Indeed, it was often in their best interests to underplay this intervening time. Whiston thought that no great change in the fabric of the world could take place between Flood and Conflagration. Woodward, again, claimed that no significant geological vicissitude had taken place since the Flood, because he too wished to dispense with the slow workings of nature and replace them with his miraculous diluvian catastrophe. This, countered Arbuthnot, was Woodward's error, and with him erred the other World Makers.

For in fact there was a long geographical tradition that had emphasised Aristotelian-Senecan vicissitude as an inherently gradual process, capable of effecting great changes over long periods of time. We commonly read that it was James Hutton (1726–97), working long after this period, who came up with the idea of the continuous, gradual vicissitude of the earth's surface. This is quite wrong, as the notion is as old as Aristotle. What has obscured vicissitude to historians in most of its pre-Huttonian guises is that in a biblically limited environment it takes place too quickly for either its Aristotelian origin or its Huttonian destination to be immediately recognisable. The overriding impression of the founding text of stratigraphy, Nicolaus Steno's *Prodromus*

(1669), for instance, is of a very busy earth. Steno accepted a strictly biblical chronology, and the result is that the ruins he saw around him were evidence that the earth was flexing all the time. The achievements of Robert Hooke in his geological lectures are best seen too as the culmination of an academic geographical tradition of vicissitude. Whereas the World Makers started with the great biblical miracles of Creation and Flood, and tried to align geographical and geological theory with them, Hooke worked in the opposite direction; and if the World Makers wreaked havoc with the notion of miracle, Hooke, and in collaboration with him Halley, all but disconnected biblical narrative from their researches. Before discussing their landmark innovations, however, we shall survey the problem of vicissitude as it was received by later seventeenth-century theorists.

In the academic tradition the seventeenth century witnessed the gradual dominance of the distinction of geographical study into *special* versus *general* geography. This distinction was copied from the textbook division of Aristotelian physics, *general* physics dealing with principles common to all matter, and *special* physics with specific applications of the former principles to meteors, say, or animals, or the heavens, or the soul. The influential German educator Bartholomäus Keckermann (1571/3–1608), whose various textbooks were especially popular in Cambridge University, explained in his standard crib on geography that his subject differed from cosmography in its more precise and restricted coverage. Whereas the latter is of broad application, covering matters physical, astronomical, and geographical, geography proper deals with solely the terrestrial globe, that is, the sea and the land. Keckermann claimed that the distinction originated in the classical geographer Ptolemy himself, under the headings of 'geography' versus 'chorography'. After Keckermann, geography could now confine itself to mathematical, mensural matters and the unlocalised physics of the globe (how seas, rivers, mountains, earthquakes, and so forth function), while special geography performed the task of describing particular places, including their human aspects (manners, customs, local history).[1]

The major figure to implement this distribution was the Dutchman Bernhard Varen or Varenius (1622–50). Varenius lived and worked in Leiden and Amsterdam, and had contacts in the world of practical geography, notably the cartographical family of Blaeu. In 1649 the Elzeviers of Amsterdam produced in their popular 'Republics' series Varenius' *Descriptio Regni Japoniæ et Siam* (Description of the Kingdom of Japan and Siam), a group of essays in special geography. The following year they brought out Varenius' complementary *Geographia Generalis* (General Geography), a squat little duodecimo of some eight hundred pages, destined to shape European geographical theory for well over a century.

Varenius described geography, as Keckermann had, as a branch of 'mixed mathematics', and provided a breakdown of its two parts in some fold-out tables. Special geography he divided into 'terrestrial', 'celestial', and 'human' parts. Terrestrial geography dealt with location and figure, hence matters such as the names and heights of mountains, the swiftness of specific rivers, and so forth. Celestial geography treated climates and zones, meteorological phenomena, the rising and setting of the stars, and the motion of the Earth, 'following the Copernican hypothesis'. Human geography examined the customs, morals, habits, language, politics, and history of given peoples. Hence at all times, special geography was written with respect to given places. General geography turned to more global and theoretical matters, and its interest in specific places was only illustrative. It was organised into 'absolute', 'respective', and 'comparative' sections, themselves minutely subdivided. Absolute geography examined the shape of the whole Earth, its material, its motion, and its astronomical place in the universe. It then descended to an examination of land masses and water, of the properties of mountains, woods and deserts. Next, 'hydrography' treated of all water-based geography, embracing oceans, rivers, streams, lakes, and springs. A further chapter dealt with the atmosphere and the various winds. Respective geography addressed phenomena 'with respect to' the heavens, in other words the mathematics of latitudes, longitudes, zones, time difference, and so forth. Comparative geography, finally, compared place with place, and discussed how to get from one to another, especially by ship. General geography thus provided the researcher with all the tools that would be needed to compile a given special geography. Varenius had separated out the mathematics of measurement and the physics of the landscape from the different mental activities of collecting testimonies from travellers or undergoing that experience oneself. Although his fame rests on the former activity, Varenius was sensitive to the claims of the latter, and Varenian geography therefore operates as two complementary, interlocking activities.[2]

Varenius was the authoritative theorist of vicissitude. In his chapter 'On the transformation of dry places into wet, and vice versa', Varenius asserted that the shape of the Earth changes over time, as Aristotle had said, and that land can become sea and sea land. Varenius also proposed that the Earth by the natural wearing down of mountains and silting of troughs might in time revert to its state at creation, a sphere of earth entirely covered by water. Earlier English geographers too, such as Nathanael Carpenter, noted that Genesis 14:3 had described 'the vale of Siddim' as (now) 'the salt sea', and hence some swapping of land and sea had taken place between the time of Abraham and the time of Moses. Medieval academic geographers had speculated that the Earth's centre might shift as matter is redistributed around the globe, and these discussions were current in contemporary commentaries on the *Meteorologica*, such as the 1646 work of the magnetician Nicolaus Cabeus, a copy of which sat in Hooke's library. Furthermore, all recalled well-known schoolroom passages from Ovid's *Metamorphoses* and Seneca's tragedy *Hippolytus*, in the fourth act of which a Messenger talks of islands suddenly appearing out of the sea. Ovid had testified to such changes in the final book of the *Metamorphoses*, in a section that mentioned fossils too. This is the passage, in George Sandys's popular contemporary translation:

> For nothing long continues in one mould.
> You Ages, you to Silver grew from Gold;
> To Brass from Silver; and to Iron from Brass.
> Even places oft such change of fortunes pass:
> Where once was solid land, Seas have I seen;
> And solid land, where once deep Seas have been.
> Shells, far from Seas, like quarries in the ground;
> And anchors have on mountain tops been found.
> Torrents have made a valley of a plain;
> High hills by deluges borne to the Main.
> Deep standing lakes sucked dry by thirsty sand;
> And on late thirsty earth now lakes do stand.
> Here Nature, in her changes manifold,
> Sends forth new fountains; there, shuts up the old.
> Streams, with impetuous earthquake, heretofore
> Have broken forth; or sunk, and run no more.

In Thomas Farnaby's standard schoolroom edition of the *Metamorphoses* (1650, 1677), this passage was glossed with references to the relevant portions of not only Aristotle, Pliny the Elder, and Seneca's *Natural Questions*, but also Lucretius' scientific poem *De Rerum Natura* (On the Nature of Things). Poetry, science, and scientific poetry all cross-linked at such moments.[3]

Hence the notion of a more radical vicissitude than the silting up of the occasional river was a constant presence in geographical speculation. It also helped people to think about how lands unknown to the Ancients could be discovered by the Moderns, as in Michel de Montaigne's famous essay 'Des Cannibales' (On the Cannibals). Four decades later in England, Robert Burton (1577–1640) in an Ovidian mood opened the question in his *Anatomy of Melancholy* (1621), and, in a set of ever-widening circles, typically did not close his enquiry:

> … how come fir trees to be digged out from the tops of hills, as in our mosses, and marshes all over Europe? How come they to dig up fish bones, shells, beams, iron works, many fathoms under ground, and anchors in mountains far remote from all seas? Anno 1460 at Berna [Berne] in Switzerland 50. fathom deep a ship was digged out of a mountain, where they got metal ore, in which were 48 carcasses of men, with other merchandise. That such things are ordinarily found in tops of hills Aristotle insinuates in his meteors, Pomponius Mela in his first book, cap. *de Numidia*, and familiarly in the Alps, saith Blancanus the Jesuit, the like is to be seen; came this from earthquakes, or from Noah's flood, as Christians suppose, or is there a vicissitude of sea and land, as Anaximenes held of old, the mountains of Thessaly would become seas, and seas again mountains? The whole world belike should be new moulded, when it seemed good to those all-commanding Powers, and turned inside out, as we do hay-cocks in harvest, top to bottom, or bottom to top: or as we turn apples to the fire, move the world upon his centre; that which is under the poles now, should be translated to the equinoctial, and that which is under the torrid zone to the circle arctic and antarctic another while, and so be reciprocally warmed by the sun: or if the worlds be infinite, and every star a fixed sun, with his compassing planets (as Brunus and Campanella conclude) cast three or four worlds into one; or else of one old world, make three or four new, as it shall seem to them best.

Yet the most influential English affirmation of the principle of vicissitude was George Hakewill's *An Apologie or Declaration of the Power and Providence of God* (1627, 1630, 1635), an encyclopedic polemic arguing against the thesis that both mankind and his environment were in moral, intellectual, and physical decay. Hakewill instead affirmed the text from Solomon that all things go round in a circle, that 'What has been will be again, / what has been done will be done again (Eccles 1:9). His fusion of a biblical affirmation of circularity and Aristotelian vicissitude was the major post-Baconian apology for the new science, and Hakewill's thesis was cited by a long list of scientific innovators, including John Wilkins, Samuel Hartlib, Thomas Lawrence, Henry Power, John Ray, and William Whiston, often as an authority for the thesis of geographical vicissitude within a stable cosmology.[4]

Varenius, then, was taking a well-known but religiously problematic tradition – note how Burton opposed 'Christian' interpretations to Anaximenes' vicissitude – and supplying it with the best scholarly credentials of his age. As we noted, he moved the question whether the entire Earth might in time be covered with waters, a theory commonly encountered after the Jesuit Josephus Blancanus (1566–1624) claimed in *Sphæra Mundi* (1620) that the Earth was slowly being worn flat, and would at length become submerged, as it was at the Creation. The passage would later be translated and printed by John Ray in one of his physico-theological works. Although Varenius accepted that there was nothing in theory to prevent this happening naturally, as opposed to supernaturally, it was extremely unlikely to take place because of the height of mountains and the compaction of land masses. Nevertheless Varenius had opened up geography to the reality of a sliding scale of change, in which complete submersion was improbable, but now only the extreme terminus of a series of processes that can and do take place, gradually, daily.[5]

The *Geographia Generalis* had a vigorous life in England. In 1683 it was translated and tied to a twin work of special geography, as the full title of this joint publication shows (we may note too both the persistence of 'cosmography' as a classifier, and the cartographical additions): *Cosmography and Geography in Two Parts: The first containing the general and absolute part of cosmography and geography being a translation from … Varenius … the second part being a geographical description of all the world taken from the notes and works of the famous Monsieur Sanson … Illustrated with Maps* (London, 1683). But 'the accurate Varenius', as Robert Boyle dubbed him in 1660, had already made his mark on the English scene. In 1654 his book was already being recommended to John Aubrey by his sometime tutor at Trinity College, Oxford, as containing the best epitome of navigation available. Years later, in 1671, George Hough of St John's College, Cambridge, sent a presentation manuscript of diagrams designed to accompany Varenius's text to Aubrey's friend Robert Hooke in London, begging him to arrange for an English edition of Varenius, to be accompanied by Hough's diagrams. In a 1667 meeting of the Royal Society – though Hough did not know this – Hooke had invoked Varenius' authority in a discussion of earthquakes, in the context of Hooke's own research into the shells of his native Isle of Wight: 'Mr. HOOKE related out of VARENIUS'S geography, that in China, a lake of thirty leagues over was made by an earthquake, the earth then sinking; and in another place, for the space of forty leagues, the earth shook all at the same time.'

Hooke, however, did not act on the obscure Hough's request. This was presumably because in 1672 the young Lucasian Professor of Mathematics in Cambridge, Isaac Newton, published his first signed work, an edition of Varenius with Newton's own commentary. It was in this year, too, that Hooke and Newton first badly quarrelled. Newton's Varenius would have a long life: it was revised and republished in 1681, and in 1712 Newton's disciple James Jurin, with help from fellow Newtonians Roger Coates and Edmond Halley, brought the work up to date for a new century; finally, in 1733 the Jurin edition was translated into English. Sir John Evelyn, grandson to the more famous Evelyn, wrote regularly to his grandfather while he was a student at Oxford, and one of his letters shows that in 1700 Varenius was doubling as an Oxonian textbook for geography and physics: 'The tutor reads Varenius' *General Geography* to us, which contains under that title much relevant to physics; and every day we dispute physical questions.' Thus the Varenian tradition came to dominate English geography, especially after it received the powerful patronage of the Newtonians, who shackled it to their cause for the best part of a century. This kind of geography, although no longer based on Aristotelian physics, nevertheless kept alive the old Aristotelian maxim that 'sea replaces what was once dry land, and where there is now sea there is at another time land'.[6]

The most important beneficiary of the new geography was the Dane Nils Stensen, Latinised as Nicolaus Steno, whom we have already briefly encountered. Steno travelled throughout western Europe, and in 1665 he was in Montpellier exactly when Martin Lister, John Ray, and various other English naturalists were visiting. As Lister recalled in his manuscript memoranda, he had 'the honour to assist at an Anatomy Lecture or some particular dissections, made by Mr Steno the Dane'. Visiting Steno afterwards for further conversation, Lister found him 'infinitely taking and agreeable'. Steno's first important work came in the mid-1660s, when he worked on *glossopetræ* or tongue-stones. But his most significant work appeared in 1669, the *De solido intra solidum naturaliter contento dissertationis prodromus* (Forerunner of a dissertation on a solid naturally contained within a solid); the fuller work, which Steno promised to write in Tuscan, never appeared, as Steno abandoned research for the Church. The *Prodromus* was translated into English just two years later by Henry Oldenburg, Secretary to the Royal

Society, and Robert Boyle considered this translation important enough to reprint it with his own *Essay about the Origin of Gems* (1672).

Steno presented his work in a highly methodical manner, as a chain of theorems and corollaries, problems set and solved. As Oldenburg chose to subtitle his translation, this was to be a 'foundation' for 'a rational accompt [account]', not a collection of studiedly miscellaneous observations and conjectures, which was more the English vogue. Conversely, Steno sounded rigorous, continental, and Cartesian, setting himself the following governing problem: 'A body of a certain Figure, and naturally produced, being given, to find in the Body it self Arguments, discovering the Place and Manner of its Production.' This he solved in three successive propositions. First, if one solid body is contained in another, the one contained was the first one to solidify; or, more generally, the one that leaves the impression of its surface on the other was the prior solidification. Secondly, if one solid body is exactly like another in surface and substance, then the manner and place of its production must be the same too. Finally, all such solid bodies arise at first out of fluids. Steno had therefore replaced the usual question of 'what kind of thing is this particular stone?' with the more fundamental query 'how are solids formed?'. This question could apply equally to stones, fossils in the modern sense, metals, and crystals. Steno accordingly presented his ideas on the growth of crystals and shells together, noting that the geometrical regularity of the former was quite unlike the asymmetry of the latter. Shells, unlike metals or gems, followed the forms of the living things they enclosed, and in this fossilised shells invariably followed them. Thus did Steno prove the organic origin of fossils.

Steno founded upon these observations a theory of stratification. Perished organic forms must have been first exposed only to water or to air. Subsequently, these original organic forms became covered in sediment, both at length petrifying. Such sedimentation, because originating in liquid processes, settled at first into horizontal layers. We might imagine some shells at the bottom of a quarry becoming covered gradually by water and mud. As with all such liquids, the surface of the puddle must lie parallel to the horizon. This mixture subsequently hardens and petrifies. Yet it is obvious from looking at modern strata that they do not all maintain a horizontal orientation, but jut this way and that. Since we can deduce the original and observe the current orientations, we should be able to deduce the intermediary stages too. This is the achievement for which Steno is remembered: the landscape could now be read much more precisely than ever before, and its language was that of sedimentation.

This language in turn led Steno to perceive that the shape of the Earth had been transformed many times. He offered a case history of Tuscany, accompanied by illustrations of cross-sections of the local strata at different points in their history. Steno, of course, pegged this local history to biblical time. Stratigraphy shows that Etruria has been twice fluid, twice plane and dry, and twice scabrous and craggy. This Steno proposed was true of the whole Earth too. As for the first stage (fluid), Scripture and nature agree that the whole earth was covered with water at first. We know from Scripture that the Earth then became plane and dry. Steno's evidence then suggested a third stage in which the earth was craggy. Next came the Flood, which again both Scripture and nature teach us. (Steno also proposed various physical models for the Flood.) Following the Flood, in its fifth stage, the land became dry once more, and in its sixth, erosion rendered the surface craggy again. These processes involving the collapse of strata took place by undermining, sometimes caused by earthquakes.

Steno's Earth was therefore highly dynamic, something he could demonstrate by applying reason to observation. He also argued that we should respect what ancient reports of change we do have, an approach Hooke too would advocate: 'That Mountains may be overturned and whole Fields transferred; the tops of Hills be raised and depressed; grounds opened, and closed again; and the like things happen, which in the reading of Histories are counted fabulous by those, that will not be taken for credulous.'

Steno was willing to accept the one-time severance of the Mediterranean from the Atlantic; the existence of an ancient passage from the Mediterranean into the Red Sea; and the ancient submersion of a continent called Atlantis. We know, and therefore may expect to see again, that 'whole Fields with their Trees and Houses do by degrees subside, or are swallowed unawares, so that there come to be vast Lakes, where formerly stood Towns'. It was this dynamism, rather than Steno's by then familiar hypothesis of the organic origin of fossils, that disturbed as well as impressed his contemporaries. As an early eighteenth-century commentator protested, Steno presented 'such strange and until then unheard of Paradoxes and Inconsistencies, that nothing less that a total dissolution of the Terrestrial Frame must be admitted to establish the Conclusion'. Steno's system took a while to catch on, but even Woodward's apparently original *Essay towards a Natural History of the Earth*, as we saw, was quickly exposed as highly derivative of Steno. Although his longer book never appeared, Steno's *Forerunner* presented in elegant brevity not only a demonstration reasoned from general terms, but a research programme of how to apply his method to other locations: Steno's case study of Tuscany could be repeated for any other location where there were visible rock strata, and this was accomplished by Gottfried Wilhelm Leibniz in his *Protogaea* (1691–3), in origin a study of the Harz silver mines where Leibniz had been attempting to implement various doomed mechanical innovations. Leibniz offered his text as a contribution to the new field of what he termed 'Natural Geography'.[7]

In England over the decades in which Varenius and Steno were read, criticised, and translated, and in which Robert Hooke delivered his own lectures on fossils and earthquakes, we should also recall that there were many reported seismic events around the world, prompting a general interest in the subject of earthquakes that spread far outside the walls of Gresham College. In 1650, for example, there had been a massive volcanic eruption at Santorini, north of Crete. Nearer to home, in 1665 an earthquake toppled the cathedral spire in Coventry. In 1683 one was felt in Oxford, reported in the *Philosophical Transactions* by Hooke's acquaintance the young don Thomas Pigot (1657–86), and in 1692 another shook the south of England in the same year as there was a massive eruption of Etna. The historical record was full of similar accounts too: the most spectacular anecdote, often repeated, concerned Markley (now known as Marcle) Hill in Herefordshire, which in 1575 'with a great noise removed itself from its place, and went continually for three days together, overthrowing Kinaston Chapel, bearing the earth 400 yards before it', as one Norfolk fossilologist recalled almost a century later. The vogue for earthquake studies swiftly generated its own subscholarly literature, for instance the handy 1694 *The General History of Earthquakes* of hack writer Nathaniel Crouch, a chronologically ordered list of all the notable examples working through biblical and subsequent history from the Creation to the present day. There was a strong providentialist strain to much of this literature. Charles Hallywell, for instance, writing on the 1692 English earthquake, adopted secondary, physical causes of exploding subterranean fires, but also emphasised that earthquakes were God's means 'by which to chastise a wicked and Atheistical people, and to manifest his Power over not only the upper but lower Regions'. This was not a tone most natural philosophers adopted.[8]

Hooke developed his ideas on earthquakes initially in the late 1660s as a consequence of his initial work on fossils. In 1678, in an appendix to his published lectures on 'spring', Hooke reaffirmed his Aristotelian hypothesis that 'Mountains have been sunk into Plains, and Plains have been raised into Mountains'. Polar wandering over the ages has forced the great oceans themselves to shift their locations. Mountains are caused by earthquakes, and although such massive disruptions may not be so frequent now, they were very common in the early days of the world, a hypothesis forced on Hooke by biblical pressures on chronology. Indeed, Hooke associated his study of fossils so strongly with his new and consuming interest in earthquakes that he considered them two sides of one coin. His contemporaries did not, and we too will consider the latter first. Throughout the 1680s, the terms of the debate had shifted following Burnet's publications, and although Burnet had nothing to say about fossils, he was retailing grand theories of planetary tectonics clearly rubbing plates with Hooke. The earlier entries of Hooke's later journal, maintained from 1688, are full of references to Hooke's reading of Burnet, and reporting back his short book reviews to the Royal Society in session. Hooke, despite his initial rupture with Isaac Newton in the 1670s, was also aware in the late 1680s that Newton's forthcoming *magnum opus* might support his geomorphological ideas. In a March 1687 meeting of the Society, just before Hooke discoursed on the equatorial bulge of the Earth, the Society first heard a 'paragraph' of Newton's forthcoming *Principia Mathematica* – read out by Halley? – in which it was demonstrated that the addition of new matter to a spinning globe would indeed cause axial shift. Newton and Hooke agreed that the Earth was very slightly ovaloid, but with its longer axis passing through the equator, not through the poles as Burnet had proposed.[9]

In this climate of renewed interest in geomorphology, Hooke therefore resumed lecturing on the Earth in 1686 and kept on doing so right up to 1700. In the 1660s he had presented his ideas on fossils and earthquakes in a fairly positive manner. But his tactics changed over time. His 1686-7 lectures are distinctly defensive, reaffirming his theory of fossils with the exasperated admonishment that he had provided 'all the Evidence the Matter is capable of'. (This comment connects the theoretical status of Hooke's work to the epistemology developed by the Anglican rational theologians, who taught that one must not demand too high a standard of evidence in non-mathematical enquiries.) Hooke also deployed his two governing metaphors for field research: fossils are 'Medals of Nature' and also parts of 'Nature's Grammar', to be collected like coins and read like texts. Yet his interests had shifted to 'the Figure of the Earth', and it was this aspect that would dominate his arguments over the next three decades. Hooke, following Newton, argued that if a spinning globe bulged out at its sides, gravity should diminish the further one went away from the poles, reaching a minimum at the equator. That was why Edmond Halley's pendulum had slowed down on St Helena. Hooke further argued in his lectures that if this were to be combined with a theory of wandering poles, then the equatorial bulge must travel too, and here was a powerful motor for his undulating Earth. Hooke then ransacked the historical record for evidence – might the orientation of the Egyptian pyramids help, he wondered? – but it is clear that he found little support. His ideas were also again met with coolness in the Society itself, as he grumbled. In an initially surprising move he therefore turned for help to pagan mythology, to Plato's story of the lost continent of Atlantis, to Hesiod's *Theogony*, and especially to Ovid's *Metamorphoses.*[10]

This appeal to poetry and mythology was in fact a respectable if still a curious move. Francis Bacon himself had published in 1609 *De sapientia veterum* (On the Wisdom of the Ancients), a collection of 31 ancient myths complete with exegeses of their allegories. On the Continent, the great geographer Abraham Ortelius (1527–98), in a passage discreetly tucked away in a 1596 dictionary of classical toponyms and hence unspotted at the time, argued from Plato's *Atlantis* and *Critias* that America, Europe, and Africa had been shorn from one another in a primeval cataclysm by flood and earthquake. Turning to the heavens, Kepler had also made some startling claims about the Hellenistic ironist Lucian's satirical fictions as veiling genuine astronomical learning. The use of allegory, especially of Ovid, also had good precedent. The sixteenth-century Italian experimentalist Giovanni Battista della Porta had detected the doctrine of spontaneous generation in Ovid's fable of Pytho, and John Aubrey later recorded that the FRS Francis Potter (1594–1678) derived the idea of blood transfusion in the 1640s from Ovid's tale of Jason and Medea. Hooke may have disagreed with Burnet's *Sacred Theory*, but he appreciated Burnet's *Archæologiæ Philosophicæ*, and explicitly endorsed in his earthquake lectures Burnet's method of seeking for ancient truths concerning Creation in pagan as well as sacred sources. Indeed, admiration of Burnet's criticism yoked to confutation of his physics seems to have been a taste in Hooke's circle. His friend John Beaumont's *Considerations on a Book Entitled The Theory of the Earth* (1693), dedicated to Hooke, was especially provocative. As John Ray disapprovingly observed, Beaumont indeed confuted Burnet's physics, but subjoined a good deal of puff about the mystical, allegorical, and even numerological physics of the Ancients that Ray found both obscurantist and heterodox. Hooke was therefore not an incomprehensible voice when he explained to the Royal Society in 1693 that the Rape of Proserpine was nothing other than a huge earthquake in Sicily at the dawn of time, and that Jupiter white-hot with anger signified erupting volcanoes. Hooke also poured into his lectures any ancient travel accounts he could find, notably the tiny *Periplus* of Hanno the Carthaginian, the fifth-century BC explorer. Hanno had witnessed rivers of fire pouring into the ocean off the west coast of Africa, exactly where Hooke located the lost continent of Atlantis, beyond the Pillars of Hercules. Hooke was also stung by criticism from Oxford that his theories were impious, and in 1688 launched into a long exegesis of the opening verses of Genesis, to which we will return. Right up to the turn of the century, Hooke would not let go. As he admitted in 1699, he had long since convinced himself if not others, and there were even those, he snapped, who were indeed privately convinced, but pretended they weren't, simply to annoy the increasingly elderly and melancholic Hooke.[11]

We can see now that the component of Hooke's theory that had the power to cause the most damage to the biblical model was his notion of the Earth changing over time in ways that were too various to be comprehended under the model of a unique catastrophe, and which had escaped the record of written history. In propounding this theory, Hooke was burning some intellectual bridges. In the preface to the *Micrographia*, Hooke had praised, as thirty-year-old scholars on the make are wont, his intellectual father-figure, John Wilkins. Yet Wilkins too cannot have approved of his protégé's subsequent geomorphological studies. As one of the earlier proponents of physico-theology, Wilkins had developed the leading strategy of showing that the world had a beginning and was not eternal. This insistence was typically coupled to an endorsement of the biblical view of world history as extending no further back than six thousand years or so, and coterminous with the history of man. By implication, attempts to tamper with the age of the Earth, to propose recurring floods or disappearing nations, could easily be construed as interfering with the piety of physico-theological arguments. Thus Wilkins' *Of the Principles and Duties of Natural Religion* (1675) insisted that the world had a beginning, dated to roughly when Moses said so. Wilkins rebutted recurrent flooding, war, famine, and pestilence in terms that evoke the arguments of not just Aristotle, but also Hooke. He was very probably writing the *Principles and Duties* in the years immediately following Hooke's 1668 lectures, and we may be sure that he knew precisely what his erstwhile student had been proposing, as the two men remained close until Wilkins' death. Hooke's later Oxonian opponent was John Wallis, the Savilian Professor of Geometry, who attacked Hooke's theories in 1687, pointing out that Hooke's period of extreme seismological instability could only have taken place 'before Adam', given that both sacred and secular history were otherwise silent on the matter. As Wallis assumed that was there was no time before Adam, his insinuation was clear.[12]

A more involved and reciprocal engagement, however, took place between Hooke and Edmond Halley, and this phase belonged strictly to the later courses of lectures Hooke delivered. In 1687, the same year in which Wallis was attacking Hooke, Halley presented an account of the German astronomer Johann Philipp von Wurtzelbaur's observations on the latitude of Nuremburg, which was found to have remained, *pace* Hooke's theories, static over two centuries. His intent here was to question Hooke's hypothesis of polar wandering. As he commented, 'if these [i.e. Hooke's] inundations are produced by any regular motion of the Poles, it would require a prodigious number of Ages to effect those changes we may be certain have been'. Tradition and Scripture tell us that this was a catastrophe, not a gradual wandering, so Halley proposed instead the impact of a comet or some other space-borne body.

In late 1694 Halley turned to the problem of the Flood itself. Conscious of the theological sensitivity of his lectures, he refrained from publishing them until over three decades later. In his first lecture, he declared that the biblical account was itself textually unsatisfactory, bearing the marks of later accretions, and at any rate inadequate as a physical description. Here we can see the contemporary biblical criticism of Richard Simon directly influencing scientific work. Halley then pointed out that in terms of gravity, wandering poles cannot cause physical change, but rather physical change (that is, a redistribution of mass) might cause variation in axial tilt and period of rotation. The ruins of the old world show that this has happened before, 'at least once' in Halley's words, and hence his paper advanced a theory of periodic catastrophism. Here Hooke and Halley were in accord. A week later, after conversations with 'a Person whose Judgment I have great Reason to Respect' – presumably Hooke – Halley proposed some further variations on the problem of harmonising Scripture with periodic catastrophism. Now, he pushed back the time of his primal catastrophes to a point before man was created, and certainly before the Flood, all but attributing this innovation to Hooke. Indeed, Halley reported that his interlocutor had proposed that these changes preceded the Chaos – in other words, that there was a world before this one, and that Genesis therefore recorded the creation of a new geography out of an old landscape. As William Buckland was to say well over a century later, 'there is nothing … inconsistent with the Mosaic declaration' if we were to affirm that 'the present system of this planet is built on the wreck and ruins of one more ancient'. In the 1690s this was extremely heterodox exegesis of Genesis.

At the time, Halley was certainly suspected of theological aberrancy: in 1691 he wrote to Abraham Hill complaining that he, Halley, was under the suspicion of 'asserting the eternity of the world'. Hooke's lectures, too, had to wait until two years after his own death before their publication by Richard Waller. When Halley finally printed his two papers, he took occasion to note that his theory of cometary impact had preceded William Whiston's similar suggestion, and his insinuation is clearly that Whiston copied him. Yet quite unlike Whiston, who also published on technical chronology, Hooke and Halley were developing a theory of catastrophism that had chronologically disconnected itself from biblical exegesis: the events they saw recorded in nature were not recorded by Scripture, because they had happened too early. This was to dismantle one of the assumptions on which early-modern historiography was based – that Earth history and human history shared a common time-frame. As Halley stated at the opening of his lecture on salinity:

> There have been many Attempts made and Proposals offered, to ascertain from the Appearances of Nature, what may have been the Antiquity of this Globe of *Earth*; on which, by the Evidence of Sacred Writ, *Mankind* has dwelt about 6000 Years; or according to the *Septuagint* above 7000. But whereas we are there told that the formation of *Man* was the last Act of the *Creator*, 'tis no where revealed in Scripture how long the *Earth* had existed before this last Creation, nor how long those five Days that preceeded it may be accounted; since we are elsewhere told, that in respect of the Almighty a thousand Years is as one Day, being equally no part of *Eternity*; Nor can it well be conceived how those Days should be to be understood of natural Days, since they are mentioned as Measures of Time before the Creation of the Sun, which was not till the Fourth Day. And 'tis certain *Adam* found the *Eerth* [sic], at his first Production, fully replenished with other sorts of *Animals*.

It was Halley, therefore, not Buckland, who first articulated the notion that the 'days' of Genesis might have taken thousands of years.[13]

Halley and Hooke were not intentionally anti-biblical. There is no reason to doubt Hooke's sincerity when he maintained that later accounts of creation 'were some way or other fetched' from Moses' text. Yet Hooke was not led by the concerns of biblical exegesis, and he tethered his biblical comments to the scientific business at hand. This priority powered his heterodoxy. Indeed, Hooke's use of biblical data was opportunistic in the sense that he was not primarily interested in establishing biblical truth, though of course happy to claim that he had biblical support. He used as his working bible the London Polyglot (1654–7), and Hooke's superficial knowledge, in Latin paraphrase, of the Samaritan, Arabic, Syriac, and Targum (often termed the 'Chaldee paraphrase') readings of the opening of Genesis, for instance, derives simply from the opening page of Walton's Polyglot, and should not trick us into suspecting any independent linguistic skill. Indeed, Hooke sometimes used biblical allusion for rhetorical, literary effect, in order to bolster principles that others would declare unbiblical. In his peroration against the proponents of fossils as merely tricks of nature, Hooke adopted a dialect immediately if incongruously recognisable as that of God thundering at Job:

> And those Persons that will needs be so over confident of their Omniscience of all that has been done in the World, or that could be, may, if they will vouchsafe, suffer themselves to be asked a Question, Who informed them? Who told them where England was before the Flood; nay, even where it was before the Roman Conquest for about four or five thousand Years, and perhaps much longer; much more where did they ever read or hear of what Changes and Transpositions there have been of the parts of it before that? What History informs us of the burying of those Trees in Cheshire and Anglesey? Who can tell when Tenerife was made?

'Where wast thou when I laid the foundations of the earth? declare, if thou hast understanding' (Job 38:4), demanded God of Job; Hooke returned the question to his opponents. Within his strictly physical discussions, Hooke drew Genesis into the orbit of his argumentation, but in a manner that we must distinguish from the bibliocentrism of many of his contemporaries.

We can expose the ambiguity of Hooke's relationship to the biblical Creation narrative by examining one word in the text of Genesis which Hooke addressed at three different times, and for which he provided three different glosses: the Greek word *stereoma* (= Latin *firmamentum* or 'heaven', as in 'the waters under the heaven'). In 1668, at the end of his first lecture cycle on earthquakes, he interpreted *stereoma* as signifying the atmosphere. When he delivered his lectures on comets in 1682, he returned in an incidental section to philological exegesis of Genesis. Addressing 'the two fundamental and primary Powers, to wit, that of Matter, and that of Motion', Hooke subdivided this latter power into the laws of light and of gravity, and then argued that this was conformable to Genesis 1. Now *firmamentum* has changed its meaning: 'And God said, Let there be an Expansum, or a Firmament, and let it divide the Waters from the Waters. This seems to signify the second general and grand Rule of Natural Motion, namely, Gravity'; 'And this Expansion or Firmament, which was the extensive Power of Gravitation, was that which caused those Effects'. By 1682, then, the firmament had become a force not a zone. In his 1688 attempted rapprochement with Genesis, Hooke finally decided that *stereoma* signified what we would today call the crust (*stereoma* from *stereos*, 'firm' or 'solid'), the hard layer which, in the process of Creation, separated the waters under the crust (what we term the mantle) from the waters over it. Flexion in this crust produced peaks and troughs, and hence the Earth's landscape, as the waters over the crust flowed off the new mountains, and settled into the new hollows. Floods are produced by further flexions. In the space of twenty years, therefore, Hooke's 'firmament' had progressed from an aerial zone, to a force, to a physical layer – a change in each case motivated by Hooke's larger physical arguments, and forgetful of any previous decision. Hooke was not openly sceptical of biblical evidence, but his theory treated such evidence as largely mute or at best ancillary to the geomorphology that Hooke believed had nonetheless taken place.

Hooke's theories received some support, though this dwindled as he pushed through from the thin thesis of organic fossils to the thick thesis of an Earth tumbling along its orbit, racked by indigestion. His disciple John Aubrey however was one consistent convert: as the eighth chapter of his *Natural History of Wiltshire*, cut by his nineteenth-century editor, Aubrey included 'An Hypothesis of the Terraqueous globe'. This chapter, immediately following a discussion of fossils, presented a few Hookian remarks on Earth history, affirming that water once covered all the Earth, that fish were the oldest species, and '[t]hat this World is much older, than is commonly supposed'. Aubrey would consistently posit earthquakes for most puzzling geological formations. He remembered that when he and the poet Edmund Waller (1606–87) had walked over the Alps in their youth, Waller had mused 'that at the Creation, those Mountains were the Sweepings or Rubbish of the World heaped up together'. He also conjectured axial shift, quoting liberally from Ovid to support his case. Returning to his manuscript in 1691, he recorded Halley's thesis, to be discussed later, of a secondary, interior Earth. Aubrey then sent the work to John Ray for review. Ray wrote back, urging Aubrey to publish, but to cut the Hookian material: 'I find but one thing that may give any just offence and that is the Hypothesis of the Terraqueous Globe, wherewith I must confess my self not to be satisfied.' Aubrey was privately angered by this response. Against the instruction to excise the digression, Aubrey placed a rebuttal, never returned to Ray: 'This hypothesis is Mr Hooke's: I say so: and 'tis the best thing in the Book it (indeed) does interfere with the 1 chap. of Genesis.' Here, stung into action by what he clearly perceived were misgivings fuelled by traditional biblical chronology, Aubrey disclaimed any interest in harmonising his Hookian 'hypothesis' with conventional biblical chronology or even exegesis. Hooke could not say this in public lectures, but his chief imitator did in private manuscript, and interpreted it as Hooke's real position.[14]

Hooke's attitude to the past transcended biblical and eventually all written evidence. In Hooke's phrase, 'the Orthography, Etymologia, Syntaxis, and Prosodia of Nature's Grammar' existed as phenomena embedded in the current form of the Earth. The naturalist had to learn to 'read' such evidence as a form of history, much as the geographer read the new grammar of stratigraphy, much as the chronologist used known astronomical events to stabilise terrestrial history, and much as the geologist was to affirm, 'For us, nature thus stands in place of history'. Hooke may have superficially agreed with Burnet that there was once an ancient form of wisdom, but Hooke's endorsement of antediluvian learning again served a different purpose. Burnet argued that his terrestrial theory was compatible with a *prisca theologia*, currently garbled, but not entirely lost: that, once, people had believed as he did about Creation, and that this was the divine doctrine. Hooke also thought that there had been lost truths, naming 'Atomical Philosophy' and Copernicanism as two schools of thought apparently known to the Ancients. He elsewhere stated that the problem of longitude had 'lain hid some thousands of years already'. For Hooke, however, a theory was not right because it had been shared by the Ancients. Rather, he recognised that the past probably contained civilisations of which no trace remains, civilisations which had lighted upon the truth merely by exercising their native ingenuity.

Hooke's point was unsettling. Given that the learning of many cultures has probably been lost to us, including the very knowledge that such cultures once existed, it is likely that what we consider innovation is often just rediscovery. In an eerie passage, Hooke meditated on the devastations of time:

> 'Tis not impossible but that there may have been a preceding learned Age wherein possibly as many things may have been known as are now, and perhaps many more, all the Arts cultivated and brought to the greatest Perfection, Mathematics, Mechanics, Literature, Music, Optics, &c. reduced to their highest pitch, and all these annihilated, destroyed and lost by succeeding Devastations.

For Hooke, there was no *prisca theologia* of a hieratic, mystical kind, a golden chain reaching back to the mouth of Noah, and perhaps threaded to Adam conversing with God in Eden. There was merely once potentially correct reasoning, subsequently 'annihilated, destroyed and lost'. Strabo, Pliny, Ovid, Hanno the Carthaginian, early biblical history, were all valuable because in their different ways they happened to preserve, amidst general ruin and decline, historical data that Hooke's geomorphological theory required. Hooke's theory of culture, then, was based on loss and not persistence: time, he said in the Greek formula, falls into unknown, mythical, and historical periods. When mythical and historical accounts fail, the natural historian, treading into the realms of the unknown, had to trade and trust in only the coin of nature.[15]

9

Fossils and Extinction

I shall leave it to the *Reader* to judge, whether it be likely that *Providence* which took so much care to secure the works of the Creation in *Noah's Flood*, should either then, or since, have been so unmindful … as to suffer any one *species* to be lost.

— ROBERT PLOT (1677)

'Fossil' derives from the Latin *fossilis*, 'something dug up', and such substances in early-modern classifications ranged from things puzzlingly non-mineral in form, such as petrified leaves and shells, to less controversial substances such as flints, marbles, gems, and metals. The task of later seventeenth-century discussions was to articulate the difference between fossils mineral in substance and form, and fossils mineral in substance but seemingly not in form, and to explain how the difference had come about. As it has been well expressed, this involves explaining three things: the *substance*, the *form*, and the *position* of the class of fossils that looked as if these three attributes might not be in harmony: why is it, for instance, that one can find mineral *substances* in the *shape* of seashells at the *top* of mountains?[1]

For many there were Aristotelian explanations already at hand, and there was hence no problem to be solved. 'Stones' in this tradition were closer to organic matter than we might assume. Standard physics textbooks repeated the Aristotelian idea that stones were 'mixed with a certain liquid oiliness, by length of time cemented together by the force of heat and cold, and by mineral power'. Petrifaction took place through the presence of vapours or fluids, and hence stones were grown rather than having existed unchanged over time. This is the principle behind the many anecdotes of self-renewing mines in the period. And if, for example, a fish seed were to be washed into a rocky place by accident, it is possible that the *virtus* of the stone might latch onto this seed and the information it contains on the form of the fish, and grow the stone-fish *in situ*. So for those who believed the boundaries between the mineral, plant, and animal kingdoms to be permeable, there was not necessarily a mystery to be solved when stones in the form of 'higher' existents were encountered. Likewise, those swayed by Neoplatonic or Paracelsian ideas were attuned to fossils as the sports of nature: as everything in the macrocosm has its counterpart in the microcosm, and as the universe is a huge network of imitations and correspondences, it is to be expected that the mineral kingdom imitates organic forms in stone, and even man-made objects. Hence the motley list in Robert Burton's *Anatomy of Melancholy* of stones dug up in the form of 'Birds, Beasts, Fishes, crowns, swords, saws, pots, &c.', to say nothing of Athanasius Kircher's illustrations of stones dug up not only in the form of natural and artificial objects, but even with various alphabets and magical symbols inscribed upon them. (Kircher was as ever too much for most English naturalists: 'As for Father Kircher I count him a credulous person', John Ray commented upon the passage.) Nevertheless, that the Paracelsian interpretation survived the period is witnessed by a 1705 attack on the 'Theorists' of the age:

> And truly in this regard I can see no reason why those people that daily observe the many and some very exact resemblances in the parts of Vegetables, to the parts and members of Animal Bodies; of which there are Multitudes of instances in *Oswaldus Crolius* his Tract of Signatures; can yet by no means prevail with their Faculties to believe that there might be the like Analogies and Similitudes in the parts of Stones and Minerals, with the said parts of Animal Bodies, without making them to be the true and genuine parts of some of those Bodies they resemble.[2]

Nor need these 'old' theories of purely mineral origin be entirely displaced by the 'new' hypothesis of organic origin and subsequent petrifaction. Geographically convenient fossils – fossilised shellfish very near a shore, for instance – might easily be treated as fossils in the modern sense, while more puzzling objects such as the stone versions of creatures no longer extant could be explained on the mineral hypothesis. Martin Lister, Robert Plot, and John Ray, three of the major contributors to the debate, all ran both Aristotelian and organic theories in parallel at various points in their careers.

In 1698 the second Keeper of the Ashmolean Museum, Edward Lhuyd, wrote to fellow collector John Archer, affirming that 'all Star stones derived their origin from Star-fishes', but that the belemnite was 'a mere mineral stone'. It would be almost two centuries before these were identified as the skeletons of an extinct cephalopod.[3]

The organic hypothesis had been debated long before Robert Hooke rendered it a matter of urgency following his published espousal in the *Micrographia* (1665). As far back as 1589, for instance, the geographers Richard Hakluyt (1552?–1616) and Abraham Ortelius, and Ortelius' nephew the London-based merchant-scholar Jacob Colius (1562–1628), discussed the matter in their letters. Colius supported an organic interpretation. At first, Ortelius demurred, but he remarked that he had once seen in Antwerp a fossilised, coiled 'slug' (*limax*, presumably an ammonite) so large and so obviously not represented by a living species that on reflection he must admit 'metamorphosis' in nature. Indeed, and unsurprisingly, a good deal of the later English discussions of fossils drew on continental sources, notably essays by Girolamo Fracastoro (1478?–1553) and Fabio Colonna (1567–1640). Fracastoro, the humanist doctor remembered for his poem on syphilis, had already maintained in the early sixteenth century that the presence of petrified shellfish on high mountains can be explained neither by the Flood nor by Aristotelian notions of growth *in situ*. He proposed instead that mountains took their origin from the seas slowly retreating from them, leaving maritime samples behind to petrify. Colonna performed chemical experiments: he affirmed the organic origin of petrified shark's teeth as a result of his method of burning various substances and inferring their origins from the stages they pass through in the fire, and the residue they leave. These sharks' teeth, also known as tongue-stones or *glossopetræ*, were among the most famous of fossil 'problems', not helped by Pliny the Elder's report that 'in the eclipse of the moon' such stones fall 'from heaven', and were deemed by some to possess magical properties.[4]

The most significant continental figures for the Royal Society naturalists were Paulo Boccone (1633–1704), who took the name Sylvio after joining Cistercians, the painter-by-training Agostino Scilla (1629–1700), and the stratigrapher Steno. Boccone himself visited London, where in 1673 he attended a meeting of the Royal Society and presented them with 'a certain leafy stone' from Sicily. The next year he published his *Recherches et Observations Naturelles* (Natural Researches and Observations) in Amsterdam, a collection of letters (including ones addressed directly to Hooke and to Ray), often subsequently referenced by English naturalists. Boccone affirmed once again the organic origins of the *glossopetræ* and other Sicilian fossils. As for their positions, he argued, we know that major rivers overflow their banks now and then, and when materials are found at problematically high points, we can also invoke sedimentation and earthquakes. Whole islands, as the classical poets and historians testify, have arisen and disappeared in this way. In distinction to Colonna, whom Boccone also cites, he believed that the Flood alone could not account for this. Joining the distinguished chorus of his time, Boccone affirmed that 'even since the Flood, the earth has been covered by water in many places, and has been uncovered in others'. Boccone donated boxes of his shells to the Royal Society, and was recorded consequently as a donor to their Repository; the copy of his *Recherches* now in the Lister collection in the Bodleian was a friendly gift to Ray himself, 'A Monsr John Wray pour une marque d'estime et d'amitie'. Scilla's richly illustrated *La Vana Speculazione Disingannata dal Senso* (Vain Speculation Undeceived by Sense; Naples, 1670) was abstracted in the *Philosophical Transactions* for 1695 by William Wotton, and Scilla had collected his fossils in the hills of Sicily with Boccone himself. Finally, the most important continental for all European nascent palaeontology was Steno. As we have seen, his 1669 manifesto on stratigraphy not only affirmed the organic origin of fossils, but offered a rigorous model of how to interpret the larger geological formations in which they were found.[5]

Despite these strong continental spurs in the 1670s, the Royal Society had long since discussed the organic hypothesis. In one meeting in late May 1663, for instance, the following round-the-table exchange took place. William Brereton (1631–80), aristocrat and natural philosopher, intervening in a discussion on trees, noted that in Cheshire there were oak and fir trees found buried underground; the gentleman barrister Philip Packer (1620–86) then commented that he had seen a tree cut to the root in Berkshire that was part petrified; so the lawyer Sir John Hoskins (1634–1705) moved that they find out more about the subject for their next meeting. At this point Hooke presented some microscopic observations on ants, gnats, and needle-points, later to appear in his *Micrographia*. The others then turned back to petrifactions. The veteran experimentalist and Oxonian Jonathan Goddard (1617–75) produced a piece of petrified wood, which was given over to Hooke to examine, perhaps the trigger for his initial discussion in the *Micrographia*. Next meeting, it was Goddard again who commented that grey marble appears to be made out of 'cockles and other shells compacted by intercurrent stony juices', and the physician Francis Glisson (1599?–1677) added that such juices filling the pores of wood caused its petrifaction too. Hooke then duly produced Goddard's petrified wood and described its appearance under the microscope. Goddard and Glisson, therefore, were proposing explicitly organic theories for both petrified wood and shells, and Goddard even spoke of their 'continual permeation ... through the earth, whereby the several parts thereof are strangely shifted from one place to another'.

So Hooke was sent off to think about it further. When he published his results in the *Micrographia*, he had already settled on the theory that he would defend intermittently for almost four further decades. Examining under the microscope not just petrified woods but also cockles and ammonites, he concluded:

> I cannot but think, that all these, and most other kinds of stony bodies which are found thus strangely figured, do owe their formation and figuration, not to any kind of Plastic virtue inherent in the earth, but to the Shells of certain Shell-fishes, which, either by some Deluge, Inundation, Earthquake, or some such other means, came to be thrown to that place, and there to be filled with some kind of Mud or Clay, or petrifying Water, or some other substance, which in tract of time has been settled together and hardened in those shelly moulds into those shaped substances we now find them; that the great and thin end of these Shells by that Earthquake, or what ever other extraordinary cause it was that brought them thither, was broken off; and that many others were otherwise broken, bruised and disfigured; that these Shells which are thus spiralled and separated with Diaphragms, were some kind of Nautili or Porcelain shells; and that others were shells of Cockles, Muscles, Periwinkles, Scallops, &c. of various sorts; that these Shells in many, from the particular nature of the containing or enclosed Earth, or some other cause, have in tract of time rotted and mouldered away, and only left their impressions, both on the containing and contained substances; and so left them pretty loose one within another, so that they may be easily separated by a knock or two of a Hammer.

So Hooke by 1665 had settled on explanations for the three crucial questions of form, substance, and position. Stony substances are in the form of organic matter because such organic matter was once genuinely present; petrifaction accounts for the change in substance; floods and earthquakes for the change in position. Nevertheless, as we can see, comparison of the Society's minutes with the *Micrographia* reveals that Hooke was working from hints proposed by his colleagues and employers, and the evolution from the May 1663 discussions to the only apparently sole-authored *Micrographia* of 1665 is an excellent example of the collaborative possibilities and exchanges the format of the Royal Society encouraged. At this point, Hooke had little more to say than what Goddard and Glisson had hinted; no mention yet of the problem of extinction, nor yet an advanced theory of seismic disturbance. The formal integration of all these arguments would come later.[6]

Hooke however did advance the latter of these discussions in the *Micrographia* – but, interestingly, in terms of the *Moon*'s surface. Hooke's last observation reported how he had simulated the texture of the Moon's surface on the Earth experimentally. He first dropped bullets into wet pipe-clay, noting that the results looked like facsimile lunar craters. He next boiled alabaster, and let it set, producing near-identical-looking craters. Hooke then moved a candle around his alabaster cast in a darkened room to simulate the various aspects of the Moon in the night sky. Because Hooke had no notion of meteorites, he preferred his alabaster experiment as the 'most notable', as it suggested that the Moon, like the Earth, had been wracked over the ages by internal fires and vapours. Hooke, we now know, was mostly wrong about the Moon, but he was mostly right about the Earth, and this would become a dominant strain of his work.[7]

Steno was working on his own ideas a little after this date, and we saw that Lister and Ray met him in Montpellier at the time Hooke was publishing the *Micrographia* in London; Hooke himself never left England. Steno's *Prodromus* only appeared in 1669, and then in Oldenburg's English two years later. This has led to various accusations about intellectual misappropriation. John Aubrey, who displayed an almost canine loyalty to Hooke, wrote on the inner front board of his copy of Oldenburg's Steno that Oldenburg 'by stealth sent a copy of Mr Hooke's Lectures of Solids in Solids read about 1664, to Mr Steno, who printed Mr Hooke's excellent Notions in Italy and Mr H. Oldenburg translated them into English'. Not content with this private judgment, Aubrey also wrote in his circulated *Natural History of Wiltshire* manuscript that Hooke had started lecturing on his theory of fossils in '1663, or 1664', and therefore Steno, through Oldenburg's perfidy, was a plagiary. Hooke undoubtedly reached his position independently of Steno, and could easily have done so by 1663. But that Steno subsequently relied on a surreptitious missive from Oldenburg is unlikely and unnecessary. Steno's own work breathes a different intellectual atmosphere, and the notion of the organic origins of fossils was common. Steno also presented his work in a quasi-geometrical

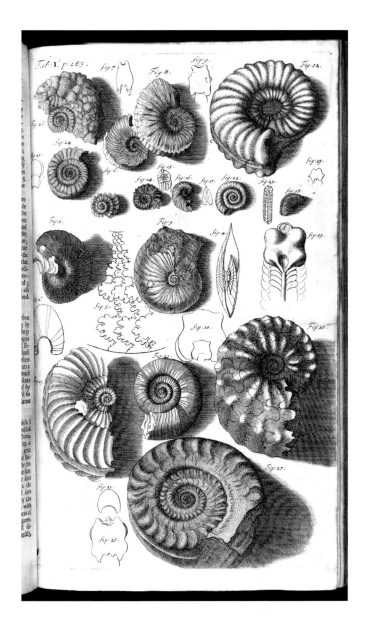

Figure 6. Robert Hooke, *Posthumous Works* (London, 1705),
table 1: fossils collected and illustrated by Hooke. With the permission of
the President and Fellows of Magdalen College, Oxford.

fashion, quite unlike Hooke's carnival of microscopical wonders. Oldenburg himself had been quite open in both the *Philosophical Transactions* and his Steno translation that Hooke was doing equally valuable work, and the blame for this particular priority squabble rests with Hooke: behind Aubrey's two comments his master's voice can be heard clearly. Rather, we have dwelt on the whole quarrel because it illuminates the problem of both the nature and the ascription of scientific priority at the time: as we have seen, Hooke himself was prompted by the chemical observations of Goddard and Glisson, volunteered in a scheduled but not a scripted discussion between a group of like-minded naturalists. This was a crucial social function of the early Royal Society's organisation: regular meetings fostered the exchanges of the naturalists in ways that defy exclusivist notions of intellectual property. In contrast, such a social format could not easily assist the more advanced mathematical theorists, whose very subject-matter resisted conversational extrapolation.[8]

Regardless of the help he received, Hooke's achievement was to systematise a theory of fossils, and he did this in a string of lectures delivered in 1667–8, accompanied by examples of the fossils themselves from the Royal Society's Repository, and his own drawings of other specimens (see Figure 6). Hooke gathered together as many examples and anecdotes as he could of the bewildering range of fossil types, of their differing substances, and their differing locations. He extracted out of Varenius an account that would also be recalled by John Ray and John Arbuthnot of a well dug at Amsterdam, where 99 feet below the city a four-foot-thick layer of sand and shells was discovered. Hooke then collected his thoughts into eleven systematic propositions. (1) Fossils representing animal or vegetable substances were once those very substances, now transformed by petrifying liquids, 'locked up and cemented together in their Natural Position and contexture'. (2) Such petrifaction must have required an external 'extraordinary Cause' or a number of such causes. (3) These were fourfold: 'fiery exhalations' raised by earthquakes; saline juices; a glutinous or bituminous agent; or 'very long continuation' under cold and high pressure. (4) Water itself may petrify over time. (5) Likewise other fluids. (6) What is now land was once sea; what was once sea is now land. (7) Hence Great Britain once 'had Fishes swimming over it'. (8) The receding of waters may be effected either by a change in the centre of the Earth's gravity, or by earthquakes and internal fires. (9) The highest mountains, such as the Alps, have been underwater, and probably owe their current prominence to earthquakes. (10) Indeed, most of the inequalities of the earth's surface have been effected by earthquakes. (11) Finally, many species have been lost; many more species are new.[9]

Hooke's eleven propositions were daring – 'at the first hearing they may seem somewhat paradoxical', he conceded in advance. But he moved from one consequence to the next with speed and assurance. He commenced with a minute discussion of figured stones, accompanied by drawings of 29 samples microscopically discussed. There followed further discussions and annotated drawings of a giant nautilus, various echini or 'helmet-stones', fossilised crabs and teeth, and what we would term today belemnites and crinoids. Hooke insisted on the organic origins of such fossils, ultimately invoking the theological argument, first used in the *Micrographia*, that nature does nothing in vain: '... it is contrary to all the other acts of Nature, that does nothing in vain, but always aims at an end, to make two Bodies exactly of the same Substance and Figure, and one of them to be wholly useless, or at least without any design that we can with any plausibility imagine'. He then worked down through his chain of consequences; and within one compact lecture cycle, examination of the tiniest sutures of shells had exploded into a total theory of the Earth, constantly knocked about by its own internal explosions, with what are now the north and south poles having once drifted through the equator, whole species perishing in their wake. As Hooke commented wryly in 1688, 'some may say, I have turned the World upside down for the sake of a shell'.[10]

When, by late 1668, Hooke had concluded his first series of lectures, he had not won over all his auditors – nor would he. That fossils might be organic in origin was hardly a novel idea, though Hooke's absolute claims were, as we shall see, controversial. But to assert the total vicissitude of the earth's surface as a corollary was to assert too much. In the minds of his auditors, Hooke's extreme version of Varenian geographical vicissitude stepped close to the Aristotelian version, in which vicissitude worked upon an eternal Earth. Hooke underscored this lineage by quoting again and again from the relevant sections of Aristotle and Seneca. His final proposition that earthquakes might upset the centre of the Earth's gravity, unfix her poles, and extinguish some of her species was the most radical idea in the earth sciences of the age.

Hooke was becoming dangerously unbiblical. Even in his earliest lectures he had dismissed the biblical Flood as an adequate motor for the current position of fossils. Instead, the Flood was itself caused by Hooke's prized earthquakes, *Deo volente*, and it was only one of many such deluges. Other major floods have been and will be so caused, he added, and this is the true glint of history lying behind the floods of pagan mythology. The catastrophe of Sodom and Gomorrah, for instance, was an earthquake; the long lives of the patriarchs can be explained by supposing that the Earth once span faster and hence the days and years were shorter; the giants of even the pagans' *gigantomachiæ* are, yet again, said Hooke, primal earthquakes – and the real giants of the Old Testament demonstrate the possibility of the extinction of an entire species.

Before we move on to discuss the reception of Hooke's geological theories, it is worth pausing to digress on his final claim: extinction of species. This claim has long excited scholars, and has even been referred to as an astonishingly early theory of 'Biological Evolution'. This is clearly worth assessing, but to be able to do this we need to understand more about contemporary theories of species variation. We have seen that detailed analyses of the Flood mobilised geometrical and zoological experts. These analyses, however, presupposed the endurance and fixity of species: all the species God created in the beginning still exist today, with no additions or diminutions. Hence the notions of both the extinction of some species and the creation of some new ones were typically rejected as an insult to the divine economy. When God rested on the seventh day, as most commentators affirmed, creation was complete, perfect, and God, as Sir Walter Ralegh (1554–1618) commented, 'did not then after create any new species'. To allow otherwise 'would argue an imperfection in the first Creation, which should produce any one Species more than what was absolutely necessary to its present and future State, and so would be a great derogation from the Wisdom and Power of the Omnipotent Creator', as Hooke rehearsed the standard objection. It would be highly unlikely, added Robert Plot, 'that Providence which took so much care to secure the works of the Creation in Noah's Flood, should either then, or since, have been so unmindful … as to suffer any one species to be lost'. This, agreed John Ray, would amount to 'the dismembering of the Universe, and rendering it imperfect: whereas … the Divine Providence is especially concerned to secure and preserve the Works of Creation.' Such statements would remain common for over a century. It is true therefore that Hooke's age was not comfortable with the notion of extinction, and this aspect of his thesis is indeed bold.[11]

The idea of variation *within* species, however, was commonly endorsed, based on climatic theories with a long pedigree extending back to Aristotle, Theophrastus, and Hippocrates, and receiving new impetus as a result of the apparently unrecognisable flora and fauna of the New World. Climatic ideas were espoused by Matthew Hale in his *The Primitive Origination of Mankind*, where he noted that the English mastiff lost its courage when transplanted to France, and that Barbary horses likewise degenerate in the first or second generation if removed from their home soil. Such environmental ideas were also applied to humans. Hale further noted the difference in 'colour, Figure, Stature, Complexion, Humor' between the peoples of different nationalities: the Spaniard is haughty, the Frenchman sprightly and sudden, those of the northern nations fair, strong, and courageous. Sir William Petty composed a carefully restricted manuscript titled 'Of the Scale of Creatures' in which he likewise eroded the absolute boundary between man and the beasts. Aristotle had declared the temperate zone the only inhabitable band of Earth precisely for climatic reasons. Athanasius Kircher too said that men born in the torrid zone were typically stupid, deceitful, shifty, violent, debauched, and superstitious; conversely, in the frigid zone men were stolid, insensate, sluggish, timid, obtuse, and workshy. Hence only those from the temperate zone are properly adjusted for human society. Less conventionally, Kircher elsewhere related the tale, repeated in England, of the Sicilian diver Nicolaus, dubbed *Pescecola* (i.e. 'Fish-colas', from *Pesce* and *Nicola*), whose long periods of diving had turned him into an amphibian with webbed feet and expanded lungs. Hale noted variation in skin colour within his discussion of climate-induced variation, and John Aubrey likewise encompassed humans in his environmental thought. 'Quaere [i.e. enquire] if Aborigines of one Country being transplanted to another, will not after some generations degenerate, or the contrary, according to the soil?' he asked. Elsewhere he noted that the English in Ireland became as lazy as the Irish after living there for seven years.[12]

None of this counts as proper variation *of* species, and indeed variation *within* species was often opposed to variation *of* species. As Sir Walter Ralegh again cautioned, 'if colour or magnitude made a difference of Species, then were the Negroes, which we call the Black-mores *nòn animalia rationalia* not men, but some kind of strange beasts'. So although there was a counter-tradition that espoused true variation of species, usually of plants (endorsed by Francis Bacon, for instance), extended sometimes to animals (by Giovanni Battista della Porta, for instance, whom Bacon only dared to imitate on plants), the discussion stopped short of human beings for the obvious soteriological reason. If climate could change species, then men could be unmanned, and hence ejected from the economy of salvation. Towards the end of the century, a cautious minimalism was probably the most common position. The FRS and Oxford botanist Robert Sharrock, for instance, studying with Boyle in the

Botanic Gardens, conceded that change was possible in the vegetable kingdom, but was restricted to silkworms and caterpillars in the animal kingdom. Variation because of climate would also necessarily be affected by variation *of* climate, as cosmological discussions of the precession of the equinox noted. So the many discussions in the period that at first look as if they are teetering on the brink of full variation are doing so only with this one major restriction. As it was still in practice impossible to decouple zoology from theology, variation was based upon environmental and climatic influences, might genuinely produce species change within the lower kingdoms, but only accidental and not substantial change in human beings themselves. If the human being in the tradition of Christianised Aristotelianism is defined as a rational animal, it is the faculty of reason, and not skin colour or physical dimensions, which controls access to heaven. Ironically, an age that happily traded in slaves had no biological theory of racism, other than in some extreme interpretations of La Peyrère's Preadamism. Finally, the later, crucial Darwinian notion of competition was easily available through the Epicurean philosophy of Lucretius, enjoying a revival at the time.

> Besides, the Earth produced a numerous train
> Of Monsters, Those her labour wrought in vain;
> Some without hands, or feet, or mouth, or eyes;
> Some shapeless lumps, Nature's Absurdities. […]
> A Thousand such in vain arose from Earth;
> For Nature frighted at the ugly birth,
> Their strength and life to narrow bounds confined,
> Denied them food, or to increase their Kind. […]
> But more, these years must numerous Kinds deface,
> They could not all preserve their feeble race:
> For those we see remain, and bear their young,
> Craft, strength, and swiftness hath preserved so long.

Some species therefore perished through being misformed, unable to feed or procreate, or lacking in the requisite cunning and courage. But later in the same section, Lucretius explicitly rejected variation of species:

> Yet nothing proves, that things of different Kind,
> That disagreeing Natures should be joined, [   ]
> But each arising from its proper Cause
> Remains distinct, and follows Nature's laws.

To conclude the digression, despite the availability of both the hypotheses of Aristotelian variation and Epicurean competition, these notions were not explicitly linked in the seventeenth century, and it is hence at best an anachronism to refer to any theory of 'evolution' in the period.[13]

We can now appreciate that Hooke too treats extinction as caused by environmental change, not by competition between species. He indeed claims that new species may be created, but all his subsequent remarks on changes in species are not 'evolutionary' but belong, as we have seen, to conventional ideas of environmentally caused variation within a given species. Change in climate, soil, and nourishment may produce 'divers new varieties … of the same Species'. Hooke's orthodox origins here are confirmed by his subsequent sentence, in which I italicise the pertinent terms: ''tis not to be doubted but that *alterations* also of this Nature may cause a very great change in the shape, and other *accidents* of an animated Body. And this I imagine to be the reason of that great variety of Creatures that do *properly belong* to one Species.'

Hooke's originality lies not in voicing variation, then, but in combining it with his rarer views on extinctions and new creations. Some of this originality can be seen by comparison with Hale's *Primitive Origination of Mankind* again, which contains a section on the migration of the original communities, land and sea vicissitude, fossil origin, the stocking of America with flora and fauna, and the diversity within species caused by climatic influence and cross-breeding. Hale even recounted a Gloucestershire fossil-collecting ramble of his youth, just as Hooke had recalled in his lectures his own childhood walks, combing the fossil beaches of the Isle of Wight. One wonders if Hale had heard some of Hooke's lectures, or obtained a text of them. But Hale, unlike Hooke, nowhere says that entire species have become extinct.[14]

If Hooke's hypothesis of extinction, now known to be correct, was unlikely to receive much support, his organicist theory of fossils was received coolly too. For, given that there were workable Aristotelian and Paracelsian explanations for fossils as self-generated stones, there was no theoretical vacuum urgently in need of filling. Hooke's major opponents proved to be the physician Martin Lister and the naturalist Robert Plot, two of his most influential and well-connected colleagues. The early papers of John Beaumont, too, supported a non-organic interpretation, which he described using Paracelsian vocabulary in the *Philosophical Transactions* in 1676. Lister, great-nephew to the famous physician of that name, had travelled on the continent in the 1660s, spending time in the celebrated academe of Montpellier, and joining John Ray and his companion Philip Skippon to survey the local flora and fauna. We have seen that Steno was there at this time too. Ray and Lister remained regular correspondents on natural matters for many years. Lister was made an FRS in 1671, and sat on the council in the 1680s and 1690s. Plot had been part of the Boyle set and then of the Thomas Willis set in interregnum Oxford and later achieved fame in 1677 with his *Natural History of Oxford-Shire*, becoming an FRS the same year; he took over as one of the Society's secretaries after Hooke's resignation in 1682, and therefore presided over the resuscitation of the *Philosophical Transactions* that Hooke himself had suspended. Plot and Lister were natural allies, and in 1682 Lister cemented this bond by presenting a large number of books, manuscripts, and objects to Plot's citadel, the newly opened Ashmolean Museum.[15]

Although he had not yet published anything substantial on the matter, Lister regarded stones, earths, indeed all minerals and shells as his territory. When, therefore, he heard of Hooke's theories, he prepared a short response, which appeared in the *Philosophical Transactions* in 1671 in the form of a letter to Henry Oldenburg composed a few months before his election to the Society. Lister did not dispute the organic nature of the Italian shells discussed by Steno: 'particularly along the shores of the Mediterranean Sea, there may all manner of Sea shells be found promiscuously included in Rocks or Earth, and at good distances too from the Sea'. The problem arose when one tried to transfer this theory to the inland English quarries discussed by Hooke. Lister had two major reservations. First, he observed that different quarries yield different shells, both in substance and form, and the well-travelled Lister had so far encountered no significant overlap. This did not bode well for the theory of organic origin, where one might expect more regularity throughout the land; instead, so Lister thought, it pointed to extremely localised processes of fossil production, and so to non-organic origins. Secondly, Lister had searched along shores and in fresh water looking for examples of these inland shells, and had so far failed to pair up any specimens from the living and the fossil worlds. His conclusion could only be that these were discontinuous realms. He objected to 'those persons, that think it not worth the while exactly and minutely to distinguish the several species of the things of nature, but are content to acquiesce in figure, resemblance, kind, and such general notions'.

To Lister, a leather-soled naturalist, Hooke's and indeed Steno's arguments from analogy seemed sloppy and even cloistered.[16]

Plot turned to the issue in his *Natural History of Oxford-Shire*, a work deeply informed by Plot's chemical researches: 'If any body doubt whether stones, and so petrifications arise from Salts, let him but consult the Chymists, and ask, Whether they find not all indurated Bodies, such as stone, bones, shells, and the like, most highly sated with the saline principle?' 'Salt' in this chemical tradition was one of the three ultimate elements of things, and Plot maintained the familiar theory that such saline juices could transform non-stony into stony substances over time. But when Plot addressed the vexed issue of 'formed' stones (i.e. fossils), he sided explicitly with Lister, against Hooke and even John Ray, whom he interpreted as holding the 'hard' organicist position at this date. Lister held that figured stones were '*lapides sui generis*', stones of their own kind; Hooke and Ray that they were 'formed in an Animal mould'. 'Upon mature deliberation', Plot adjudicated, 'the latter opinion appear[s] at present to be pressed with far more, and more insuperable difficulties than the former.'

Plot reasoned that the Flood and earthquakes were the two mechanisms that could account for the positions of the more troublesome figured stones. But in a moment of surprising heterodoxy, Plot endorsed Stillingfleet's partial flooding, commenting that the biblical deluge 'seems not to have been universal', and had extended only as far as the outer borders of the biblical lands. Were northern flooding to be granted, it must have been either gradual, or violent. If gradual, most of the shellfish would not have moved; if violent, they would have been scattered indifferently and would not be found in the puzzlingly regular distributions that we see. If we turn to earthquakes, they are too weak in these northern regions, 'unless we shall groundlessly grant' (as Hooke had indeed argued) that in the infancy of the world earthquakes were more frequent than now. Nor can we have recourse to extinction: God could never 'have been so unmindful of some shell-fish (and of no other Animals) as to suffer any one species to be lost'. Plot agreed with Lister that petrified, semi-petrified, and unpetrified shells near the shore or on flats near the coast pose no problem. He then marked his man by excerpting a long passage from the *Micrographia* on how we should not make nature do things in vain. But, riposted Plot, the *lapides sui generis* certainly beautify creation, and may have as yet unexploited medical uses. Within the parameters of his age, Plot's four-pronged argument was strong. His comment, especially, on Hooke's 'groundless' hypothesis of more vigorous seismic activity in a previous age demonstrates how very difficult it was to move towards a fully organic hypothesis within the constraints of biblical time. As long as the only option was to increase the frequency of geomorphological events rather than lengthen the whole chronological bracket, the position of Lister and Plot was almost unassailable.[17]

The anxieties the best naturalists faced here are exemplified by John Ray. Plot treated Ray, we saw, as on Hooke's side. In 1677 this was true, but Ray, who had set out his thoughts on the matter in his 1673 *Observations Topographical, Moral, and Physiological*, was nevertheless always unsettled by the problem. In the preface to his book, he warmly acknowledged some corrections offered to him by Lister, who had reclassified some of Ray's fossils as imitating parts of vegetables rather than parts of fish, as Ray had initially proposed. But he interpreted this as evidence favouring Hooke's position, though evidence that itself raised further questions for Ray:

> Wherefore unless we will grant them to be primary and immediate productions of Nature, as they are in the form of stones; we must embrace Mr. Hooke's opinion, that they were the roots of some Plants; though I confess I never as yet saw any Roots or Branches shaped and jointed in that manner. Perhaps there may be or have been such kind of submarine Plants or Roots which have hitherto escaped my knowledge.

In his later discussion in the body of the work, Ray excerpted all the material he could gather from Goropius Becanus, William Camden, and others, on fossils that resembled organisms. Many of these were the striking 'snake stones' or *cornua ammonis*. (Ray even suggested that 'Adderbury' outside Oxford took its name from the prevalence of such fossils there.) He again sided explicitly with Steno and Hooke: 'to me the most probable Opinion is that they [such fossils] were originally the Shells or Bones of living Fishes and other Animals bred in the Sea.' This was what classical authorities taught; this was what Steno had proposed afresh; and this too was Hooke's position in the *Micrographia*. But how could Ray account for the position of such objects if they were indeed marine in origin? Here he too denied that the Flood could meet the problem. Fossils at the top of mountains would be washed by the torrential rain down from, not up onto, the summit, an objection first raised by Fracastoro. If subterranean waters broke out too, then they should have scattered matter everywhere, and cannot account for localised, concentrated seams of fossils. So both Plot and Ray, though they disagreed about the origin of the figured stones, agreed that the Flood will not help either side out. Earthquakes would not suffice either, as Ray held that 'in general since the most ancient times recorded in History, the face of the Earth hath suffered little change'. This, we recall, was the position of the World Makers too.

Ray was nevertheless sympathetic to some of Lister's objections. The entire Earth cannot have been covered by sea in the deluge long enough for adequate fossil distribution. The problem of fossils 'which are not at this day that we know of anywhere to be found' among the living species encouraged the hypothesis of extinction, 'a dismembering of the Universe and rendering it imperfect', intolerable for Ray. Yet even here Ray vacillates slightly: 'granting that some few Species might be lost', he concedes, the fossil record is still too diverse to be tamed. Ray therefore ended up in a rather ambiguous position. He confessed that the English inland quarries may contain '*lapides sui generis*', only to brand the double-theory of some fossils organic in origin, others not, as merely 'a shift and refuge to avoid trouble' – a 'refuge' he himself had just taken. All Ray could conclude at this date was that he wished someone would solve the problem for him. He, too, could glimpse that behind the whole issue lay the chronological problem, one from which he shied away: 'if the Mountains were not from the beginning, ... the World is a great deal older than is imagined or believed, there being an incredible space of time required to work such changes'.[18]

Ray kept returning to the matter, both in his correspondence with fellow naturalists such as Lister himself and Plot's assistant and eventual successor Edward Lhuyd, and in his printed works. Thomas Burnet had so churned up the waters for the naturalists by the 1690s that Ray felt moved to publish a string of scientific apologetics in the early years of that decade, namely his *The Wisdom of God Manifested in the Works of the Creation* (1691), and his *Miscellaneous Discourses Concerning the Dissolution and Changes of the World* (1692), reworked and expanded as *Three Physico-Theological Discourses* (1693). These semi-devotional works had a long history of republication stretching through the next century. It is in the *Three Physico-Theological Discourses* that Ray provided a summation of his thoughts on 'formed Stones' in the aftermath of Burnet. His basic position remained that of the 1673 work. What had changed was that in twenty years a good deal of new collection and discussion had taken place. Ray now opened his discussion by noting that 'formed Stones' is the *new* term for what were once just called 'petrified Shells', an indication that the organic hypothesis had been unexceptionable until the attacks of Lister and Plot rendered naturalists sensitive to the issue. Confirmation that the organic hypothesis was coming to be seen as the older interpretation is provided by John Woodward's identical remark in 1695, branding the notion of fossils as 'mere Sportings' as the 'new Expedient'. (So the modern historiographical assumption that the organic position supplanted the *lusus naturæ* interpretation, surprisingly, now needs inverting: it was *denial* of the organic origin that seemed to prominent contemporary experts the 'new' stance.) Ray rehearsed Hooke's position and Plot's animadversions, replying to Plot's comments on the beauty of fossils that all other natural 'ornaments' serve living things, and have a functional as well as an aesthetic role. The notion that God would bother making shells that never held living things in their embrace 'is indeed so contrary to that innate *Prolepsis* we have of the Prudence of Nature' that Ray must once again agree with Hooke that *Natura nihil facit frustra*, 'Nature does nothing in vain'.[19]

Nevertheless, Ray still preferred to class some fossils as examples that 'Nature doth sometimes *ludere* [play]', citing the impressions of plant-leaves in coal sent to him by Lhuyd. He also agreed that there are 'strange and seemingly absurd Consequences … hardly reconcilable to Scripture, or indeed to sober Reason' if one were fully to endorse the organicist position, and he revisited the problems of the missing flood or floods, and of extinction. Ray also commented that despite the huge numbers of marine and vegetable fossils known to him and his naturalist friends, no one had yet produced a convincing fossilised piece of a land animal. We know today that this is because land animals die in the open, and tend to rot or be weathered away, or simply eaten. Sea dwellers, in contrast, have a much higher chance of sedimenting. But Ray's claim is a still little puzzling, as his age did not know this, and many candidates for land fossils had been put forward. Most European 'cabinets of curiosities', in addition, contained objects that were claimed as pieces of giants' skeletons. Plot, for one, had interpreted many huge English bones as pieces of giants, for instance the bone found when St Mary Woolchurch was pulled down after the Fire of London, and in Plot's day hanging in the King's Head tavern in Greenwich, said to be part of a giant woman. The Irish natural philosopher Sir Thomas Molyneaux (1661–1733) published 'An Essay concerning Giants' in the *Philosophical Transactions* for 1700 in which he calculated that the famous Leiden giant forehead bone came from a man about eleven or twelve feet tall, possibly from Brazil, and that the biblical giants were no larger than well-attested modern versions. Molyneaux, however, rejected the organic origin of fossils.[20]

The fossilised 'snakestones' or 'ophiomorphites' (i.e. ammonites) puzzled Ray most of all. They had been found 'as broad as a Coach wheel' in fossil form, but Ray was not prepared to admit that such a massive shellfish had ever existed, and preferred to class them as some kind of as-yet-undetected land creature. Yet even here, as he threw up his hands in desperation, Ray had to admit that the Bristol collector William Cole (c. 1622–1701) had found ophiomorphites covered in shells, a sure sign of marine origin. Ray, then, was left to posit a number of factors that depart or are simply omitted from biblical history. Like others before him he enlisted non-miraculous floods, both those known and unknown to history. Some fossils are in such strange positions that he revived the notion that all waterways are connected under the earth, and might have worked like giant fire-hoses during the biblical Flood, spraying out ambient marine matter too. In a striking *mise-en-abîme*, pondering the aesthetic appeal of fossils, Ray even speculated whether current fossil-hunters have been stymied by earlier fossil-hunters, whose own abandoned collections are therefore signs of man, rather than nature, playing with man. In his final writings on the matter, a series of private letters to Edward Lhuyd, Ray eventually confessed that the 'tricks of nature' hypothesis ought to be entirely retired, and that he now supposed that subterranean fires lit by God at the dawn of time first pushed the land masses out of the water. Ray had finally defected entirely to Hooke.

Ray was always extremely diligent in weighing his arguments. Despite his friendship with Lister and Lhuyd, he sided with Hooke; but despite his appreciation of Hooke's providential argument that God does not sport with nature, he refused to dissemble the problems into which Hooke cheerfully led his more religiously cautious colleagues. Ray too could see that chronology was the major obstacle. Yet all these 1690s works of Ray's, we must recall, originated in sermons delivered in earlier years, some as far back as the 1650s – now sermons transmuted by the passage of time into broken, stratified objects, rather like the fossils that so puzzled Ray, most pious of English naturalists.

10

Meteorology, Cartography, and Globes

… [the Earth] seemed unto me no other then a huge Mathematicall Globe, leasurely turned before me, wherein successively, all the Countries of our earthly world within the compasse of 24 howers were represented to my sight. And this was all the meanes I had now to number the dayes, and take reckoning of time.

— DOMINGO GONZALES, the first astronaut (1638)

Stillingfleet in the earlier versions of his book was concerned mainly with the origin and earliest history of the Earth, and we will conclude with a discussion of its end and final destruction. Nor was Stillingfleet immediately concerned with the current state of the globe, but we must first pause to discuss some seventeenth-century advances in the description of the seventeenth-century present geocosm: how its weather was recorded and theorised, and how its features were to be mapped and modelled. Finally, the study of terrestrial magnetism was one of the most popular topics in the early Royal Society, and advances in magnetic theory fed directly into Newtonian notions of gravity, notions that proved so successful that their prehistory in magnetic enquiries is now largely forgotten.

The weather was naturally a prominent concern for any experimentalist interested in the general structure and behaviour of the Earth. In the textbook tradition winds, meteors, and earthquakes were all part of the same branch of Aristotelian physics; and in cross-disciplinary terms consideration of the atmosphere was linked to the study of epidemic disease, especially the plague. The Restoration soon had its plague; and in 1703 came 'The Wonder', the greatest storm recorded to have hit Britain, resulting in, among other things, the loss of Henry Winstanley (1644–1703) along with his celebrated off-shore engineering feat, the Eddystone lighthouse. Regular monitoring of the weather had meanwhile become a more common activity. Thomas Ax (d. 1691) of Somerset commenced his daily weather tables in 1661, later handing them to John Aubrey for his *Natural History of Wiltshire*; Robert Hooke's first diary commenced in March 1672 as a weather log, and only gradually metamorphosed into autobiography; and from around the middle of 1666 right up to 1703, the year before his death, John Locke maintained daily tables, with some gaps, of meteorological observations. Locke's weather log commenced as part of his 'Adversaria Physica', or his commonplace book on physics, an indication of the intellectual origin of such pursuits. Such activities were prompting commercial innovation too, notably the monthly 'WEATHER JOURNAL' sheets engraved by John Warner in 1685 for logging daily meteorological observations.[1]

Meanwhile, philosophical tracts on meteorology, as it was now coming to be termed in English, began to appear. In 1663 the philologist Isaac Vossius published his Latin *De motu marium et ventorum liber* (A book on the motion of the seas and winds), and was subsequently elected to the Royal Society; *De motu* itself was translated into English in 1677 by a future opponent of Thomas Burnet, Archibald Lovell. Vossius, leaning on the Senecan thesis that the Sun causes most meteorological variations, unluckily dismissed the Moon from any influence whatsoever on the tides. The more interesting meteorological theorist of the time was Ralph Bohun, Fellow of New College, Oxford. At first sight, Bohun appears somewhat reactionary. We have encountered his support for curricular Aristotelianism; and like many other scientifically involved academicians, Bohun was initially ambivalent about the London-based Royal Society, which he at first suspiciously termed 'a Learned Conventicle'. But Bohun soon warmed to the fledgling Society, and his advocacy of the structure of an Aristotelian education was not therefore an endorsement of its content. In his seminal *Discourse concerning the Origine and Properties of Wind* (1671) Bohun overturned Aristotelian meteorology, insisting 'this Philosophy is not to be had in Colleges or Books, but must be fetch't from both *Indies*'. Indeed his original preface had evidently praised the Royal Society's own meteorological researches in too positive terms, as in a remarkable intervention the *Discourse* was stopped in the press by the university authorities, and censored. The published text is less offensively modernist, explaining that that 'which we call the *New Philosophy*' was not 'Invented, but only Reviv'd' by the Moderns from ancient sources.[2]

Such an apology sits uncomfortably next to Bohun's equal insistence that his book superseded previous work. Bohun privileged materials from the sea-captains he had interviewed at Deptford while in service to the Evelyns, and his work owed more to these travellers and to the modern researches of Bacon and Vossius and especially Boyle, who also interviewed divers and travellers, than it did to the *Meteorologica* and its commentators. Like many other meteorologists, however, Bohun did refer often to Seneca's *Natural Questions*. Bohun, like Hooke and Vossius (and indeed Seneca), saw that hydrography and meteorology were analogous disciplines, both relying on fluid dynamics: 'the Currents of Air imitate the Motions of water'. He also defined the planetary atmosphere using metaphors drawn from machines: 'a kind of perpetuall *Automat*' (i.e. automaton), or 'one Immense *AEolipile*'. (The 'aeolipile' is Hero of Alexander's famous steam-engine, the water-filled sphere which when heated spins on its bearing by ejecting steam from angled tip-jets.) The aeolipile metaphor for the atmosphere would be repeated a number of times over the next few decades. Following Boyle, Bohun likewise stressed the air's quantifiable elasticity: Descartes had thought that air could expand fourfold; Mersenne had conducted experiments that greatly increased this factor; but Boyle in his trials of the rarefaction of air, so Bohun related, had extrapolated in his air-pump the staggering result of a 13,000-fold expansion – 13,769-fold to be precise.[3]

Boyle's air-pump, perfected by Hooke, is an indication that meteorology had become a matter of mechanical measurement. The landmark 1648 French Puy-de-Dôme experiment had confirmed that the height of a column of mercury varied with altitude, but variation in stationary columns was soon being discussed too. Vossius later noted that a column maintained at one altitude varied with the approaching weather: half a year's recorded weather observations had confirmed for him that a sudden drop in the level of 'Quicksilver' heralded a coming storm.[4] Hooke had long before developed his wheel-barometer, in which the small variation in the height of a stick-barometer was translated into the greater and hence more observable movement of a pointer on a dial. Hooke was particularly exercised by atmospheric interference with astronomical measurements – atmospheric refraction bent phenomena to an ever higher apparent altitude the nearer one's line of sight dropped to the horizon, a meteorological distortion that could create apparently impossible astronomical phenomena, such as the horizontal eclipse, which Hooke correctly explained.[5] Hooke also developed instruments for measuring air pressure, temperature, humidity, rainfall, and wind strength and direction, and he realised an old idea of Christopher Wren's when he combined all these in late 1678 into a 'Weather-Wiser', a weather station producing a clock-driven punched-paper printout each quarter-hour. This was placed in the Royal Society's Repository, and described in the 1681 Repository catalogue thus:

> … it hath six or seven Motions … First a *Pendulum* Clock, which goes with ¾ of
> a 100 *lib.* weight, and moves the greatest part of the work. With this, a *Barometre*,
> a *Thermometre*; a *Rain-Measure* … a *Weather-Cock*, to which subserves a piece
> of Wheel-Work analogous to a way *Wiser*; and a *Hygroscope*. Each of which have
> their *Regester*, and the *Weather-Cock* hath two; one for the *Points*, the other for
> the *Strength* of the Wind. All working upon a Paper falling off of a *Rowler* which
> the *Clock* also turns.[6]

Hooke also prepared an early paper on standardising both instruments and observations so that independent researches could be compared; Hooke's mechanical innovations were as ever integrated into a larger, rationalised intellectual project.[7] In the preface to his *Micrographia*, Hooke claimed, in a tacit allusion to both Bacon and Wilkins, that humans could overcome the epistemological consequences of the Fall of Adam by curing sensory defects with artificial instruments. It is therefore interesting to note that Hooke's earliest hygroscope is a kind of equivalent plant cyborg: Hooke plugged a beard of wild oat into an output device that amplified tiny organic motions through – just like his wheel barometer – the larger sweep of a pointer on a dial.[8]

Hooke was also keen to advance oceanography or 'hydrography', one of the divisions of Varenian geography. In 1686 he drew up a large Varenian 'Hydrography' chart, arranging 'the History and description of the Nature and use of Waters' into distinct headings embracing everything from the history of ancient shipping to the study of magnetism. The chart survives both in Hooke's own papers and, appropriately, in Samuel Pepys' manuscripts; Pepys was the naval expert among this group, contributing tables of maritime terminology to John Wilkins' artificial language, and eventually publishing an economic study of the navy.[9] Their friend and colleague Sir Anthony Deane, FRS, was the best ship-builder in the period; he wrote a manuscript 'Doctrine of Naval Architecture' for Pepys – and also prepared a 1683 paper on the dimensions of Noah's Ark.[10] Hooke again developed an array of devices for investigating 'hydrography'. He proposed depth-sounders with self-releasing floats which bore deep samples to the surface; measurers of submarine pressure, sounders or waywisers that recorded the number of revolutions of attached vanes as they sank; even sounders with two metered vanes, one to record the descent and one the ascent. Even if many of these contrivances were unoriginal or impractical, the importance of Hooke's efforts lay in his full and illustrated technical descriptions, which were widely reproduced in the following century.[11]

If the concepts for meteorological instrumentation in the period often outstripped practicality, innovation was more successfully implemented in cartography. English map-making in the period could still not compete in quality with Dutch enterprises. But quantity was not lacking: between 1668 and the end of the century, over three hundred advertisements appeared for new maps for sale in the *London Gazette* alone. Some adverts now bore attestations by prominent researchers including Wren, Vossius, and Hooke.[12] All these men were also closely involved in the bookseller Moses Pitt's notorious 'English Atlas' project, an overambitious plan to publish a twelve-volume, rather derivative world atlas; it stalled one-third of the way through, ruining Pitt.[13] But several technical innovations were beginning to appear in English cartography, such as road maps and straight-line distance maps.[14] After the Restoration, the publisher and globe-maker Joseph Moxon (1627–91) cornered the mathematical market, publishing over thirty popular scientific and technical handbooks. He was appointed Hydrographer Royal in 1662, a post that had been in abeyance for over a century, 'for the making of Globes, Maps and Sea-Platts'; this in turn secured him a fellowship of the Royal Society, although his status as a tradesman proved socially controversial within the Society. Moxon was also the first London seller to publish a regular list of paper instruments for sale, a reminder of the importance of this now almost entirely perished class of mathematical instrument. He performed important lexicographical work in mathematics as the first publisher of a mathematical dictionary, *Mathematicks Made Easie* (1679, six editions to 1705), containing explanations of technological and geographical words too.

Even here, however, the biblical was never far off: Moxon, who had spent his youth in Delft and Rotterdam, published various pieces of scriptural cartography imitated from similar publications from the Low Countries. He translated from the Dutch *Sacred Geographie, or Scriptural Mapps* (1671, 1691), which he dedicated to the two universities. These maps, beginning with one of Creation and one of Paradise, were accompanied by a commentary offering a précis of Genesis through Creation, Fall, and Flood and tracing the subsequent population dispersal. The commentary noted, for instance, that Americans must derive from Noah, 'the likeliest probability' being settlement of the continent by the sons of Japheth. In around 1670 Moxon also issued a 'Map of all the Earth and how after the Flood it was divided among the Sons of Noah' overlaid with all the names of Noah's offspring from Genesis 10, and surrounded by engravings derived from Wenceslaus Hollar depicting Creation, Fall, Flood, Babel, Crucifixion, and the New Jerusalem. This map literally encircled geographical space with the notion of biblical time.[15]

More ambitious cartographical innovations were proposed too. John Aubrey opened his county history of Wiltshire, substantially completed in 1685, with an expressed desire: 'I have oftentimes wished for a mappe of England coloured according to the colours of the earth; with markes of the fossiles and minerals.'[16] Earlier, in 1683, Martin Lister published a paper in the *Philosophical Transactions* similarly proposing 'a *Soil* or *Mineral Map*', in which soils were to be distinguished by colours or varied hatching. Claiming long precedence for his own proposals, Lister also took occasion to reaffirm his distrust of the organic hypothesis of fossils, and to agree with William Gilbert that the inside of the Earth was probably iron, proposing additionally that sand was the Earth's original topsoil.[17] Thomas Burnet, too, in his *Sacred Theory* had called for 'natural' as well as 'civil' maps, which would 'represent the Earth as it would be if there was not an Inhabitant upon it'.[18] The most impressive contributions to the emerging notion of thematic cartography, however, were made by Edmond Halley. In 1686 he published in the *Philosophical Transactions* the earliest meteorological chart, a map of the trade winds. He later released as separate items an isogonic map of magnetic declination for the Atlantic (1701); followed by a declination map for the whole world (1702); then a tide chart for the English Channel (1702); and finally – before it had taken place – a map showing the path of the shadow of the Moon as it was to cross England during the 1715 eclipse.[19] Halley had introduced cartography to both meteorology and oceanography.

Closely associated with maps were globes. In the seventeenth century, use of the two globes was evidently part of the basic arts training in the universities, as extant Latin manuscript curricular cribs often contain sections on the celestial and terrestrial globes.[20] Manuals for using the globes were soon vernacularised. The celebrated Elizabethan geographer and voyager Robert Hues' 1594 textbook on the globes had been translated swiftly from Latin into Dutch and German, and it remained current in England too for the best part of a century, thanks not only to Latin republication (1651, 1663,

1668) but also to the Oxonian Edmund Chilmead's English translation (1639, 1659). Hues' treatise was originally published to accompany the 2-foot 2-inch terrestrial and celestial globes made in 1592 by Emery Molyneux. Joseph Moxon again was the major designer and retailer of globes in the Restoration, ranging from his own 2-foot 2-inch pair to his 3-inch portable nested globes, in which a terrestrial globe was protected by a case, on the inside of which was painted in concave the celestial globe.[21] He too designed globes and manuals to be sold and used in tandem. But whereas the Molyneux-Hues system was Ptolemaic in assumption, Moxon advertised both Ptolemaic and Copernican globes. (English globes were, however, dwarfed by the contemporary 3½-foot printed and 15-foot manuscript globes, constructed for Louis XIV by Vincenzo Coronelli.)

Moxon's contemporaries made some suggestions for modifying globes too. In the *Sacred Theory*, for instance, Thomas Burnet proposed the construction of 'a *rough Globe*, expressing all the considerable inequalities that are upon the Earth', but none appears to have been undertaken, and the earliest reported relief globe dates from almost a century later. This is hardly surprising given the difficulty of assembling the requisite information.[22] In fact the first recorded early-modern relief globe was of the Moon: at royal command, in 1661 Christopher Wren constructed 'a globe which so accurately represents the Moon that on it are visible all the Moon's inequalities, heights, depths, seas, rivers, islands, continents, etc., exactly as Mr. Wren saw all these things with the telescope during one whole lunation' – a far easier task to undertake for at least the visible side of the Moon than to construct its terrestrial equivalent. This globe was presented to the king, and the French visiting *savant* Samuel Sorbière remembered being shown it 'dans le cabinet du Roy' as a testament to both the theoretical ambitions and the practical skills of the English experimentalists. Presumably Wren had taken his hint from the Bohemian astronomer Johannes Hevelius' *Selenographia*, in which Hevelius had proposed a (non-relief) lunar globe, but unfortunately Wren's own globe, which was still in his family's possession in 1750, has since disappeared. But all is not lost – the globe still has a partial life through portraiture: it can be seen tucked into the bottom right-hand corner of a large portrait of Wren in his old age, now hanging on the east wall of the Sheldonian Theatre, Oxford, a building which Wren of course designed.[23]

11

Magnetism and its Survival

Magneticall Philosophy is not neglected here ... it is a reall designe amongst us, wanting only some assistance for execution, to erect a Magneticall, Mechanicall, and Optick Schoole, furnished with the best Instruments, and Adapted for the most usefull experiments in all those faculties.

— SETH WARD on the Oxford experimentalists (1654)

In 1654 the preacher, physician and metallurgist John Webster (1611–82) published an attack on Oxford and Cambridge universities. Webster portrayed them as dormitories for backward conservatives, either hostile to or unaware of major contemporary advances in learning. One area in particular was emphasised:

… what shall I say of that wonderful and most beneficial discovery of the Magnetical Philosophy, by our worthy, learned, and industrious Countryman Doctor Gilbert? what rare and unheard-of mysteries doth it disclose? what huge light, and advantage doth it bring to Natural Philosophy, and the Mathematics? What helps to Navigation, and almost all other arts, and trades?[1]

William Gilbert of Colchester (1544–1603), physician to Elizabeth I, was in the eyes of many seventeenth-century scholars at home and abroad the father of modern English science. An anti-Aristotelian polemicist and reformer of scientific method, he had published in 1600 his *De magnete, magneticisque corporibus, et de magno magnete tellure, physiologia nova* (A new physics on the magnet, magnetic bodies, and the great terrestrial magnet). Boasting in its preface 'a new style of philosophising', the *De magnete* attracted the attention

of Galileo and Kepler on the Continent, as well as some tepid comments
from Francis Bacon. 'Philosophy is for the few', Gilbert warned, and unlike
many of his mathematical and maritime collaborators, Gilbert wrote solely
in Latin. Yet his manner of expression was in explicit opposition to that
of the secretive alchemists. He talked his reader through each step of his
magnetic experiments, employing an imperative grammar – *fac tibi*, 'make
for yourself' – reminiscent of the recipe book rather than the lecture theatre.
He explained about the lodestone, iron, polarity, how to make pointers or
versoria, how to make floating pointers using wires pushed through corks,
how to 'arm' magnets with iron caps, the use of the 'little earth' or *terrella*, a
spherical magnet, the properties of deformed or fragmented magnets, how
to stroke needles, what happens when magnets are heated, what magnetic
'declination' (variation) is, and how to measure it (see Figure 7). Although
few readers could have possessed the money, time, or dexterity to replicate
Gilbert's experiments, Gilbert employed grammar that treated them as if they
did. In this, he stood alongside his more publicised contemporary Francis
Bacon.

Gilbert was offering not just an experimental programme but a whole
new physics (*physiologia*), flowing from and unifying his researches, a physics
that was Copernican in its larger orientation. Just like the magnet, Gilbert
proposed, 'the earth has a fixed verticity, and necessarily revolves with an
innate whirling motion'. Magnets are a privileged type of object, because they
share in the very essence of the Earth itself. The poles, the equator, latitudes,
and longitudes were no longer simply convenient abstractions projected
from the heavens onto the Earth, but physically meaningful points, lines, and
curves. The giant magnet of the Earth spun round, once every day, hence the
apparent retrograde motion of the heavens in the same period. Gilbert had
supplied Copernicanism with a physical reason for diurnal rotation, and in
turn Kepler was to adapt Gilbert's extension of this power of 'verticity' to all
celestial bodies in order to explain how the Sun managed to sweep around
its attendant planetary satellites. This Gilbertian-Keplerian explanation
was adopted in the great cosmological epic of the early Restoration, John
Milton's *Paradise Lost* (1667), in a moment where Milton's largely conservative
cosmology teetered on the brink of heliocentrism. Milton is describing the
planets and the Sun:

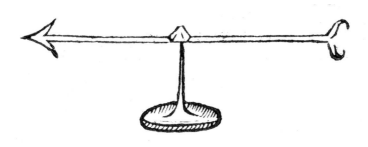

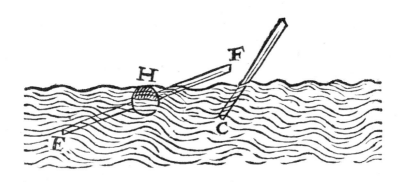

Figure 7. William Gilbert, *De magnete* (London, 1600), pp. 49, 57: a *versorium* and a floating pointer. Courtesy of the Warden and Fellows of New College, Oxford.

... they as they move
Their Starry dance in numbers that compute
Days, months, & years, towards his all-cheering Lamp
Turn swift their various motions, or are turned
By his Magnetic beam, that gently warms
The Universe, and to each inward part
With gentle penetration, though unseen,
Shoots invisible virtue even to the deep ...

Gilbert was not explicitly a full Copernican. He praised Copernicus as the 'restorer of astronomy', identified the Sun the 'chief inciter of action in nature', and set most of the heavenly bodies in motion around it. Yet he carefully restricted himself to discussion of the Earth's rotation alone, and this compromise position, in which the Earth revolves, but may not trace a curve in space, became the dominant position among cautiously progressive English philosophers for the two generations following Gilbert's publication. Gilbert's main idiosyncrasy, however, lay in his advocacy of the ancient thesis of the pre-Socratic philosopher Thales of Miletus that magnets possess souls. Gilbert started from the Aristotelian position that all bodies are composed of form and matter. He then proposed that magnetism flowed from the *forma* (as opposed to the *materia*) of things. Now the form of a human, as all agreed, was the soul, and Gilbert simply applied this to the whole Earth, which therefore moves 'with a certain high intelligence', possessing a *magnetica astrea mens*, a 'starry, magnetic mind'. Strictly speaking, therefore, the Earth is a living being, even one that possesses reason. This is true for all self-moving celestial bodies.[2]

These conclusions were controversial long before Webster accused the universities of neglecting Gilbert's work. The medic Mark Ridley and the cleric William Barlow, for instance, both styling themselves Gilbert's heirs, had clashed in the 1610s over the authenticity of Gilbert's sixth book, the medic championing 'full' Gilbertianism, and the cleric dismissing the moving, animistic Earth as heretical. Gilbertian magnetism soon made it into the lecture hall and the university textbook tradition with Nathanael Carpenter's *Geographie Delineated* (1625, 1635), although Carpenter dodged the Copernican application, and deflected the problem of the magnetic world-soul by turning it into a figure of speech: 'so that *by an apt Trope* it hath been called of many, the Magnetical soul of the Earth.'[3]

So, unsurprisingly, when they received Webster's polemic, the universities were stung, as they rightly felt that Webster's criticisms were exaggerated. The authors of the reply, *Vindiciæ Academiarum* (1654), were John Wilkins and Seth Ward, respectively the Warden of Wadham and the Savilian Professor of Astronomy, and both future architects of the Royal Society. As they countered, 'there is scarce any Hypothesis, which hath been formerly or lately entertained by Judicious men ... but hath here its strenuous Assertors, as the Atomical and Magnetical in Philosophy, the Copernican in Astronomy &c.' It is important to note here the division by the 1650s of modern 'philosophy' into two wings: one working on the 'Atomical' hypothesis, the other on the 'Magnetical', and both had indeed made important inroads into English education by this point. We have encountered the influence of 'Atomical' physics in either its Cartesian or Gassendist forms in discussions of Creation. Yet the significance of ongoing experimentation in and theorising about Gilbertian magnetism is less often recognised. One reason for this is that Newtonian universal gravity came to replace magnetism as the force understood to control the motions of all bodies. Gilbert's planetary magnetism, moreover, cast its envelope to a fixed radius, whereas Newton's gravity knew no bounds. But the lasting importance of Gilbertian magnetism lay rather in the experimental investigation of a force that was immaterial and which could act at a distance.

When Wilkins said that Oxonians studied the 'Atomical' and the 'Magnetical' hypotheses, he was gesturing towards the distinction between the Cartesian or Gassendist hypotheses of infinitesimal corpuscles of matter in constant contact or occasional impact, and the English investigation of an intangible planetary force that could be exploited to allow mariners to sail on course through storms and darkness. When Isaac Newton published in the *Principia Mathematica* (1687) a mathematical description of matter's behaviour, he notoriously forbore to explain *how* a tiny particle billions of miles away could exert a quantifiable influence upon the whole mass of the Earth – action at a distance was not mechanically explained. As we earlier saw, Newton privately considered alchemical models of micro-matter to account for this action, but for most of his followers, lack of discussion of ultimate causes was literally a saving grace – it left space for Providence, and a God who does more than merely turn on the universal machine. In the construction of Newtonianism, the older magnetical philosophy itself had acted, at a distance. It was this studied failure to provide a full physical explanation of gravity that so enraged most of Newton's continental readers.[4]

Although some late Paracelsian-influenced theorists would continue to promote animistic theories of the earth, almost all English philosophers and naturalists after Gilbert quietly retired talk of world-souls. Nevertheless Gilbert's methodology of direct experimentation resting on the notion of forces acting at a distance proved a crucial component within English speculation, serving in the eyes of some to distinguish it from the more dangerously exclusive materialism associated with the continental corpuscular philosophies. Christopher Wren, for instance, in his inaugural lecture as Gresham Professor of Astronomy in 1657, when he was merely 25 years old, praised Gilbert as 'the Father of the new Philosophy; Cartesius being but a Builder upon his Experiments'. Somewhat surprisingly for conventional historical accounts of this period, Wren altogether omitted mention of Francis Bacon.[5]

In the early decades of the Royal Society, magnetic experiments were popular, and magnetism was treated as an especial area of expertise of Boyle, Hooke, and the astronomer William Ball (c. 1631–90). The Society had its own *terrella* and dipping-needles for demonstrations, and when the veteran member Theodore Haak presented his portrait to the Society, he had himself painted pointing to his own magnet. The Halifax medic and microscopist Henry Power (1626–68) sent in an early report suggesting that magnetic fields propagate through objects 'as light through a burning-glass', rather than emanate from them. In 1664 Boyle proposed magnetic experiments at the bottom and then the top of St Paul's steeple, for 'determining the difficulties about the magnetical virtue of the earth, especially in reference to gravity', but these were cancelled on the grounds that the iron in the fabric was predicted to interfere.

In 1666 Hooke was again asked to investigate 'whether gravitation be something magnetical'; Hooke had earlier enquired whether, if the connection between gravity and magnetism were genuine, gravity too therefore increased at the poles. Other types of variation were discussed: Hooke thought magnets might be weaker in winter, and possibly affected by thick or thin air. A supposedly four-poled *terrella* was displayed by Ball in 1664, and it was suggested that this might in reality be two magnets compacted into one. This four-poled *terrella* was to have a surprising theoretical afterlife, as we shall see. In 1670 Oldenburg published a translation of a letter on secular variation from Adrian Auzout, a French astronomer in Rome, and orders were given to produce revised meridian tables for England to check whether the supposed eastward drift of declination had indeed changed direction, as Auzout had conjectured. In 1674 Hooke devised the now familiar experiment of drawing iron filings across paper or parchment by moving a magnet underneath. The filings formed into a set of concentric ovaloids, magnetic field lines visible for the first time. Soon afterwards Hooke announced his theory that the magnetic pole itself wandered around geographical north at a distance of 10°, with a period of 370 years. In 1683 the chemist Thomas Henshaw (1618–1700) presented a *versorium*-and-bar experiment that plausibly 'confirm[ed] the opinion of Dr. Gilbert, that the whole globe of the earth is a great magnet; and of Mons. Des Cartes, that the magnetical effluvia of the earth are carried in certain lines from one pole of the magnetism to the other.' William Petty speculated on the material nature of atoms in his lecture on duplicate proportion of 1674, supposing that each atom was 'like the Earths Globe or Magnet', possessing 'such Motions as *Copernicus* attributes to the Earth, or more'. Once again, biblical texts were applied, and Petty gendered his atoms into male and female, interpreting the text of Genesis 'Male and female He created them' as extending down to even 'the smallest parts of the *first Matter*'. Magnetic research had some unexpected offshoots too. In 1669 Hooke introduced a magnet into the design of his pocket-watch as a motion regulator, and it was eloquently observed in the Society's minutes that if the magnetically regulated watch were successful, magnetism 'would then furnish the navigator with the longitude, as well as it hath hitherto served him with the latitude'. Such horological success proved elusive.[6]

We could easily expand this motley list of anecdotes, but the most important subset of magnetic speculations was that concerned with the ongoing investigation of the relation of magnetism to gravity. Thirteen years before Newton published his *Principia*, Hooke proposed three famous 'suppositions' for a new 'System of the World': that all celestial bodies 'have an attraction or gravitating power towards their own Centres'; that all bodies will move in straight lines unless deflected; and that a body's attraction varies with distance. Hooke later asserted that attraction and distance were related as an inverse square. But Hooke, as was so often his habit, presented his three initial suppositions as a passing comment on the last two pages of his 1674 *Attempt to Prove the Motion of the Earth*, a mere 'hint' towards the system that he would pursue properly in due course. The notorious tangle that has ensued between historians over the differing claims to priority for the inverse square law of Hooke, Wren, Halley, and Newton need not concern us here. Nevertheless, at the date of Hooke's three suppositions, Newton's cosmology was still substantially Cartesian, assuming a *plenum* of vortices; whereas

Hooke's new 'System' worked on the notion of attractive forces working across potentially empty space. Furthermore, in Cartesian systems gravity is modelled by matter being *pushed* towards a given centre by matter further from that centre, whereas Hooke's gravitic centre *draws* matter towards it. In other words, it was Hooke's debt to magnetism that enabled him to frame his initial 'System' as he did, a debt obvious in his phrase that bodies attract 'within the sphere of their own activity'. It is unlikely that Hooke simply equated gravity with magnetism, however, as Wilkins had earlier explicitly treated the two forces as analogous but not identical. But the immediate genealogy, rooted in magnetism, of Hooke's 'System' is clear.[7]

As in cartography, the greatest practical work on terrestrial magnetism was carried out by Edmond Halley. Halley had picked up an interest in astronomy and magnetism while still a schoolboy at St Paul's School. Abandoning Oxford before he had taken his degree, Halley then voyaged to St Helena to observe the transit of Mercury predicted for late 1677. Despite troubles and delays arising from international wars, weather, and on one occasion mutiny, Halley put to sea again at various points throughout his life to realise his plan to chart global magnetic declination. We have encountered the resulting charts of 'Halleyan' lines, and these also witness to the enduring presence in the English scientific programme of Gilbert's terrestrial force, a force which also lay behind many of Halley's scientific papers of the 1680s and 1690s.

In the mid-1680s, when Hooke recommenced his earthquake lectures, he concentrated on finding evidence for his hypothesis of wandering poles, and here Hooke's thoughts kindled Halley's interest too. In the Gilbertian world, geographical and magnetic poles were identical; the declination of the magnetic needle was caused by the influence of nearby land masses twisting the needle aside. But in 1634–5 the Gresham Professor of Astronomy Henry Gellibrand (1597–1637) had discovered secular magnetic variation, or 'variation of variation'; from the year of Hooke's birth, therefore, it was known that magnetic variation changed over time as well as space, and so the two types of poles had now become distinct phenomena. Hooke was suggesting, with only the scantest of evidential support, that *both* magnetic *and* geographic poles wandered. Such claims led Halley to propound a system of almost science-fictional ingenuity.

In 1680 the FRS and master of the mathematical school at Christ's Hospital Peter Perkins (d. 1680) had suggested in a paper before the Royal Society that there were 'six meridians, in which the needle did not vary, three in the north, and three in the south'. By 1683 Halley had posited instead four magnetic poles in the earth, irregularly spaced and with asynchronic variation. This he deduced from tables of magnetic variation, some perhaps obtained from Perkins' papers, as Flamsteed darkly suspected. Halley at first claimed that it would take at least a century to work out an adequate theory to explain such an effect on the global scale.[8]

As it turned out, Halley himself proposed a solution within the decade, announcing his theory of the hollow earth in the *Philosophical Transactions* in 1692. Here Halley accounted for multiple magnetic poles by hypothesising an independently rotating *terrella*, possibly more than one, within the planet. His two or more dipoles could therefore be fully uncoupled from one another, as each dipole emanated from independent planetoids nested inside one another. To the objection that no such thing had been encountered in nature before, Halley proposed that Saturn and its rings were an analogous construction, and we have seen that Burnet too appealed to the form of Saturn to support his own theories.

Halley was proud enough of his theory of the nested earths to be painted holding a sketch of it (see Figure 8). What one cannot tell from the sketch of the nested earths, though, is that in his paper itself, Halley proposed that an unknown race of men lived on the surface of this interior earth, lit by strange aerial lights or by luminous materials attached to the great concave arches that replaced the terrestrial sky. Athanasius Kircher had, in his uncritical fashion, retailed various anecdotes in his eagerly awaited and fabulously expensive *Mundus Subterraneus* (1665, 1678) of strange green children crawling out of caves, as had happened in England, in Woolpit, Suffolk in the reign of King Stephen. This very story had been incorporated into the first work of English science fiction, Bishop Francis Godwin's *The Man in the Moone* (1638), a work dependent on Gilbert's *De magnete* for its own scientific underpinnings, and which in turn influenced both John Wilkins and Robert Hooke. Godwin's aliens lived on the moon, exiling their reject children to the earth. Halley proposed the idea of indigenous internal aliens by invoking the philosophical principle of 'plenitude of being', the idea that all realms of existence are populated by suitable forms of life. To the objection that a dark, uninhabited world turning within our own was an insult to the divine economy, Halley replied that all the planets 'are with reason supposed Habitable', and that this must extend to the internal as well as to the external planets in order for full plenitude to be upheld. That the other planets were inhabited too was a note heard with increasing frequency

Figure 8. Portrait of Edmond Halley holding a diagram of his system of concentric Earths (1737, original 1270 × 1016 mm). Courtesy of the Royal Society of London.

in the latter half of the century. As John Ray had preached to the students in the chapel of Trinity College, Cambridge in around 1658,

> Every fixt Star in the now received Hypothesis [i.e. Copernicanism] is a Sun or Sunlike body, and in like manner encircled with a Chorus of Planets moving about it … Each of these Planets is in all likelihood furnished with as great variety of corporeal Creatures animate and inanimate as the Earth is, and all as different in Nature as they are in Place from each other.[9]

Halley therefore yoked the growing acceptance among natural philosophers of extraterrestrial life to his new model of terrestrial magnetism. Although for once Halley was wrong, his paper is a reminder of the metaphysical and providential problems that such experimental research both encountered and embraced.

12

Conflagration and Millennium

… at the glorious appearance of our Saviour, the Conflagration will begin
at the City of *Rome* and the *Roman* Territory.

— THOMAS BURNET (1689)

One topic Stillingfleet's *Origines Sacræ* avoided was the end of the world.
Given that Stillingfleet's business was the origin of the world, this omission is
generically defensible. We cannot ignore this final topic, however, as despite
the reticence of many divines in this matter, discussions of the Conflagration
and possible Millennium embracing theological, physical, and chronological
concerns remained rife until the end of the century, and models not just of
Creation and Flood, but of Conflagration and Millennium too, were proposed
by almost all the major World Makers. Indeed, it is no exaggeration to say
that millenarian belief was the norm and not the exception among the early
Fellows of the Royal Society, despite the quiescence of many divines of
Stillingfleet's stamp.

Theories of the Conflagration were controversial because of a slightly
different set of reasons than those informing the reception of allied proposals
on Creation and Flood. Belief in the Conflagration itself was universal and
unproblematic: 'a Subject own'd by all, and out of dispute', as Thomas Burnet
assumed. But common too was belief in a two-stage millennial or 'chiliastic'
(from the Greek *chilias*, 'one thousand') model, whereby the arrival of King
Jesus shall precede the Final Judgment by one thousand years, between which
dates a purified Earth shall be given over to Christ and his saints. There were
thus two destructions, one preceding and one following the Millennium, and
likewise two resurrections, the first only of the just, the second of all. Despite

its scant scriptural base, Millenarianism was a common belief in the patristic age. Revived in the early Reformation, it was swiftly adapted for radical political application: prophecy of this nature was central, for instance, to Paracelsian evangelism.[1] In the mid-seventeenth century, chiliastic ideas in some quarters became associated with philosemitic hopes, on the hypothesis that the recall of the Jews would herald their conversion and hence the Second Coming. However, in order to understand the complex inheritance of later seventeenth-century English discussions of Conflagration and/or Millennium, we need to turn first to two earlier Caroline traditions.

The first tradition is exemplified by George Hakewill's *Apologie*, a work that also addressed the problem of the Millennium. On the physical side, Hakewill insisted against the position of theorists, including Blancanus and Godfrey Goodman (1583–1656), that the end of the world must occur by physical catastrophe, and not as the final result of a slow, incremental process. This catastrophe, as both pagan and Christian philosophers had always taught, will be by fire. The difference is that some pagan philosophies, notably Stoic, taught not 'one onely Conflagration of the World, but diverse *periodicall* Conflagrations and Deluges at certaine times and by turnes succeeding each other', a view that can easily be confounded with Aristotle's notion of perpetual geographical vicissitude. Hakewill rejected this fantasy, as well as many later Christian hypotheses, opting for the brusque solution that at the last day all things bar heaven, hell, angels, and men, will be annihilated back to the nothingness whence they were first summoned. Theologically, Hakewill did not reject the Millennium as such, but he preferred to think of it as a period of final ecclesiastical peace and prosperity, and not a material renovation of the Earth's fabric. His was a moral, not a physical Millennium. When the actual Conflagration came, it would come but once. Hakewill was unwilling, too, to discuss the dating of his one-off Conflagration.[2]

Hakewill was writing in the midst of the Thirty Years War, and his doctrinal minimalism was one strategy for forestalling politically sensitive speculation on the Millennium, currently rife on the Continent. Such speculation would be transferred to England in the decades of the civil war and interregnum. This time, physical Millenarianism was aided by another English publication, *Clavis Apocalyptica* (Apocalyptic Key; 1627) by the Cambridge academician Joseph Mede (1586–1638), a work that would exert a huge influence in England after Mede's death. Mede initially hoped that he would be able to follow his English predecessor on the topic, Thomas Brightman (1562–1607), who had proclaimed the Millennium already in progress, synchronising its inception with the pre-Reformation labours of John Wyclif. However, Mede eventually decided that the Millennium had not yet commenced, and identified the Fourth Vial of Revelation 16:8 with the Protestant hero, King Gustavus Adolphus of Sweden: 'there is now at length come from the *North* Gods revenger of wrongs, to succour afflicted and distressed Germany; a godly King, happy, and which way soever he cometh, a conquerour, whose prosperous progresse is wonderfull speedy. Is not this he, whom the Lord of Hosts hath destinated to execute the worke of this Phyall?' The Long Parliament gave order for Mede's book to be published in English translation, which appeared in 1643, and thereafter Mede's Millenarianism was pushed to ever more radical application. Long after the Restoration, in more politically quiescent days, Mede's work was still being cited appreciatively.

Hakewill and Mede may stand as two different exemplars of the problems associated with millenary speculation: Hakewill rejected a physical Millennium, while Mede's support for it was at first enlisted for causes more politically radical than the gentle academic could have espoused. Mede would also influence subsequent commentary through the publications of his student Henry More, who was particularly exercised in *An Explanation of the Grand Mystery of Godliness* (1660) to defend his old teacher against the novel continental 'preterist' exegesis of Hugo Grotius. Preterism worked on the presumption that the events of Revelation referred to identifiable events in the *earliest* decades of Christian history, and therefore possessed no predictive power in the modern world. This was to take the wind out of the sails of prophecy, by granting its truth, but then relegating it to the closed cabinet of the past – such prophecies had already come to pass. More, in opposition, promoted Mede's method of 'synchronisms', the detection of purely internal symbolic parallelisms, over Grotius' externalist chronology, which understandably struggled with the task of pegging Revelation to known first-century ad events. Indeed, More championed his old master Mede's beliefs to the extent that in *The Grand Mystery* he was also content to argue, as Mede had claimed against colonial evangelists in the 1620s and 1630s, that the Native Americans were not the sons of Adam, but of Satan, a rather peculiar argument to re-encounter in 1660. More would continue to defend Mede's exegesis right into the 1680s. Grotius' preterism, however, had been adopted as early as 1653 by Henry Hammond in his influential *Paraphrases* on the New Testament. More and Hammond therefore kept alive in the Restoration two very different academic, exegetical traditions of Caroline or continental origin for reading biblical prophecy. More, for instance, exerted influence over writers such as Glanvill and Burnet; and John Ray engaged openly with Hammond's preterism in his physico-theological publications of the 1690s.[3]

Chiliasts assumed that the end of the world was nigh, indeed usually datable, and such chronological analysts were therefore assuming for themselves a prophetic role. In England in the aftermath of the civil war, such 'enthusiasm' posed a social as well as an intellectual threat. On several occasions, even spreading into the Restoration, socially quiescent academic works on the Millennium were cited by radical activists to justify not only evangelism but actual violence. Most notoriously, in early January 1661, the cooper Thomas Venner led fifty Fifth Monarchists in 'Venner's Rising', an attempt to replace King Charles II with King Jesus, whom they were expecting to join them in person. Their manifesto, *A Door of Hope*, liberally cited Joseph Mede, and announced the Fifth Monarchists' intention, 'having led our Captivity Captive', to prosecute their Holy War across the Continent to Rome itself. After some fighting in the capital, Venner and many of his men were taken, tried, and hanged, drawn, and quartered. Venner died unrepentant, telling the crowd as the rope was around his neck that the Fourth Monarchy was now, and that it was everyone's duty to usher in the Fifth. Heavily wounded, he was delighted that he had nevertheless made it alive to the scaffold, so that he might die a martyr.

In the next year, also the year of the Royal Society's official incorporation, the scientific apologist Joseph Glanvill published his *Lux Orientalis*, ostensibly a defence of the pre-existence of the soul. He dedicated it to John Ray's patron and collaborator, the aristocratic naturalist and FRS Francis Willughby. Glanvill concluded his tract with a terse and vigorous account of both Conflagration and Millennium, explicitly fusing together the theories of Descartes and Henry More. Glanvill offered two sequential models. The first runs thus. Already, the previous damned are confined within this hollow, hot globe: the deeper, the wickeder. There, they lie chained 'by a kind of fatal *Magnetisme*'. At the time of Conflagration, the fire inside the Earth will rage its hottest, igniting the planetary surface. The righteous, struggling to fly off the surface, will find themselves mired by the impurities of their bodies, until Christ appears, hovering in the skies. The sight of the Redeemer will so enthuse the righteous with joy that their bodies will melt into flame, and their souls will be freed to rise up and travel on to heaven. Meantime, the not-so-just on the Earth's surface will at length be annihilated or at least left in quiescence. The Earth will then burn itself back into a comet, and wander out of the solar system until it joins another vortex. Glanvill's second stage reprises his first, but with the initial temperature reduced a little, so that the Earth does not leave its new orbit. In this second phase, the sooty vapours rising from the hot globe will descend again to revivify the Earth, which will grow into a second paradise, with new, purer bodies for the sleeping souls to rejoin. At the end of this phase, a final destruction will occur, probably by the death of the Sun. Occurring sequentially, Glanvill's two phases meet exactly the needs of a chiliastic model: a conflagration, a renewal, and a final destruction.[4]

Glanvill was perhaps not fully aware of how maverick his work looked in the immediate Restoration, and his ideas were not received with much sympathy – indeed, at this point he was probably more of a minor embarrassment than a major asset to the experimentalists, whom he had courted with *The Vanity of Dogmatizing* the previous year. Nevertheless, Glanvill's basic model of Conflagration and Millennium was later taken up in a more auspicious climate by Thomas Burnet in his two eagerly anticipated final books of the *Sacred Theory* (Latin 1689, English version 1690). Burnet appears to have been concerned about gaining a licence for the latter half of his complete *Theory*, as he recounted to correspondents in 1688 that it was being held up at Lambeth Palace awaiting the censor's approval, until in late September he could report that 'My Booke has, at length, passt ye pikes at Lambeth, and is now in ye press.' Given Burnet's apocalyptic subject, it is important to remember that William of Orange was to land at Torbay the following 5 November, and by the time the public were reading Burnet's new instalment, the Stuart dynasty, against which Burnet had already taken a prominent stand, had collapsed.

The reticence of the ecclesiastical censor is understandable. Indeed, Burnet's initial Latin text was far more outspoken than his subsequent English version, expressing more open dissatisfaction with the current political regime, and looking forward with greater urgency to a Millennium close at hand; these issues are rather more vague in the English text. The initial Latin version also appears to have been written hurriedly, and in its uncharacteristic grammatical slips one can perhaps sense Burnet's growing anxiety at the Papist threat. 1685 marked both the ascendency of the Catholic James II and the Revocation of the Edict of Nantes in France; and by 1687 Burnet himself had been drawn into direct conflict with the Crown over James's attempted intrusion of a Catholic as a Pensioner of Burnet's Charterhouse. Most modern commentators have followed Burnet's 1680s critics, who necessarily treated

Burnet as a World and a Flood Maker. However the publication of his complete system coincided exactly with the Glorious Revolution itself, and it was this second phase that Burnet worked over in his manuscript notes to his own copy. We should therefore think of Burnet not just as a World Maker but as a chiliast and a World Destroyer, and after 1689 this latter role was for a time much the more prominent of the two.[5]

Burnet brought to the Cartesian Conflagration his customary attention to detail and quantification. He again found the material necessary for a total combustion of the Earth close at hand, and dismissed the need for any large-scale miracles. At the time of the Conflagration, Burnet argued, volcanoes worldwide will be ready to burst in concert, diminishing and consuming the seas, throwing down and melting the mountains, and impregnating the air with sulphurous fumes and flaming debris. Earthquakes too will break out, and the whole surface of the earth will burn; 'A World is sooner destroyed than made.' In order to substantiate his claims about volcanoes quantitatively, Burnet adduced the recent account of Etna by Giovani Alfonso Borelli (1608–79), a founder member of the Accademia del Cimeto, the short-lived Italian analogue of the Royal Society. Borelli's account was itself commissioned by the Royal Society, on the occasion of the 1669 eruption of Etna, which partially overran the city of Catania. (Catania was to be completely overrun by lava in 1693.) Borelli's luridly illustrated *Historia, et meteorologia incendii Aetnaei anni 1669* (The history and meteorology of the eruption of Etna in 1669; 1670) provided Burnet with the statistic that the eruption threw out 93,838,750 'cubical paces' of matter, of which about two-thirds emerged as flowing lava. This had formed a rolling stream sometimes six to seven miles broad, sometimes ten to fifteen fathoms deep. Burnet asked his readers to imagine the quantities of material that would be thrown up if all the volcanoes in the world erupted simultaneously, and this provided the mechanism for his Conflagration.

With relish, Burnet recognised too that as Italy is the seat of Antichrist, so is it the most volcanic nation; God has intended all along to ignite the Conflagration from within the Papacy itself.

> *Italy* ... by all accounts, ancient and modern, is a store-house of fire; as if it were condemn'd to that fate by God and Nature, and to be an Incendiary, as it were, to the rest of the World. And seeing *Mystical Babylon*, the Seat of Antichrist, is the same Rome, and its Territory ... you see both out lines meet in this point; And there is a fairness, on both hands, to conclude, that, at the glorious appearance

of our Saviour, the Conflagration will begin at the City of *Rome* and the *Roman* Territory.

This general Conflagration will however be a mechanism for the purification rather than the utter annihilation of the world. Polar tilt will be cancelled, the Earth will resume its antediluvian orientation to the Sun, and 'when the external region of the Earth is melted into a fluor, like molten glass, or running metal; it will, according to the nature of other Fluids, fill all vacuities and depressions, and fall into a regular surface, at an equal distance, every where, from its center.' The Earth, in other words, will be restored to the initial state that Burnet had established in his second book. This Conflagration will be presided over by Christ appearing in the skies on his throne, flanked by thousands of angels, who will manipulate nature to ensure exactly the right degree of destruction. The Millennium itself will follow, where the blessed will live with Christ and his angels in a government 'neither Humane, nor Angelical, but peculiarly Theocratical'. There will therefore be a two-fold Resurrection: first of the just at the beginning of the Millennium; and then of everyone else at its end for the Last Judgment. The Millennium itself will be spent largely in devotion and contemplation, but highlights will include getting to learn the true astronomy from angelic teachers, communicating with the inhabitants of the other planets, and even perhaps establishing contact with the great alien lord who sits in the middle of the Sun. At the end of all, the Earth itself will be transformed into a Sun, depart its orbit, 'and, with a lofty flight, take its seat amongst the Stars'.

Burnet's final two books possess shocking charge, because whereas in his first two books he dealt with a past that was completed and closed, Burnet assumed in his closing books that he and his readers will experience personally the events he described – in one resurrection or the other. Nevertheless, many of the problems we detected in Burnet's first two books persist in his apocalyptic speculations. Once again, Burnet could not find all the proof texts he needed in the Bible itself, so he had recourse to piling up non-biblical witnesses to support his case. Secondly, and more importantly, Burnet used the sheer magnitude of his envisaged destruction to affirm that God's thoughts are not like our thoughts. But all Burnet really means is that God does things on a very large scale, and his whole strategy relies on the analogy, rather than the discontinuity, between human and divine processes. Burnet's conviction that providence best expresses itself through natural processes remains strong, and, accordingly, God is not allowed much of a role in the physics of his final books at all. Burnet instead insisted that what can be done by lesser powers (angels) should not be undertaken by omnipotence: 'And as to the power of Angels, I am of opinion that it is very great as to the Changes and Modifications of Natural Bodies; that they can dissolve a Marble as easily as we can crumble Earth and Moulds, or fix any liquor, in a moment, into a substance as hard as Crystal' (3.8). But these Angels of Wrath no longer strike us as supernatural beings effecting incomprehensible miracles, merely as superior versions of human chemists.

In conclusion, it may appear difficult to decide whether Burnet is more a natural philosopher doing theology, or a theologian doing natural philosophy; but of course the opposition is a false one. In Burnet's Conflagration, volcanoes naturally erupt, coaxed on by angelic chemists; and in his Millennium, the blessed live under Christ, learning about cometary theory and the other occupants of the universe. It has been influentially argued that the inspiration for the Baconian movement was millenarian, looking to Bacon's utopian *New Atlantis* (1627) as the blueprint for a community of pious experimentalists. In Burnet's final books, that vision is achieved as part of prophetic history: the blessed will indeed form scientific communities.[6]

Burnet's chiliastic books received a good deal of attention, especially because of their author's new-found political prominence. Perhaps because of the nature of his subject and the nature of the times, however, Burnet's last two books were not attacked with the vigour that his earlier efforts had provoked. Chiliasm was still a widely held doctrine in mainstream circles, and the events of 1688 encouraged its reaffirmation. The Cambridge theologian Drue Cressener (1642–1718), for instance, published in 1689 his millenarian tract *The Judgments of God upon the Roman-Catholick Church*, in which he acknowledged that he had read Burnet's second part in manuscript while composing his own work. Cressener too had been taught by Henry More at Christ's College, Cambridge. Robert Boyle in his *Disquisition about the Final Causes of Natural Things*, composed earlier but published in the revolutionary year of 1688, likewise adduced Burnet's texts from St Peter on 'the Renovation and Refinement of the Present World by the last Fire, that will not only Dissolve, but, if I may so speak, Transfigure it'.[7]

The most interesting of the minor chiliastic treatises from 1688–9, however, is a short manuscript tract 'Concerning the Millennium' written by the aristocratic gardener and FRS John Evelyn. The tract was never published, but Evelyn's own manuscript is headed 'Copy of what I sent to the Countesse of Clarendon 1688', that is to Flower, Countess of Clarendon, the second wife of Henry Hyde, the second earl. That Evelyn addressed his own chiliastic meditations in a letter to a female aristocrat and the wife of one of his most powerful patrons shows how open such speculations had become. Evelyn carefully distinguished his Millennium 'in that Renewed Heaven & Earth to come' from that of the millennialists of old and the recent Fifth Monarchists, who sought the Millennium on this Earth; and Evelyn like Burnet was also unprepared to put a date on the Conflagration. Again following Burnet, Evelyn was concerned to establish as literal a model as possible for the actual events of the Conflagration and beyond. Therefore when the saints are taken up into the clouds so that the wicked can burn on the Earth, this was not for Evelyn a metaphor for going to heaven, but a literal action to protect the saints from singeing before their reign on the new Earth with Christ in his human nature could commence. Hence in the Conflagration we are to look for a physical alteration of the Earth 'as far as the Atmosphere or first Region at least about it'. After the renovation, Christians will enjoy 'a Thousand yeares Tranquility, in power, purity & eternal splendor before the Day of Judgement', a doctrine taught not just by the early Fathers but by the Moderns Cunæus, Piscator, Alsted, and Mede. The new Earth itself will be smooth all over its surface after the Conflagration, 'whence haply that of the most ingenious Author of the New Theorie' – Evelyn too, we must infer, had seen a pre-publication manuscript of Burnet. The seat of Christ's government will be at Jerusalem, again as in Burnet, and its architecture will be based on the visionary temples of Ezekiel. The Jews will be converted by the reappearance of Christ himself. Animals too will join the congregated elect, no longer subject to toil and labour.[8]

In the 1690s, the great new interest of the naturalists in London, Oxford, and elsewhere was, as we have seen, fossils. Despite the interest many of the naturalists showed towards Burnet's first two books, fossils and the Millennium had nothing intrinsically in common, and hence we find that Burnet has nothing to say about the former, and John Woodward (at least in his 1695 *Essay*) nothing to say about the latter. The only two major figures determined to match Burnet in supplying a complete theory from Creation to Conflagration and beyond, fossils included, were John Ray and William Whiston. As we may imagine, Whiston effected all his sacred catastrophes by comets: the ancient chaos was the atmosphere of a comet; a glancing blow from a comet first instituted diurnal rotation and converted the Earth's orbit into an ellipse; the near pass of comet caused the Flood, supplying the necessary waters from its tail; and so a comet, this time scoring a direct hit, will cause the Conflagration. In all probability, it will be the same comet that caused the Deluge. The Conflagration is again a purifying event, to fit the Earth 'proper to receive those Saints and Martyrs for its Inhabitants, who at the first Resurrection [are] to enter, and to live and reign a thousand years upon it, till the second Resurrection, the general Judgment, and the final consummation of all things'. A last cometary impact at the end of the Millennium will dismiss the Earth from its orbit, and it too will finally become a comet. Whiston, we can see, was entirely conventional in his conclusions: like so many other post-Revolution figures he endorsed the Millennium, the two Resurrections, even the final departure of the renewed Earth from our solar system. His idiosyncrasy is that he insisted on accomplishing all sacred catastrophes by comets; and once again this should be interpreted as a piece of Newtonian reductionism, effecting as many phenomena by as few agents as possible. As Charles Webster has commented, 'Whiston thus improved on Burnet and produced an explanation for the major parameters of universal history consistent with the economy of explanation so congenial to Newtonians.'[9]

The most significant of the chiliastic physicists, and yet the most neglected today, was John Ray. As we have seen, in the 1690s Ray embarked on a sustained publication spree in the area of physico-theology mainly resurrecting and refining old materials, but all in the service of providing an entire alternative world-system to that of Burnet. Ray is celebrated today as the greatest of the naturalists, concerned with the taxonomy of extant beings, but it was he, rather than Lister, or Plot, or Lhuyd, or Woodward, who took up the apocalyptic mantle, and his *Three Physico-Theological Treatises* (1693) addressed the Chaos, the Deluge, and the Dissolution respectively – the last treatise being the longest. Ray's work is distinguished by his clear sense of the rhetorical difficulties provided by Scripture, especially those flowing from the 'lofty and tumid Metaphors and excessive *Hyperbola's* and Aggravations' of the 'Oriental Rhetorick'. Although Ray does not acknowledge it, he is here indebted once again to the cautionary arguments of Robert Boyle, whose *Some Considerations touching the Style of the H. Scriptures* (1661 etc, one Latin and four English editions by 1693) was an important contribution by the most celebrated layman natural philosopher towards a properly historicised theory of scriptural exegesis.[10]

Ray supposed that there were four natural ways in which the world could end: by a second flood, by extinction of the Sun, by the expansion of the core fire, or by the eruption of all volcanoes at once. He rejected out of hand the fifth possibility of 'daily Consenescence' as having been exploded by George Hakewill long since. The interest of Ray's method is that he was prepared to endorse the physical possibility of a number of conflicting models. For Ray, an acceptable model is not the only physically possible solution, but the physically possible solution that is most adequately scriptural. Therefore, when addressing the possibility of a second deluge, Ray accepted at the physical level the Blancanus-Varenius thesis, whereby the globe started as a sphere of earth surrounded by a sphere of water, was then manipulated by God into the terraqueous globe, and will return at (great) length back to its original state. This would be so, Ray cautioned, were it not that we know by Scripture that God will impose conflagration by fire *before* this natural second deluge occurs. Concerning the extinction of the Sun by spots, a Cartesian suggestion of Henry More in his *Immortality of the Soul* (1659), Ray agreed that it was physically possible, but again not the required scriptural holocaust. On the explicitly Cartesian eruption of the central fire, Ray accepted that there may be a central ball of fire, but that it is at best a 'possible' not a 'probable' mechanism of conflagration. In an admonition rare among English readers of Descartes, Ray also reminded his own readers that Descartes had only claimed hypothetical status for his work, deferring at least rhetorically to Genesis. Finally, in response to the hypothesis of the desiccation and ignition of the globe, Ray rejected polar shift and denied that any amount of heating of the Earth could trigger earthquakes or dry out the seas.

Ray, in short, endorsed none of the conventional models for Conflagration, insisting merely that it will happen, by the natural means of fire, but wielded by God in a supernatural fashion. We *do* know that the process will be quick, but at an 'absolutely uncertain and indeterminable' date. Such destruction will extend to all matter, not just to Burnet's sublunary zone, even if the conflagration of the heavens will be effected by different physical means. Once again, we can see that the Deistic possibilities inherent in Burnet's method were provoking among opponents renewed recourse to miracle.

Ray's caution might lead us to suppose that he rejected the chiliasm of his contemporaries. This is not so. Discussing models of destruction versus purification, Ray unhesitatingly opted for the latter, not only respectfully signalling his opposition to Hakewill, but citing Burnet himself as a collector of testimonies in support of the Millennium. Ray does not however appear to have supported the double Resurrection. At the Conflagration, mankind will be distributed between heaven and hell, and then the Earth will be refitted for the Millennium. What, then, is this pristine, refitted globe for? Here Ray harmonised his chiliasm with one of his major philosophical preoccupations, namely the arrogance of anthropocentrism:

> We are too short-sighted to penetrate the Ends of God. There may be a new Race of rational Animals brought forth to act their parts upon this Stage, which may give the Creator as much Glory as Man ever did or could. And yet if there should be no material and visible rational Creature made to inhabit the Earth, there are spiritual and intellectual Beings, which may be as busie, and as much delighted in searching out, and contemplating the Works of God in this new Earth, and rendring him the Praise of his Wisdom and Power as Man could be.

Ray was a chiliast, then, but his Millennium was not for mankind. The purified Earth is not to be the home of the righteous, but a stage cleared for the next act in the divine drama, played by beings perhaps corporeal, perhaps incorporeal, accompanied by flora and fauna of potentially alien appearance, all quite unfathomable to us. Ray, who believed that aliens existed and that the Earth was only a very small corner of creation, had quietly turned chiliasm inside out. Chiliasm was traditionally a device for remembering and comforting the Elect, for promising them that victory on a restored, future Earth for which they so strove in an unregenerate, often hostile present. Ray's Millennium, conversely, could only commence at the very point at which humanity was finally dismissed from the cosmic drama.[11]

Belief in the Conflagration is an unavoidable consequence of a literal reading of certain biblical texts and is therefore unlikely to disappear as long as literalist believers survive. Millenarian speculation, although more controversial, will also persist, because literalist exegetes draw comfort from their predecessors, and Millenarianism is an undeniable component of the history of exegesis. Nevertheless, it is noticeable that mainstream apocalyptic thought declined in England after about 1700, and the contexts in which it survived were increasingly associated with religious and political separatism or radicalism, especially following the arrival of the millenarian Camisard exiles in London after 1706. It is noteworthy, for instance, that the first major physico-theology of the new century, Nehemiah Grew's *Cosmologia Sacra* (1701), quietly omitted any formal discussion of the last days, moving straight from this life, through the brief door of Judgment, to the next. A rough bibliography of apocalyptic writings has suggested that the number of apocalyptic writings appearing between 1701 and 1750 was less than a tenth of those appearing between 1601 and 1650, and less than an eighth of publications 1650–1700.[12]

Decline is not fall. Republication statistics of the World Makers alone suggest an ongoing interest in their entire packages. One good indicator of growing decline in the new production of such discussions, however, is provided by the Boyle Lectures, in which space given over to apocalyptic discussions diminished rapidly over the first two decades of their institution. By William Derham's Boyle Lectures of 1712–13, published as *Physico-Theology*, speculation on the timing or mechanism of the Conflagration had been all but dropped. But this is not to say that Derham found physics and the Last Judgment absolutely incompatible discussions. His equally popular *Astro-Theology* (1715 etc.), for instance, assumed once again that comets were instruments of divine providence. Indeed, Derham suggested that comets performed not only as God's ministers of destruction and famine, but perhaps literally as the prison-ships of the damned, ferrying their occupants in never-ending ellipses from extremes of cold to extremes of heat. Yet for Derham these were passing considerations, and the close union between natural philosophy and prophecy was unravelling fast.

One peculiar exception deserves mention: the *Principia Mathematica Christianæ Philosophiæ* (1699) of John Craige (c. 1663–1731), in which Craige predicted the earliest possible date for the Apocalypse using the new mathematics of fluxions as applied to probability. Craige's eccentric project was certainly intelligible, and his hopes that the new sciences might assist theology are no different from those of Whiston. Indeed, Craige was a friend of Newton, Hooke, and Halley, a contributor to Wotton's *Reflections upon Ancient and Modern Learning* (1694), and a future FRS on account of his mathematical fame. Nevertheless Craige's *Principia* was greeted at the time largely with derision, not least because his argument rested on the disturbing premise that the credibility of testimony decays over time, and what was a rational belief on the basis of extant testimony last year may not be so this year. 'Probability generates faith but destroys knowledge', Craige dangerously maintained; 'certainty, on the other hand, generates knowledge and destroys faith'. When it is no longer rational to believe in the testimony for the gospel, extrapolated Craige, then shall Christ stage his Second Coming. This impious piety won Craige inclusion in Alexander Pope's *Dunciad* (1742), and that is all that non-specialists remember today of the Scots mathematician who tried to date the Apocalypse.

Be that my task (replies a gloomy Clerk,
Sworn foe to Myst'ry, yet divinely dark;
Whose pious hope aspires to see the day
When Moral Evidence shall quite decay).[13]

Indeed, poetry itself became the new, rather tame kennel of mainstream apocalyptic speculation. Once John Milton the man was safely dead and buried, his increasingly applauded epic *Paradise Lost* could be freed from its associations with the old republican regicide, and pushed towards the centre of the English literary canon. In the eighteenth century, the most prominent description of Creation and of the Christian cosmos was not, therefore, a scientific tract or even a biblical commentary, but a blank verse epic. Yet Milton had conspicuously failed to write at any length about the Conflagration or the Millennium, mentioning the subjects only twice in his epic, and with uncharacteristic brevity; Milton was certainly a millennialist, but it appears that he did not want to talk about it much. This opened a space for pious versification on the last rather than the first things, and it was filled by numerous poetasters, of which the most pertinent here is the obscure Samuel Catherall of Oriel College, 'Mean Follower of *Great Milton*', who published his *Essay on the Conflagration in blank verse* in Oxford in 1720 ('his tendency to versification was lamentably strong', remarked his college historian). Catherall's epyllion is explicitly an attempt to complete the Miltonic project up to the Dissolution, and his verse is a somewhat sycophantic cento of Miltonic quotation. What is striking from the point of view of our subject is the frontispiece of the book, which depicts neither Catherall nor Milton – but Thomas Burnet. As Catherall explained, 'The Renown'd Dr. *Burnet* having shewn such a masterly Genius in his Account of *the Conflagration*, I was tempted to extract many of his Notions.' Catherall's *Conflagration*, therefore, was to be Burnet in substance and Milton in style. His first book comprised a dialogue between Catherall and the angel Uriel; his second book was a dream vision of the actual Conflagration, so violent, indeed, that all creation – even Oxford – lay ruined by Christ in an hour. Catherall displayed minimal intellectual engagement with his subject, and when his angel is questioned about the Millennium itself, Uriel repeats what Milton's Raphael had originally told Adam about unnecessary curiosity in astronomy: 'Joy therefore thou / In what thou knows't, and seek to know no more!' The epic verse of John Milton, radical politician and theologian, and the epic prose of Thomas Burnet, maverick ecclesiastic and natural philosopher, have been reduced into the brief, conservative work of a forgotten Oxford don, artistically uninteresting, intellectually unexplorative. In the hey-day of English natural philosophy, major FRSs considered it part of their scientific business to discuss the physics of not only Creation and Flood, but also Conflagration and Millennium, seeing nothing problematic in applying scientific considerations to biblical events, past or future. By the end of the first quarter of the eighteenth century, this union was unravelling.[14]

Conclusion

… some may say, I have turned the World upside down for the sake of a
shell.

— ROBERT HOOKE (speaking in 1688)

Now we have surveyed the whole sweep of seventeenth-century speculation on
the biblical and physical history of the world from Creation to Conflagration,
we must conclude by offering some remarks on the wider significance and
context of such discussions. What was the significance of the creation of
scientific societies? What was the legacy of the naturalists? Was there any
one 'orthodox' school by the end of the century? Was there any connection
between scientific innovation and religious heterodoxy?

By the end of the seventeenth century, institutionalised science in
Britain was on a firm footing. The Royal Society may have been financially
precarious, but the institutional, collaborative, and documentary practices
that it had formalised were there to stay. Indeed, the models of discovery and
dissemination promoted by the many nascent learned societies across Europe
were already beginning to feed back into the structures of university teaching
and research, and this is arguably the greatest legacy of the seventeenth-
century experimental societies. Nevertheless, the major preoccupation of
this book has been to demonstrate the enduring presence of the Bible in the
earlier phases of British institutionalised science, and this was of course true
across Europe. Narratives of the scientific revolution that stress primarily
developments in mathematics and astronomy often under- or misrepresent
this presence, or focus solely on the continental ecclesiastical censorship of
Copernicanism. Most people are now at least anecdotally aware that Newton
was obsessed with alchemy and biblical criticism, but if this is only voiced as
a complement to the mathematical Newton of the *Principia*, then we have still

misunderstood the wider character of scientific research in Newton's age. I have argued instead that we must appreciate the role of the 'naturalists' as well as of the 'mathematicians', and indeed in contemporary terms, the naturalists were the dominant institutional presences. This is not to undervalue the mathematical aspect of the scientific revolution, merely to insist that that interpretation is only partially true. The naturalists concerned themselves with any number of what they or we would term antiquarianism, archaeology, botany, cartography, chemistry, chronology, climatography, demography, fossilology, geography, geology, geomorphology, history, hydrography, linguistics, magnetism, meteorology, stratigraphy, topography, and zoology, and in all these areas biblical considerations impinged. They were also all areas which were comprehensible to amateurs.

A second, more methodological preoccupation of this book has been to appreciate the significance of institutional structures, archival maintenance, and the importance of reception and the nature of its documentation. The types of enquiry promoted by the Royal Society and imitative gatherings were directly shaped by the fellows' ways of going about generating, gathering, discussing, preserving, and publishing knowledge, and by the accompanying creation of bespoke repositories and museums. The invention of the learned journal, the laboratory report, the paper delivered to peers, the specialist single-subject tract, and the formalisation of certain correspondence networks were all literary phenomena that likewise not only recorded and communicated, but also embodied and controlled, new forms of information. The establishing of archives themselves anticipates but also subtly conditions future investigations and judgments. Finally, assessment of the reception of new ideas is the only way to gauge their contemporary significance and force; and reception itself can take a number of forms, from private worry or praise to printed extrapolation or refutation.

What, then, was the state of the natural sciences at the turn of the century? What relation did they have with the previously dominant pursuits of biblical exegesis and criticism? What were the elements of continuity and what of change?

From the point of view of the general scholar, what is striking about the state of natural philosophy in general at the end of the seventeenth century is its eclecticism. We have noted the persistence of traditional textbooks in the academe. Alongside such examples of immobilisation were modernist gestures, such as the decision of Samuel Clarke (1675–1729) to dispute on Newton's *Principia* in 1695 for his BA degree, a text which his examiners almost certainly could not understand. Academic eclecticism is nicely captured by some manuscript reading lists scribed onto the fly leaves of various Bodleian books. The endpapers of one copy of Sanderson's conservative Aristotelian physics of 1690, for instance, contain a dozen titles – probably recommended by a University College tutor – of a strongly modernist slant, including works by Du Hamel, Descartes, Rohault, Charleton, and 'All Mr Boyl's pieces'. A copy of the English translation of the Accademia del Cimento's experiments likewise bears a reading list dating from just after 1695 on the controversy over fossils:

> Of Shells &c lodg'd in ye bowells of ye Earth &c see Mr Rays three Physico-Theol. Disc. Steno's Prodromus, Dr Hooks Micrography Rays travels from p. 113 to p. 130. Plott of Oxfordshire If you will consult more Auth^{rs} upon this subject, you may see y^r names in a late piece call'd Two Essays sent in a letter from Oxford to a Nobleman in London &c [i.e. the Deist work by 'L. P.' published in 1695].

This eclecticism survived well into the eighteenth century, and is epitomised in the English edition of Rohault's *Physica* (in ever-expanding versions of 1697, 1702, and 1710) prepared by the same Samuel Clarke who disputed on Newton. Jacques Rohault (1618–72), whose heart was buried next to Descartes, was the leading Cartesian populist, but in Clarke's Latin edition for use in the English universities, Rohault's Cartesian physics was presented with a Newtonian commentary. This commentary intentionally trumped the text itself, and ironically Clarke's Rohault therefore contributed to the collapse of Cartesianism in England. Like Sanderson, Clarke's Rohault appears to have been sold commonly in an interleaved form, and surviving examples contain cross-references not just to conservatives such as Sanderson himself, but also to cutting-edge modern texts such as Cristiaan Huygens' *Cosmotheoros* (1698), in which the Dutch astronomer argued by analogy for the existence of aliens on all the other planets, peering back at us through their own telescopes. In 1699 the chapter on 'Natural Philosophy' in Thomas Baker's critical *Reflections on Learning* was dominated by meditation on Descartes and the three major English 'theorists' he spawned, not on traditional natural philosophy. One early eighteenth-century guide for students stipulated for fourth-year study the reading of Burnet, Woodward, Whiston, and their detractors. Hence the biblical quarrels at the heart of the debate over the 'theorists' remained central concerns for some decades after their initial publication. In continental terms, too, biblically sensitive 'theories of the earth' persisted, and the English

World Makers were soon joined by Leibniz, whose *Protogaea* appeared in various forms between 1693 and 1749; and by the subversive Benoît de Maillet (1656–1738), whose Cartesian dialogue *Telliamed* ('Demaillet' backwards) circulated in manuscript before the turn of the century. *Telliamed* argued for an Earth billions of years old, with all life springing from the ocean onto the slowly emerging mountains in transformist jumps. De Maillet's work, however, remained in manuscript until the mid-eighteenth century, and even then was doctored upon publication to make it sound a little less extreme. De Maillet thought that humans had evolved from mermaids, whereas Leibniz denied the possibility of species variation on biblical grounds.[1]

From the point of view of experimental practitioners themselves, experimental philosophy was rapidly becoming a set of specialised activities, and although general textbooks were still prepared for educational purposes, the short journal article on a precise topic had become the standard form for reporting recent work. The various terse papers of Edmond Halley exemplify how new, naturalist techniques could be applied to old questions – how, for instance, chronological issues once resolved by the appeal to texts could now be answered by natural phenomena themselves, albeit with rather different results. Nevertheless there was no swift departure from the biblical here either. The first generation of World Makers had extended their physical hypotheses into the future in order to model the biblical Conflagration and Millennium. Although prophetic science did not survive the new century in mainstream circles, throughout the same period and beyond the *Philosophical Transactions* intermittently reviewed books or printed papers on biblical matters, one late example being the 1767 'An Attempt to Account for the Universal Deluge' by the lawyer, FRS, and antiquary Edward King (1734/5–1807). Like Hooke, King invoked subterranean fires, but rather unfairly did not invoke Hooke himself. In a later publication, his millenarian *Morsels of Criticism* (1788), King, recycling theories we have encountered in Glanvill, Whiston, and Derham, proposed that the Earth in the second and final conflagration would change its orbit and become a comet, with hell at its core, on a collision course with the Sun.[2]

Despite such biblical endurance, by the late seventeenth century certain important problems concerning the relation between natural philosophical endeavour and biblical exegesis had nevertheless manifested themselves, and they would not now go away. The Royal Society was itself attacked in its earliest days as religiously suspect, provoking a flurry of defences that insisted on the piety of experimental philosophy. Both laity and clergy alike within the ranks of the experimentalists went straight to the printing press. Sprat, for instance, declared it 'the most solemn' part of his 'whole *undertaking*' to show how institutionalised science buttressed institutionalised religion. But this was a predictable, indeed inevitable reaction, and does not tell the whole truth. Many natural philosophers did indeed have heterodox leanings, sometimes apparently unconnected to their scientific work, sometimes arising directly from it. In the former category, for instance, Francis Willughby, a man whose piety seems beyond reproach, penned at an unknown date a short manuscript entitled 'Objections against the Scripture', now tucked into his commonplace book. Willughby listed moral objections to the Old Testament God: some commands given to the Israelites, for instance, 'seem contrary to moral Honesty'. Just because Willughby both composed or copied this manuscript and also worked on plant and fish taxonomy does not however imply any connection here between heterodoxy and zoology themselves. Again, in 1683 the less pious Samuel Pepys sailed to Tangier on government business with the cleric Thomas Ken (1637–1711), and on the journey Pepys occupied himself by rereading Hooke's *Micrographia* and debating with Ken about the existence or otherwise of the spirit world. Clergyman Ken considered ghosts and spirits real; Pepys, as he recorded in his private diary, did not. The next year Pepys was elected President of the Royal Society. Once more, this is interesting evidence of semi-private or at least socially restricted scepticism, but it does not necessarily illuminate Pepys' role as a virtuoso.[3]

All the same, a good deal of religious heterodoxy *was* powered by scientific concerns. Isaac Newton's secret antitrinitarianism and his interest in alchemy flow from the same vision of God that informed his published natural philosophy. Thomas Burnet deployed a dangerously radical theory of biblical criticism precisely to justify his new Cartesian physics. William Whiston's cometography was prefaced by an essay in biblical interpretation. William Wotton tried to put an end to deriving all languages from biblical Hebrew by appealing to biblical miracle. The mainly theological heresy of La Peyrère was mutated by his English readers into an intervention in physics and historiography. Francis Lodwick embraced a long, indefinite world chronology after reading La Peyrère; Hooke's geological theories, although formally reticent on the matter, beg a long chronology too; and Hooke and Halley developed an exegesis of the biblical Chaos that furnished them with one. Again, Hooke promoted his theory of extinction by trumping one theological principle with another. We could multiply such examples, but this suffices to show that behind some purely casual concurrences of heterodoxy and scientific endeavour there stand a number of important encounters in which the two were mutually implicated.

If the priorities of experimental research were prompting some awkward questions and indeed awkward answers in the spheres of theology and biblical exegesis, it might be suspected that there is merit in the 'science versus religion' thesis, in which something called science is inherently antagonistic towards something called religion. This unhistorical formulation would have made no sense to the natural philosophers discussed in this book, most of whom thought that their research at worst would not interfere with, and at best bolster, Christian piety. The problems that we have seen, rather, stemmed from within biblical criticism itself. Such criticism was now generating material that was drifting out of kilter with the increasingly shrill tones of Calvinist dogmaticians, and the lighter mumblings of Anglicans and Roman Catholics. Queries about the accuracy and authorship of the received biblical text were, however, in the end not particularly damaging – textual emendation could be performed, and even if Moses proved not to be the author of the Pentateuch, God could easily have inspired someone else.

Far more significant was Spinoza's paradigm-breaking proposal that the Bible was just another ancient text, and that there was therefore no point in trying to do science with it. The partially compatible, older view of 'accommodation', whereby God condescends in Scripture to limited human understanding, was replaced by the view that God had little to do with it: biblical text speaks only in the accent and understanding of its historical authors. Thomas Burnet may have believed that he was doing Christianity a service when he adopted this approach to the opening of Genesis, but he was mistaken; and the Spinozistic disconnection of the Bible from modern philosophy, natural or moral, was the path soon taken by Deist writers. Indeed, reading Voltaire's articles on 'Babel', 'Le Ciel des Anciens', 'Genèse', or 'Moïse' in his celebrated *Philosophical Dictionary* (1764), one might well be back in England in the 1680s and 1690s, when the conclusions indirectly sanctioned by Voltaire first prompted explosive controversy. That is the legacy of the late-seventeenth–century English encounter between emergent scientific research and biblical exegesis, and that is its enduring historical importance.

Finally, it might be suspected that a book emphasising the importance of biblical considerations across the formative decades for British science might itself be a covert apology for some continued relevance of the Bible in such studies. This is not so. There is nothing inconsistent about respecting that a theory or attitude may be rational in 1700 and ridiculous in 2000. To deny this would be to envisage the occupants of history as living in a kind of mental hospital. It is no longer reasonable to think that we can do physics from the Bible, or that Genesis tells us anything pertinent about the origins of the Earth, or Revelation about human destiny. Since the days of Halley and Hooke, developments in science and implosions in theology have stripped such positions of credibility. A simple test of this is that even nominally religious Anglophones, excepting those living in educationally backward parts of America and (alas!) even Britain, find the idea of basing a scientific research or educational programme on biblical exegesis a hideous category mistake. It would be absurd to wish that seventeenth-century academics taught that species change affected even humans. It is likewise absurd to teach variations of 'Mosaic Physics' in today's schools, be it branded as 'intelligent design' or some other anti-Darwinian methodology, and it is politically irresponsible of any modern state to endorse such heterodoxy. As I write this conclusion I read in the newspapers that the Royal Society's director of education, himself in holy orders, has in 2008 supported the teaching in science classes of creationist ideas as a 'world view'. Unsurprisingly, angry senior officials in the Society have immediately forced him to step down from his post. His remarks may have been interepreted out of context, but the reaction to them is a sure sign of the passions such discussions still provoke. Nevertheless, as contemporary debates between 'Creationists' and their opponents, atheist or otherwise, become increasingly repetitive, I wish that both participants and observers understood more about the historical origins of this particular quarrel. Human understanding itself has evolved over time, and in order to appreciate the achivement of modern science, we must appreciate where it has come from, what company it has kept, and what company it must shed.[4]

Appendix: Brief Lives

John Aubrey (1626–97) FRS, antiquary, pioneer archaeologist. He worked on a wide range of projects, from the creation of an artificial language to the study of megaliths. He was the first man both to survey extant megaliths using mathematical instruments and to insist upon their pre-Roman origins.

Francis Bacon (1561–1626) Lord Chancellor, lawyer, natural philosopher. His many works insisted upon the importance of scientific experiments and of organised data collection. He inspired generations of subsequent experimentalists, but perhaps more as a mascot than as an authority.

Ralph Bohun (1639–1716) Oxford don, clergyman, meteorologist. He was initially suspicious of the new Royal Society of London, thinking it would threaten the universities' monopoly on scholarship. He soon changed his mind, and his meteorological work helped articulate a new experimental discipline.

Robert Boyle (1627–1691) FRS, pious aristocrat, experimental philosopher. He published an immense number of works explaining the new science, and established the genre of the laboratory report. His wealth and class were important assets for the experimentalists, as were his many publications as a lay theologian.

Thomas Browne (1605–82) Physician, scholar, prose stylist. His works were venerated in his day, but the rich prose in which he ruminated upon fallacies of science and scholarship was itself soon regarded as inappropriate for scientific discussion. Nevertheless his sense of vicissitude influenced linguistics and archaeology.

Thomas Burnet (c. 1635–1715) Clergyman, natural philosopher, headmaster. His *Sacred Theory of the Earth* (1681) attempted to harmonise biblical history and natural philosophy. He was applauded for his prose, but his natural philosophy was attacked, and the theological implications of his arguments shocked more than they convinced.

John Craige (c. 1662–1731) FRS, clergyman, mathematician. He published the first mathematical text to employ the differential calculus of Leibniz. But he also thought that mathematics could serve theology, and hence more notoriously published an attempt to provide the mathematical principles of Christian belief.

René Descartes (1596–1650) French philosopher, physicist, geometer. He revolutionised physics following the publication of his *Principia* in 1644. But Descartes' actual system was soon found wanting by the English, on both physical and theological grounds. They turned to his countryman Gassendi instead.

Pierre Gassendi (1592–1655) French clergyman, physicist, Epicurean revivalist. He 'baptised' the atheistic atomism of classical theorists Epicurus and Lucretius, and presented to modern Europeans a system of physics that was quickly seen as more desirable than that of Descartes, especially on religious grounds.

William Gilbert (1544–1603) Medic, experimentalist, magnetician. His *De magnete* (1600) was one of the few English works to influence continental physicists. Although he scorned Aristotle and advocated a new experimentalism, he also declared that the planetary magnetic field was the Earth's soul or mind. He published only in Latin.

Joseph Glanvill (1636–80) FRS, clergyman, apologist. He defended the early Royal Society with great enthusiasm. But he also published in support of the pre-existence of the soul and of the existence of witches. Although he could enlist supporters among his colleagues, his outspoken heterodoxy was slightly embarrassing.

Nehemiah Grew (1641–1712) FRS, botanist, physician. He published the first catalogue of the Royal Society's own repository of objects in 1681, but later turned his hand to the theological applications of natural philosophy in his *Cosmologia sacra* (1701).

George Hakewill (1578–1649) Academician, clergyman, philosopher. He published a famous book in 1627 in which he argued that modern scientists and writers could equal their ancient counterparts. He viewed intellectual and creative history as cyclical. His rejection of inevitable intellectual decline enthused successors.

Edmond Halley (1656–1742) FRS, astronomer, voyager. His staggering achievements included interventions in meteorology and magnetism. Suspected, justly, of promulgating theories with sensitive religious implications, he suggested that there might be an unknown but populated planet within our hollow Earth.

Robert Hooke (1635–1703) FRS, experimental philosopher, first salaried scientist. He was the axis on which the early Royal Society turned, although not without factionalism and dissent. His most consistent and extended work was in geology. He insisted that fossils were organic in origin and that species might become extinct.

John Keill (1671–1721) FRS, mathematician, natural philosopher. He was to achieve distinction as a teacher of mathematics, but his earliest work was a demolition of the theories of the 'World Makers', mainly on mathematical grounds. Pondering the Flood, Keill argued that mathematics stopped where miracle started.

Athanasius Kircher (1601–80) Jesuit, polymath, hermetist. English scholars enjoyed his expensive and lavishly illustrated works on subjects from Coptic to palaeontology, but usually thought him superstitious, credulous, and indiscriminate. Yet his international contacts were extensive, and his data correspondingly prized.

Isaac La Peyrère (1596–1676) French scholiaster, secretary, heretic. He wrote that Adam had not been the first man, that the Earth was older than people thought, and that the early Bible only recorded Jewish history. The Frenchman's extreme heresy was read in England with interest, professed outrage, and some covert appreciation.

Edward Lhuyd (1659/60–1709) Museum curator, expert on fossils, Celtic linguist. He succeeded Plot as Keeper of the Ashmolean, and published the first catalogue of British fossils in 1699. He carried out extensive perambulations in order to survey megaliths, collect fossils and plants, and to record the surviving Celtic languages, of which he wrote a comparative grammar.

Martin Lister (1638–1712) FRS, medic, naturalist. He catalogued animals and shells, and made short but important contributions to geology. He was a valued correspondent of the early Royal Society, many members of which were more comfortable with his arguments, marshalled against Hooke, that fossils were inorganic in origin.

Francis Lodwick (1619–94) FRS, deviser of artificial languages, secret heretic. He published the first attempts in English to devise an artificial language. He amassed a huge library, wrote many private manuscript works, and was profoundly influenced by his friend Hooke. He believed La Peyrère, but seemingly kept this to himself.

Henry More (1614–87) FRS, theologian, natural philosopher. He initially celebrated Descartes as the true interpreter of the physics divinely understood by Moses in Genesis, but soon realised the dangers inherent in Descartes' project. More's strong Platonism was not always appreciated by his younger colleagues.

Joseph Moxon (1627–91) FRS, printer, geographer. He made and sold fine books, globes, maps, and instruments reflecting the most recent developments in the Royal Society and among the community of mathematical practitioners. The election to the Royal Society of a tradesman, even one as brilliant as Moxon, raised eyebrows.

Isaac Newton (1642–1727) FRS, mathematician, physicist. His *Principia* (1687) revolutionised science, but it was directly accessible to very few. Newton was also deeply involved in biblical criticism, and he developed an interpretation of Genesis that relied on alchemical models.

Henry Oldenburg (c. 1619–77) FRS, administrator, translator. He managed the Royal Society's vast correspondence and founded and edited the *Philosophical Transactions*. But the circle around Robert Hooke disliked Oldenburg and his faction, and Hooke suspected Oldenburg of leaking English ideas to foreign competitors.

Samuel Pepys (1633–1703) FRS, naval administrator, diarist. He recorded a great deal of the unofficial conversation of the early scientists in his diary, which he kept in shorthand. But he also made his own contributions, for instance to John Wilkins' artificial language. He served as President of the Royal Society.

William Petty (1623–87) FRS, inventor, statistician. A brilliant polymath, he was in many respects a religious sceptic, as his private manuscripts show. But his scepticism was certainly not atheistic, and he believed strongly that the statistics he pioneered could be used to quantify aspects of biblical history.

Robert Plot (1640–96) FRS, first Oxford professor of chemistry, first curator of the Ashmolean Museum. He was an antiquary and a chemist, whose *Natural History of Oxford-Shire* (1677) was the most prominent publication in that new genre. But he sided with Martin Lister in attacking Hooke's theories of fossils.

John Ray (1627–1705) FRS, naturalist, theologian. He was the most respected of the naturalists, as well as the most pious. Apart from his botanical publications and his work on dialect words and proverbs, he published a great deal of 'physico-theology', and these works proved very popular. He was deeply puzzled by fossils.

Robert Sanderson (1587–1663) Academician, bishop, writer of textbooks. He died before many of the characters in this book were active, but his conservative textbooks in logic and in physics were endlessly reprinted for university use. They are reminders of the persistence of Aristotelianism even amidst the new science.

Richard Simon (1638–1712) French Oratorian, philologist, biblical critic. A Roman Catholic, Simon attacked the textual coherency of the Old Testament, arguing that the Pentateuch was not the work of one writer but of many and made use of prior, now lost, documents. An immediate ban did not stop the work from reaching England.

Benedict Spinoza (1632–77) Excommunicated Dutch Jew, philosopher, lens grinder. His *Tractatus Theologico-Politicus* (1670) argued that the Bible was merely a set of culturally specific books aimed at local audiences. It was an explosive publication, for Spinoza was suggesting that the Bible contained neither revelation nor science.

Nicolaus Steno (1638–86) Danish palaeontologist, stratigrapher, Roman Catholic convert. He was the founder of stratigraphy and proved the organic origin of fossils, but the similarity of his conclusions to those of Robert Hooke led the latter, unjustly, to suspect Steno of plagiarism. He abandoned scientific research for the Church.

Edward Stillingfleet (1635–99) Bishop, historian, philosopher. His *Origines Sacræ* (1662) affirmed the truth of biblical history, but also took occasion to debate recent developments in physics and in theology. Stillingfleet later revised the book to address more directly what he perceived as the threat of atheism.

Isaac Vossius (1618–89) FRS, philologist, natural philosopher. He enjoyed the heterodox and the controversial, but was also a champion of learned, Latinate culture. Vossius was interested in the age of the Earth, which he computed using the Greek as opposed to the Hebrew text of the Bible. He also published on meteorology.

John Webb (1611–62) Architect, sinophile, Stonehenge speculator. Following his teacher Inigo Jones, he thought that Stonehenge was a Roman monument, and provided geometrical reconstructions. But he also considered that Adam spoke Chinese, and that Noah had built and landed the Ark in China too.

John Webster (1611–82) Preacher, polemicist, chemist. His early and ill-judged attack on the universities provoked strong rebuttal. But after the Restoration he published important work in mineralogy and even managed to secure a Royal Society *imprimatur* for his book arguing against the existence of witches.

William Whiston (1667–1752) FRS, mathematician, theologian. He opened his career by proposing a Newtonian cometography in which cometary impacts provided the external causes of the Creation and the Flood. Appointed

Newton's successor in Cambridge, he was later sacked for his antitrinitarian beliefs.

John Wilkins (1614–72) FRS, bishop, natural philosopher. Wilkins was the unofficial father of the Royal Society, and he was at the centre of the group of experimentalists who gathered in Oxford in the interregnum. A man of immense influence, he constructed an artificial language and died Bishop of Chester.

John Woodward (1665/68–1728) FRS, physician, naturalist. He argued that God lessened the force of gravity at the Flood in order to cause non-organic matter to disintegrate. He was a major collector and a man of immense energy, but he was difficult and arrogant, and was satirised on the stage for his pretensions.

William Wotton (1666–1727) FRS, linguist, theologian. His *Reflections upon Ancient and Modern Learning* (1694) argued that while the Ancients were good at the arts, the Moderns had surpassed them in what we would term the sciences. But he was also a theologian and interested in the evolution of languages.

Christopher Wren (1632–1723) FRS, natural philosopher, architect. He was a polymath and collaborated for decades with Robert Hooke. Among his many more obscure achievements were the design of a weather station, and the construction of the first lunar globe.

Notes

Introduction

1 Feingold 2001; Flamsteed in Baily 1835: 218.
2 Feingold 2005; Hunter 1981: 113–35; Malcolm 2002; Jardine 2003: 112–13; 'Clubmen' is from Hartlib 2002: 28/2/5B. The classic study of the Hartlib circle is Webster 2002.
3 Sprat 1667: 61; Boyle 1661: 36; see further Brown 1967; Hunter 1994; Feingold 1998.

1 The Physics of Creation

1 For a full study of the doctrine of Creation and the rise of science, with particular reference to the work of Robert Boyle, see Klaaren 1977.
2 Woodforde 1667: sg. c2r.
3 On the vowel-points controversy see Muller 1980; on creation *ex nihilo* see Stillingfleet 1662: 440–1; Conklin 1949: 68; Grotius 1683: book 3, ch. 13; on Hammond see Packer 1969; on Morin see Mandelbrote 2006: 74–6; Taylor 1647: 73–83, in the tradition of Hales 1659: 1–25. On biblical criticism see especially Farrar 1886, Scholder 1990, and Malcolm 2002: 383–431.
4 Simon 1682: 5; Royal Society Archives, Letter Book 8 (Copy), pp. 11–14 (Justel, undated, some time in Sept or Oct 1677). On the English publication of Simon see Ward 1946. Hill cited from British Library MSS Sloane 2891, fols. 12v; 2893, fol. 3v; 2901, fol. 135r; 2893, fol. 183v. For the reception of Simon, Spinoza, and Burnet among Hooke's friends see Poole 2006. For the larger context see Israel 2001, especially 447–76, 599–609.

5   *PT* 17 (1693): 796–812 (Hooke's review, early MS copies in Bodleian MS Eng. Misc. c.144; British Library MS Sloane 3828); Spinoza 1689: 28; Thompson 1875 (Prideaux's letter); 'L. P.' 1695: ii.

6   Hunter 1995.

7   Interleaved and annotated copies of Sanderson 1690 include Bodleian 8° Rawl. 393, 8° Rawl. 647, and Huntington Library 441102. On academic physics see Heilbron 1982. On the persistence of Aristotelianism at Oxford see Feingold in *HUO*: 400–4, whence the quotation from Bohun.

8   Funkenstein 1986: 28–9.

9   Cabeus 1646: 1.393.

10   Paracelsus, appended to Croll 1657; on Paracelsianism and its reception see Debus 1977, Webster 1982, and Trevor-Roper 1985.

11   Tymme 1605: A3r; Bacon 1620: 74–5 (Aphorism 65; compare 89), and on Bacon's cosmology see Rees 1977, Hakewill 1635: 276, and Comenius 1651. On 'Mosaic Physics' see Williams 1948 and Blair 2000.

12   Boyle 1661: 38; on Boyle see Debus 1977: 473–92 and Newman and Principe 2005. On Van Helmont and Boyle's reaction to him see Webster 1966 and Klaaren 1977: 61–4. Stillingfleet 1662: 428; Patrick 1695: 11.

13   'Eirenaeus Philalethes' 1669: 9; Newton 1960: 329–35 (letter to Burnet); Newton, manuscript of c. 1684, both cited and discussed in Dobbs 1991 (*Janus Faces*): 53, 67–8, and see also Dobbs 1982.

14   Bentley 1842: 47–52, 57–63, 69–74.

15   Webster 1671; Robinson 1694: 1, 22; Robinson 1696, and on Robinson see Rossi 1984: 9–11. On geocosmic Paracelsianism see Debus 1977: 455–63. But for Van Helmont's rather different understanding of earthquakes see Helmont 1662: 92–103. Hooke's views on alchemy can be inferred from Royal Society Early Letters, vol. P1, letters 57, 59, of the early 1680s.

16   Descartes 1644, translated in Descartes 1983; specific quotation from book 1, section 28. On Descartes' physics in context see Heilbron 1982: 22–38. Glanvill 1661: 211; Keill 1698: 14.

17   Descartes' brush with Schurman and his letters are quoted from Descartes 1897–1903: 4.698–701. On Descartes in England see Lamprecht 1935, Hunter 1981: 173–4, Harrison 2000, and Harrison 2007: 122–3.

18   Baker 1699: 97.

19   Stillingfleet 1662: 447, 466. On Stillingfleet see Rossi 1984: 25–9; on his revamped text see e.g. Stillingfleet 1709, and for remarks on it Hutton 1993.

20 Daniel 1692; Charleton 1654: 46, marginalia in Cambridge University Library Adv. a. 27. 7; Huët 2003. On the twinning of More and Huet *see* Feingold in *HUO*: 404.

21 On More's position see Gabbey 1989; Huygens 1698: 60.

22 Cudworth 1678: 12–13, 74, 150–72, 178–81; Ray 1693: 34–6; *CHSCP* 808–11; Sailor 1964.

23 On Felton see Feingold 1990: 25; there are many extant manuscripts of his work in Cambridge and London, an Oxford example being Bodleian MS Top. Oxon e. 344; Eachard 1671: 163; Whiston 1753: 32.

24 Westfall 1980: 89, 96; Eachard 1671: 162; Eachard 1670: 27; Sorbière 1664: 92; Casaubon 1999: 149–52. On the English reception of Gassendi see Frank 1980: 92–3 and Feingold in *HUO*: 405–13.

25 Evelyn 1656; Behn 1998: 240, 282; Darley 2006: 141–6; Shadwell 1676: 1.

26 Gassendi 1658: 1.162–70 (world not from eternity), 171–8 (world will end), 485 (six-day not instantaneous Creation), 2.262 (*semina*), discussed by LoLordo 2007: 28, 128–9, 197–9 and Goodrum 2002: 210–11; Charleton 1654: 14. For a summary of Gassendi's voluntarism, see Osler 1991: 155–74, and for the impact of voluntarism on English ideas of Creation see Klaaren 1977: 29–52.

27 Boyle 1663: 79; Newton 1952: 400; Boyle 1688, sg. A3r; Boyle 1666: 192. See further on Boyle Klaaren 1977: 127–84 and MacIntosh 1991; and on Newton see Dobbs 1991.

2 The Preadamite Hypothesis

1 Stillingfleet 1662: 534.

2 On La Peyrère and his influence see Hodgen 1964: 272–6, Robinson 1978, Rossi 1984: 132–40, Popkin 1987, Grafton 1991: 204–13, Malcolm 2002: 383–43, Popkin 2003: 221–30, Kidd 2006: 62–6. Details on his French and English reception are provided by Poole 2004, and on his manuscripts by Quennehen 1994 and 1995.

3 Chantilly, Château de Chantilly, Condé Museum MS 191.

4 E.g. Bodleian 8° B 257* Th, the *Præ-Adamitæ* bound with four refutations.

5 Ward 1656: 288–90; Hobbes 1994: 2.213, 214–15.

6 Pagden 1982.

7 Godwyn 1680: 15; Bodin 1945: 335.

8 de Foigny 1676, 1693, 1993; Bayle 1730, 'Sadeur'.

9 Lodwick 1972 and 2007.

10 Nottingham University Library, Middleton MS ML (i) 15, fols. 557v–9v (Willughby); Bodleian MS Rawl. A 183, fols. 1r–6v (Pepys' report, by Jeremiah Wells); Bodleian MS Rawl. A 178: fol. 71r (Petty to Southwell); Petty 1683: 22–4, 44–7 (and for two attempts to wrestle with Petty's figures see Nicholls 1696: 73–8 and Whiston 1696: 383–8); Petty 1927 2.40; Vossius 1659: 50; Hale 1677: 186; Stillingfleet 1662; Cary 1677: sg. a2v; Wilkins 1678: 73–5; Wotton 1694: sg. [A7]r–v.

11 Hooke 1935: entry for 18 Dec 1675.

12 British Library, Sloane MS 913, fols. 91v–88v (Lodwick).

13 Blount 1693: 218; L. P. 1695.

3 Chronology

1 Burnet, *Theory* 2.1. On chronology see Rossi 1984: 145–52; Barr 1985; Grafton 1991 and 1993. On 1656 see Hill 1986: 269–300 (quotation from 272).

2 Patrick 1695: 2.

3 Lydiat 1609: 1–4.

4 On the impact of Septuagint scholarship in England see Mandelbrote 2006.

5 Browne 1981: book 6, ch. 1; Browne 1658: 2. For the modern and early-modern estimates of the numbers of different creation dates see Patrides 1963 and Scholder 1990: 77.

6 Pepys 23 May 1661; Halley 1714–16, and on his paper see Biswas 1970 and Schaffer 1977; Beaumont 1693: 18; Patrick 1695: 11; Buckland 1820; Browne 1658: sg. A3r.

4 Flood and Ark

1 British Library, MS Add. 38536, fols. 36v–37r (citation of Morland's lost paper); for Harriot's 'diluvium Noachi' papers see Stedall 2002: 98; Mersenne 1644: 222; Buteo 1554: 5–30 ('De Arca Noe'); Burnet, *Theory* 1.2; on Petty and

Keill see the next chapter; Boyle 1688: 84; Croft 1685: 99; Patrick 1695: 138, 139–40; Stillingfleet 1662: 543–6. For a contemporary survey of earlier diluvial discussions see Pererius 1622: 336–66, and for modern commentary Allen 1949, Martínez and Luttikhuizen 1999, and Bennett and Mandelbrote 1998: 73–101.

2 Patrick 1695: 130.

3 Ray 1693: 4–8.

4 Lord 1630: 1–7; Hooke 1935: entry for 20 March 1689; Montanus 1670: 275, 279, 281; González de Mendoza 1588: 35–7; Acosta 1604: 79–81 (and compare Gomara in Montaigne 1613: 514–15) .

5 Wilkins 1678: 39–61; Locke 1975: 1.4.8; Nicholls 1697: 25–33, 198–9.

5 The World Makers: Burnet, Woodward, Whiston

1 Discussions of Burnet and related cosmogonical projects are legion, including the relevant chapters in or articles by Collier 1934, Adams 1938, Taylor 1948, Allen 1949, Nicolson 1959, Davies 1969, Jacob and Lockwood 1972, Rossi 1984, Levine 1991, Mandelbrote 1994, Vermij 1996, Rappaport 1997, Haycock 2002, and Richet 2007. Burnet wins chapters in histories of palaeontology (e.g. Rudwick 1985), despite the fact that he does not mention fossils; and in histories of world chronology (e.g. Albritton 1980), despite the fact that his chronology is conventional. The only full study of Burnet is Pasini 1981.

2 Keill 1698: 26; Flamsteed cited in Willmoth 1987: 42; Croft 1685: sg. A3r-v; Feingold 2002.

3 Lewis 2006.

4 Dennis 1693: 134, 139.

5 Croft 1685: sg. [a5]r.

6 Lovell 1696: 25; Keill 1698: 37.

7 An unsigned translation of the seventh chapter of the *Archæologiæ* is in British Library MS Sloane 1775, fols. 144r–55v; Benítez 1988: nos. 45, 67, 115.

8 Warren 1690, sg. [A3]r; Croft 1685: sgs. b3v–b5. On Burnet's heresy see Walker 1964: 156–66.

9 Boyle 2001: 6:214–16 (Locke, Tyrell, and Boyle); de la Bédoyère 2005: 145–6 (Evelyn and Pepys); Hooke 1705 (copy at British Library Eve. b. 48): 319, 327 (Evelyn's Hooke); Bodleian MS Rawlinson A 171, fol. 217r (Pepys).

10   Southwell's dialogue is edited from Royal Society MS 248, item 96, in Poole 2008; L. P. 1696: sg. A2v.

11   Levine 1991: 18–79; Poole 2008.

12   Le Clerc 1696: sg. A4r.

13   Arbuthnot 1697: 12 (new miracle), and see Poole 2008: 13, f.n. 92 for examples against Burnet; Nicolson 1809: 1.104; *ESO* 15.268–9 (Lhuyd to Lister, 28 March 1695); Levine 1991: 58–62, 66–72 (Baker and Edwards).

14   Ray 1928: 256.

15   Arbuthnot 1697: 51; Gay 1717: 21.

16   Newton 1960: letter 247, and Mandelbrote 2006.

17   Force 1985: 32–62.

18   Nicolson 1809: 1.104.

19   Nicholls 1697: 187–218.

20   Whiston 1696: 20.

21   Keill 1698: 177–9; Petty 1928: 21–2; Stukeley, quoted in Haycock 2002: 78.

22   Fabricius 1725: 361–6; Bodleian MS Rawlinson d 40, p. 7 (early eighteenth-century directions for students compiled by Thomas Haywood (1678–1742), fellow of St John's College, Oxford).

6   Babel and the Rise of Nations

1   Annius 1498, following the copy at Bodleian Auct. Q sub fen. II. 28, which has passed through the hands of Cardinal Lomellini, Bishop Bergonci, and Pope Pius VI. On Annius see Grafton 1990, 1991, Stephens 2004. Annius in English scholarship is discussed by Kendrick 1950: 69–76, 116–20. On Babel see Bennett and Mandelbrote 1998: 103–33.

2   Bale 1548: fols. 6r–9v; Verstegan 1605: 94–5.

3   Purchas 1626–7: 1.44. Newton's remarks on Stonehenge can be found in 'The Original of Religions', Yahuda MS 41, fol. 2v, consulted through The Newton Project (www.newtonproject.sussex.ac.uk). See Sammes 1676, and on him Parry 1995: 308–30.

4   Bibliander 1548: 31; Broughton 1612: 2–3; Verstegan 1605: 190; Stiernhielm 1671: sgs. a3r–f3r; *PC* 4 (1682): 118–21; Sheringham 1670, and on Scandinavian studies and the 'Gothic' vogue more generally in England, see Seaton 1935:

126–8, 193–4 (Robinson), 188–93 (Stiernhielm, Rudbeck, and the Royal
Society), 249–50 (Sheringham), and Kliger 1945; Wotton 1730: 28.

5   Webb 1669, on whom see Ramsey 2001; Vossius 1685: 69–85.

6   Scaliger 1612: 115–18.

7   Brerewood 1622: 42.

8   Bonfante 1953–4; Dekker 1999: 208–15.

9   Wotton 1730: 21–2.

10 Wilkins 1668: 4; Browne 1683: 129–50.

11 Wilkins 1668: 10.

12 Lewis 2007; *PT* 16 (1686–92): 63–78; Wilkins 1668: 10.

13 *PT* 300 (1705): 1993–2008; Hyde 1767: 2.517 (from British Library MS Sloane
    853).

14 Wotton 1730: 36–7.

7   Archaeology and the Silent Past

1   Verstegan 1605: 88–112; Twyne 1590: 9; Camden 1610: 1; Acosta 1604: 64–8;
    Stillingfleet 1662: 575–6; Hale 1677: 189–91, 195–7.

2   Grew 1681; Sprat 1667: 251; Aubrey's testimony is in Bodleian MS Wood F 39,
    fol. 261v. On the Repository see Hunter 1989: 123–55; on the Ashmolean see
    MacGregor 2001. Early registers of the Bodleian collections are Bodleian MSS
    Rawl. Q e 36 and Rawl. B 399*.

3   Browne 1658; Browne 1964: 4.301–27, quotation from 321, letter of 16 Nov 1659.
    On Browne see Parry 1995: 244–5, 249–50. On the Royal Society and archae-
    ology see Hunter 1971.

4   Lister in *PC* 4 (1682): 87–92 (Bodleian Lister C 148 contains Lister's own, cor-
    rected copy).

5   Aubrey 1718–19 (*Surrey*), Aubrey 1847 (*Wiltshire*), and Aubrey 1980, 1982
    (*Monumenta*). On Aubrey see Hunter 1975 and Parry 1995: 275–307.

6   Bodleian Aubrey MSS; for easy access to *Wiltshire* see Britton's edition,
    Aubrey 1847; on Lars Porsena, see Aubrey 1980, 1982 (*Monumenta*): 2.677. See
    also Aubrey 1972: 311–35, 361–3.

8   Vicissitude and Geomorphology

1   Keckermann 1617; on Keckermann see Freedman 1997.
2   Varenius 1649 and 1650; on Varenius see Baker 1955. On the English academic context see Cormack 1997.
3   Varenius 1650; Ray 1693: 307–8; Carpenter 1635: 2.184–5; Cabeus 1646: 1.52–6; Hooke 1703: 3; Sandys 1626: 311. On the medieval tradition see Kimble 1938 and Moody 1941, and on its survival see Vogel 2006.
4   Hakewill 1635: 53–5; Wilkins 1640: 43; Hartlib 1655: 137; Lawrence 1664: 11; Power 1664: 190; Ray 1692: 23, 173, 175, 181, 191, 193; Beaumont 1693: 47, 57, 59, 79, 150; Whiston 1696: 209. On Hakewill and his influence see Harris 1949 and Webster 2002: 19–20, 29.
5   Blancanus 1620: 81–5, translated in Ray 1693: 296–305.
6   Boyle 1660: 166; MS Aubrey 12, fol. 315r (John Lydall to Aubrey); MS Sloane 917 (Hough's letter and diagrams); Birch 1756–7: 2.183; de la Bédoyère 2005: 273 (Evelyn Jr). On Newton's Varenius see Warntz 1989.
7   On Steno and his reception see Scherz 1958, Albritton 1980: 20–41, and Rudwick 1985: 49–100. Lister recalled meeting Steno in 1665 in his memoranda preserved in Bodleian MS Lister 5, at fols. 224v–5r. Steno is abstracted from Steno tr. Oldenburg 1671; specific quotations from 48, 50. See also the abstract in *PT* 6 (1671): 2186–90. See Leibniz 2008: 11–13 for his *geographia naturalis*.
8   For Pigott on the Oxford earthquake, see *PT* 13 (1683): 311–21; the Norfolk fossilologist is Thomas Lawrence 1664: 45; for the Herefordshire incident see A. L. Humphreys 1915; H[allywell] 1693: 17.
9   Hooke 1678: 49; Hooke's lectures on fossils and earthquakes are printed in Hooke 1705, and edited in Drake 1996; his later Memoranda in Hooke 1935; for Hooke and Newton see Birch, *History* 4.528; what was read out was eventually published in Newton 1687 as Book 1, *propositio* 66, *corollarium* 22 (pp. 186–7).
10 Hooke's lectures are paraphrased or quoted from Hooke 1705, modern edition in Drake 1996, no further references.
11 For Ortelius on Plato, see Romm 1994; for Kepler on Lucian, see Romm 1988–9; Porta 1658: 27; Aubrey 1898: 2.166; Ray 1928: 242.
12 Wilkins 1675; for Wallis *v.* Hooke, see Oldroyd 1989.
13 Halley's papers can be found in *PT* 13 (1683): 208–21 ('A Theory of the Variation of the Magnetical Compass'); *PT* 16 (1687): 403–6 (account of

Wurtzelbaur); *PT* 16 (1692): 563–87 ('An Account of the Cause of the Change
of the Variation of the Magnetical Needle'); *PT* 29 (1714 16): 296 300 ('A
Short Account of the Cause of the Saltness of the Ocean'); *PT* 33 (1724–5):
118–23 ('Some Considerations about the Cause of the Universal Deluge'),
123–4 ('Farther Thoughts upon the Same Subject'); Buckland 1820: 24; Halley
1932: 88; for Halley in and on this paper see Schaffer 1977.

14 Aubrey and Ray quotations from Bodleian MSS Aubrey 1, fols. 13, 86–101;
Aubrey 13, fol. 174.

15 The phrase on nature in the place of history is from Leibniz 2008: 140–1.

9 Fossils and Extinction

1 Rudwick 1985; see also Rossi 1984: 3–6.
2 Scheibler 1639: 63; Stier 1647: tract. 4, p. 36; Burton 1989–2000: 2.37; Ray 1928:
210; *Account of the Origin* 1705: 35–6.
3 *ESO* 14: 367, and see further Raven 1950: 436–7.
4 Ortelius 1887: 393–5; Fracastoro in Sarayna 1540: fps. 6v–7v; Colonna 1616:
31–9; Pliny 1601: 627. For the earlier continental ideas, see Gaudant 2005:
295–310. Fracastoro is recognised as a forerunner to Steno and Hooke by e.g.
Ray 1673: 120; and Colonna by e.g. Ray 1693: 134–5.
5 Birch, *History* 3.87; Grew 1681: sg. Ddd2v. Boccone is cited from letters 26,
28, and 29 of Boccone 1674, presentation copy at Bodleian Lister A 266. Scilla
1670 was abstracted by Wotton in *PT* 19 (1695–7): 181–201, and see Robinson
1697 for a reaction.
6 Birch, *History* 1.243–4, 247–8; Hooke 1665: 111.
7 Hooke 1665: 242–6.
8 Aubrey's copy of Steno 1671 is Bodleian Ashm. C 10; his *History of Wiltshire* is
cited from Bodleian MS Aubrey 1, fol. 89r.
9 Hooke 1705: 290–1. Hooke's lectures on earthquakes 1667–1700 comprise
Hooke 1705: 279–450; Drake 1996 is a modern edition. See also Hooke 1678:
48–52. Some good studies of Hooke's lectures are Rossi 1984: 12–17, Rappaport
1986, Ito 1988, and Oldroyd 1989.
10 Hooke 1705: 318.

11   Ralegh 1614: 106; Hooke 1705: 433; Plot 1677: 114–15; Ray 1693: 147. Drake 1996
      refers to Hooke's theory of biological evolution, ultimately resting on Pavlov
      1928.
12   Hale 1677: 199–202; Petty edited in Lewis 2009; Kircher 1675: 50; Kircher 1665:
      98. The 'Nicholas the Fish' story is translated in H[allywell] 1693: 8–10. On
      climatic theories see Glacken 1967 and on evolutionary ideas see Green 1959.
      Aubrey's climatic ideas are quoted and discussed in Hunter 1975: 114–15.
13   Ralegh 1614: 111; Bacon 1627: 135–8 (6th Century, heads 518–31); Porta 1658:
      26–110 (books 2–3); Sharrock 1672: 58–63. For precession of the equinoxes,
      Gilbert 1600: 234–5 (lib. 6, cap. 8); Lucretius, *De rerum natura*, 5.837–61,
      878–82, 923–4, is quoted partially from Lucretius 1682: 165–6, 168.
14   Hooke 1705: 327–8; Hale 1677: 174–203.
15   Beaumont's two letters are in *PT* 11 (1676): 724–42; Royal Society career infor-
      mation from Hunter 1994.
16   *PT* 6 (1671): 2281–4.
17   Plot 1677: 32, 111–21.
18   Ray 1673: sg. A7r–v, 113–31.
19   Ray 1693: 127–62. On Lister and Ray see Rudwick 1985: 61–5, 81–6; on Ray see
      Raven 1950: 419–51, esp. 437–8 on Ray and Lhuyd.
20   Plot 1677: 131–9; Molyneaux in *PT* 22 (1700–1): 487–508; and see further
      Schnapper 1986.

10   Meteorology, Cartography, and Globes

1   For the textbook tradition see Prideaux [1650]: 128–34, or Sanderson 1671:
     59–68; on plague see Wear 2000: 301–2; on Winstanley and the Wonder see
     Barnes 2003; for Ax see Aubrey 1847: 14; for Hooke see Guildhall MS 1758 and
     Mulligan 1996; for Locke see MS Locke d 9; for Warner see *ESO* 12.304–5.
2   *HUO*: 401; Hunter 1981: 145–9; Bohun 1671: 3–4; *OC* 8.483.
3   Boyle 1671; McConnell 1982: 5–6; Bohun 1671: 16; Vossius 1677: 142–51; Seneca,
     Nat. Quaest., 5.1.3–4; Bohun 1671: 15, 25, 43–4, and compare Boyle 1671: 7; on
     the aeolipile see Golinski 2001: 159.
4   Vossius 1677: 185–9.
5   Hooke 1665: Observation LVIII; Poole 2007 ('Payen').
6   Hooke 1726: 41–6; Grew 1681: 358; Inwood 2002: 279–82.

7   Sprat 1667: 173–9; Frisinger 1977: 101–3.

8   Hooke 1665. 149–51.

9   Royal Society Classified Papers 20, no. 70; Bodleian MS Rawl. A 171, fol. 245;
    Wilkins 1668: 280–3; Pepys 1690.

10 Deane 1981; Royal Society MS 248, p. 45.

11 McConnell 1982: 6–11; Bennett 2003: 73–80.

12 Tyacke 1978.

13 Taylor 1940.

14 Wallis 1978; Woodward 1978.

15 Moxon 1691: 9–12; a copy of Moxon's rare c. 1670 map can be found at British
    Library Maps CC. 2. a. 12, and see also British Library Maps C. 48. e. 1 for a
    finely coloured set of the *Scripture Geography* maps. On Moxon see Jagger
    1995 and Bryden 1997.

16 Aubrey 1847: 10.

17 *PT* 14 (1684): 39–46.

18 Burnet, *Theory* 1.11.

19 *PT* 183 (1686): 155; Thrower 1978, with illustrations of all five maps.

20 E.g. Bodleian MS Rawl. D 1121, 1676 crib of Humphrey Hody (1659–1707),
    commenced three days after his matriculation.

21 Illustrated in Wallis 1978: 7.

22 Burnet, *Theory* 1.11. On early relief globes see Briesemeister 1957.

23 *OC* 1.422; Sorbière 1664: 84; Hevelius 1647: 493–5; Wren 1750: 211; Bennett
    2000.

11   Magnetism and its Survival

1   Webster 1654: 77–8.

2   Gilbert 1600: *passim*, but see especially 6.3 (diurnal rotation, but not the other
    two movements), 6.4, 6 (astral mind); Milton 1667: 3.579–86 [in the 1673
    twelve-book reorganisation]. On Gilbert and his reception see Roller 1959,
    Feingold 1984, and Pumfrey 2002. On magnetic instruments see Warner 1994.

3   Ridley 1613; Barlow 1617; *HUO*: 430 n.204; Carpenter 1625: 1.48.

4   [War]D et al. 1654: 2; on Newton's alchemical hypotheses see Dobbs 1982.

5 Robinson 1694 and 1696, on whom see Rossi 1984; Wren 1750: 204, on whose inaugural lecture and magnetic thought see Bennett 1982: 56–60, and Bennett 1999.

6 Grew 1681: 364 (*terrella* and dipping-needles); Royal Society Portrait P/0057 (Haak); Birch, *History* 1.81 (Power), 1.440 (winter magnets), 1.507 (polar gravity), 1.451 (Ball's four-poled *terrella*), 1.471 (Boyle on St Paul's), 2.109 (gravity and magnetism), 2.316 (atmosphere), 2.356 (longitude), 3.128 (iron filings), 3.131 (polar wandering), 4.202 (Henshaw); *PT* 5 (1670): 1184–7 (Auzout); Petty 1674: 18–19, 130–1.

7 Hooke 1674: 27–8; Wilkins 1640: 212–19.

8 Birch, *History* 4.18–19 (Perkins); Flamsteed 1995–2002: 2.298.

9 On Halley's magnetic researches, see Schaffer 1977, Thrower 1978, Kollerstrom 1992, and Cook 2001; for Halley's pertinent papers see *PT* 13 (1683): 208–21; *PT* 16 (1687): 403–6; *PT* 16 (1692): 563–87; *PT* 33 (1724–5): 118–23, 123–4. Hooke on Kircher is from Hooke 1705: 243; on the *Mundus Subterraneus*, see *OC* 2.207, 497, 512, 532, 549, etc. For Francis Godwin see my edition of *The Man in the Moone* (Godwin 2009). On scientific debate over the scale of nature see Lewis 2009: chs. 3–5. Ray cited from Ray 1691: 2. For the debates over extraterrestrials see McColley 1936 and Dick 1982.

12 Conflagration and Millennium

1 Webster 2005: 15–47.

2 Hakewill 1635: 559–74.

3 Mede 1643: 2.117, More 1660: 172–99. On Hakewill, Brightman, Mede, and the aftermath, see Webster 2002: 4–12, 19–20, 29, Firth 1979: 199–241, and Jue 2006. For a structural comparison of Alsted and Mede see Murrin 1984; on More and Grotius see Jue 2006: 156–63; on Mede and More's satanic Americans, see Popkin 1989.

4 Glanvill 1662: 168–90, and on Glanvill see Lewis 2006.

5 British Library Add. MS 10039, fol. 63r; British Library Add. MS 28104, fol. 16r (correspondence relating to publication); Burnet's annotated 1689 edition is Cambridge University Library Adv. c. 27. 4, excellently discussed by Jacob and Lockwood 1972.

6   Burnet, *Theory*, quotations from 3.8 (angels as chemists), 3.10 (ignition of Rome), 3.12 (would sooner destroyed, earth melted like a fluor), 4.2 (theocratical government), 4.9 (contact with extraterrestrials). On Baconian Millenarianism, see Webster 2002: 1–31.

7   On Cressener see Jacob and Lockwood 1972: 270, van den Berg 1991; Boyle 1688: 85.

8   British Library MS Add. 78369, fols. 2r–9r.

9   Whiston 1696: 209–15, 368–78; Webster 2005: 41.

10 Ray 1693: 254; Boyle 1661: 158–60, and on Boyle's biblical criticism and its influence see Pahl 1950.

11 Ray 1693: 231–406, quotations from 278, 342, 361.

12 Grew 1701: 115–20; for English apocalypticism 1660–1750, see Korshin 1984, and for the bibliography see Wittreich 1984.

13 Derham 1731: 54–5, 236–7; for a translation of Craige see Nash 1991: 53–83 (quotation from 54), and 1–7 for his reception, with the quotation from Pope (*Dunciad*, 4.459–62).

14 Milton 1667: 3.321–41, 12.451–65 [in the 1673 reorganisation]; Catherall 1720, and on Catherall and eighteenth-century conflagration poetry see Jones 1959: 48–51.

Conclusion

1   Bodleian 8° Rawlinson 647 (Sanderson, belonging to 'Usher' of University College, presumably Charles Usher, who matriculated there in 1692); 4° W 31 Jur (fossil reading list); 8° Rawlinson 229, 230 (Clarke's Rohault); MS Rawlinson d. 40 (eighteenth-century curriculum); Baker 1699: 76–86. For the continental dimension, see Leibniz 2008 and de Maillet 1968.

2   King in *PT* 57 (1767): 44–57; [King] 1788: 549–68.

3   Sprat 1667: 345. Willughby's 'Objections against the Scripture' is Nottingham University Library MS Middleton LM 15, insert, now removed and in a separate folder alongside LM 15 and marked as item '8 (p. 124)'. For Pepys and Ken, see Pepys 2004: 146, 147, 152.

4   *The Times*, 17 Sept 2008.

Bibliography

As this book is supposed to be a semi-general work, endnotes are purposively minimalist, supplying only basic references for primary quotations or allusions to secondary discussions. Occasionally some further reading is suggested. I apologise if by omission I have inadvertently insulted any scholars in the field. I have suppressed biographical references unless such material is well beyond the scope of the relevant article in *The Oxford Dictionary of National Biography*. Some unattributed anecdotal material also derives from John Aubrey's *Brief Lives*, and can be traced using the index of Andrew Clark's edition (Oxford, 1898).

The endnotes employ an 'author date: page' system, in which Hooke 1665: 124 means the book in the bibliography below written by Hooke and published in 1665, page 124. Anonymous works are cited and indexed by title. Where the work is multivolume, 2.45 means volume 2, p. 45, although in a few cases it refers to book and chapter within one complete volume (e.g. Burnet, *Theory*); where there is no pagination, signatures are used, e.g. sg. A2v means the verso of the second leaf of the signature marked A; fp. stands for folio-page and operates like signaturing; where there are further ambiguities, fuller reference is provided. Frequently referenced books are cited by special abbreviation; there is a list of these at the head of the bibliography. Manuscripts are described in the notes by location, collection, manuscript number, and folio.

Owing to the wide use of *Early English Books Online* by scholars, I have usually referenced directly to early printed editions, although when modern editions are listed, original publication or best composition dates are also provided. For reasons solely of space, papers from the *PT* or the *PC* are not included in the bibliography, but are referenced in the notes.

Abbreviations

The following are employed in the notes (full publication details can be found in the bibliography):

Birch, *History* Thomas Birch, *The History of the Royal Society of London*
Burnet, *Theory* Thomas Burnet, *The Sacred Theory of the Earth*
CHSCP Daniel Garber and Michael Ayers, eds. *The Cambridge History of Seventeenth Century Philosophy*
CHSEMS Katharine Park and Lorraine Daston, eds., *The Cambridge History of Science vol. 3: Early Modern Science*
ESO R. T. Gunther, ed., *Early Science at Oxford*
HUO Nicholas Tyacke, ed., *History of the University of Oxford: Seventeenth Century Oxford*
OC Henry Oldenburg, *The Correspondence*
PC *Philosophical Collections*
PT *Philosophical Transactions*

Manuscripts

Chantilly, Château de Chantilly
Condé Museum MS 191, La Peyrère's *Des Juifs Elus, Rejetes, et Rapeles*

London, British Library
MS Add. 38536, Sir Robert Southwell's shelf-list for his manuscript archive
MS Add. 78369, containing John Evelyn's paper on the Millennium
MS Sloane 853, Latin/Chinese commonplace book of Thomas Hyde
MS Sloane 913, theological tracts and utopia of Francis Lodwick
MS Sloane 917, John Hough's additions to Varenius
MS Sloane 1775, fols. 144r–155v, translation of the seventh chapter of Thomas Burnet's *Archæologiæ*
MSS Sloane 2891–2902, commonplace books and papers of Abraham Hill
MS Sloane 3828, papers of Sir Robert Southwell

London, Guildhall Library
MS 1758, Robert Hooke's earlier memoranda

London, Royal Society
Classified Papers 20, papers of Robert Hooke
Early Letters P1, containing letters of Andrew Paschall to Robert Hooke
MS 248, papers of Sir Robert Southwell

Nottingham, Nottingham University Library
Middleton MS ML (i) 15, commonplace book of Francis Willughby

Oxford, Bodleian Library
MSS Aubrey, papers of John Aubrey
MS Eng. Misc. c. 144, papers of Sir Robert Southwell
MS Lister 5, travel journal of Martin Lister
MS Locke d 9, John Locke's weather tables
MS Rawl. A 171, containing Samuel Pepys' 'Notes from Discourses touching Religion'
MS Rawl. A 178, containing copy of letter from Sir William Petty to Sir Robert Southwell
MS Rawl. A 183, containing Jeremiah Wells' report for Samuel Pepys on La Peyrère
MS Rawl. B 399*, Thomas Hearne's catalogue of the Oxford Anatomy School collection
MS Rawl. D 40, Thomas Haywood's directions for students
MS Rawl. D 1121, Aristotelian curricular skeleton copied by Humphrey Hody
MS Rawl. Q e 36, Thomas Hearne's gift register for the Oxford Anatomy School collection
MS Top Oxon e 344, John Felton's Cartesian digest
MS Wood F 39, containing correspondence of Anthony Wood and John Aubrey

Annotated Books

Cambridge, Cambridge University Library
Adv. a. 27. 7, William Brouncker's copy of Charleton 1654
Adv. c. 27. 4, Thomas Burnet's copy of Burnet 1689

Oxford, Bodleian Library
4 W 31 Jur, with MS fossil reading list
8 Rawl. 229, 230, annotated example of Clarke's Rohault
8 Rawl. 393, 8 Rawl. 647, interleaved and annotated copies of Sanderson 1690
Ashm. C 10, John Aubrey's copy of Steno 1671
Lister C 148, Martin Lister's copy of Hooke's printed works and *Philosophical Collections*

Pasadena, Huntington Library
441102, interleaved and annotated copy of Sanderson 1690

Primary Printed Texts

An Account of the Origin and Formation of Fossil-Shells &c. London: James Knapton, 1705.
Acosta, José de. *The Naturall and Morall Historie of the East and West Indies.* London: Edward Blount and William Aspley, 1604.
Amerpoel, Johannes. *Cartesius Mosaizans seu Evidens et facilis Philosophiæ Cartesii cum historiâ Creationis primo capite Geneseos per Mosem traditâ.* Leeuwarden: the heirs of Thomas Luyrtsma, 1669.
Annius of Viterbo. *Comentaria ... super opera diversorum auctorum.* Rome: E. Silber, 1498.
Arbuthnot, John. *An Examination of Dr. Woodward's Account of the Deluge, &c.* London: C. Bateman, 1697.
Aubrey, John. *The Natural History and Antiquities of the County of Surrey*, ed. and rev. Richard Rawlinson. 5 vols., London: E. Curll, 1718–19.

Aubrey, John. *The Natural History of Wiltshire*, ed. John Britton. Wiltshire: Wiltshire Topographical Society, 1847.

Aubrey, John. *Brief Lives, chiefly of contemporaries, set down by John Aubrey, between the years 1669 and 1696*, ed. Andrew Clark. 2 vols., Oxford: Clarendon Press, 1898.

Aubrey, John. *Three Prose Works*, ed. John Buchanan-Brown. Fontwell: Centaur Press, 1972.

Aubrey, John. *Monumenta Britannica*, 3 parts in 2 vols., ed. John Fowles and annot. Rodney Legg. Sherborne: Dorset Publishing Company, 1980, 1982.

Bacon, Francis. *Instauratio Magna*. London: John Bill, 1620.

Bacon, Francis. *Sylva Sylvarum*. London: William Lee, 1627.

Baker, Thomas. *Reflections upon Learning*. London: A. Bosvile, 1699.

Bale, John. *Illustrium Maioris Britannie scriptorum … summarium*. Wesel: John Overton, 1548.

Barlow, William. *Magneticall Advertisements*. London: Timothy Barlow, 1617.

Bayle, Pierre. *Dictionaire Historique et Critique*. 4th edn., Amsterdam, 1730.

Beaumont, John. *Considerations on a Book Entituled the Theory of the Earth*. London: for the author, 1693.

Behn, Aphra. *Oroonoko and Other Writings*. Oxford: Oxford University Press, 1998.

Bentley, Richard. *The Correspondence of Richard Bentley*, ed. C. Wordsworth. London: J. Murray, 1842.

Bibliander, Theodore. *De ratione communi omnium linguarum*. Zürich: Christoph Froschauer, 1548.

Birch, Thomas, ed. *The History of the Royal Society of London for Improving of Natural Knowledge*. 4 vols., London: A. Millar, 1756–7.

Blancanus, Josephus. *Sphæra mundi*. Bologna: S. Bonomius, 1620.

Blount, Henry. *The Oracles of Reason*. London: s.n., 1693.

Boccone, Paulo. *Recherches et Observations Naturelles De Monsieur Boccone Gentilhomme Sicilien*. Amsterdam: Jean Jansson a Waesberge, 1674.

Bodin, Jean. *Method for the Easy Comprehension of History*, tr. Beatrice Reynolds. New York: Columbia University Press, 1945.

Bohun, Ralph. *A Discourse concerning the Origine and Properties of Wind*. Oxford: Thomas Bowman, 1671.

Boyle, Robert. *New Experiments Physico-Mechanicall*. Oxford: Henry Hall, 1660.

Boyle, Robert. *Some Considerations touching the Style of the H. Scriptures*. London: Henry Herringman, 1661.

Boyle, Robert. *Certain Physiological Essays*. London: Henry Herringman, 1661.

Boyle, Robert. *Some Considerations touching the Usefulnesse of Experimental Naturall Philosophy*. Oxford: Richard Davis, 1663.

Boyle, Robert. *The Origine of Formes and Qualities*. Oxford: Richard Davies, 1666.

Boyle, Robert. *Tracts written by the Honourable Robert Boyle ... of a discovery of the admirable rarefaction of the air* [etc]. London: Henry Herringman, 1671.

Boyle, Robert. *A Discourse of Things Above Reason*. London: Jonathan Robinson, 1681.

Boyle, Robert. *A Disquisition about the Final Causes of Natural Things*. London: John Taylor, 1688.

Boyle, Robert. *The Correspondence*, ed. Michael Hunter, Antonio Clericuzio, and Lawrence Principe. 6 vols., London: Pickering and Chatto, 2001.

Brerewood, Edward. *Enquiries touching the Diversity of Languages, and Religions, through the chiefe parts of the world*. London: John Bill, 1622.

Broughton, Hugh. *Observations upon the First Ten Fathers*. London: W. White, 1612.

Browne, Thomas. *Pseudodoxia Epidemica*, ed. Robin Robbins. 2 vols., Oxford: Clarendon Press, 1981 [1646 etc.].

Browne, Thomas. *Hydriotaphia ... Together with the garden of Cyrus*. London: Henry Brome, 1658.

Browne, Thomas. *Certain Miscellany Tracts*. London: Charles Mearn, 1683.

Browne, Thomas. *The Works of Sir Thomas Browne*, ed. Geoffrey Keynes. 4 vols., London: Faber and Faber, 1964.

Buckland, William. *Vindiciæ Geologicæ*. Oxford: at the University Press, 1820.

Burnet, Thomas. *The Sacred Theory of the Earth*. London: The Centaur Press, 1965 [based on 1690/1 English text].

Burnet, Thomas. *Archæologiæ Philosophicæ*. London: Walter Kettilby, 1692.

Burton, Robert. *The Anatomy of Melancholy*. 6 vols., Oxford: Clarendon Press, 1989–2000 [1621].

Buteo, Johannes. *Opera Geometrica*. Lyons: T. Bertellus, 1554.

Cabeus, Nicolaus. *In quatuor libros Meteorologicorum Aristotelis commentaria et quaestiones.* 2 vols., Rome: the heirs of F. Corbeletti, 1646.

Camden, William. *Britain,* tr. Philemon Holland. London: George Bishop and John Norton, 1610.

Carpenter, Nathanael. *Geographie Delineated.* Oxford: John Lichfield and William Turner, 1625.

Cary, Robert. *Palæologia Chronica.* London: Richard Chiswell, 1677.

Casaubon, Meric. *Of Generall Learning,* ed. Richard Serjeantson. Cambridge: RTM, 1999.

Catherall, Samuel. *Essay on the Conflagration in blank verse.* Oxford: at the Theatre, 1720.

Charleton, Walter. *Physiologia Epicuro-Gassendo-Charletoniana.* London: Thomas Heath, 1654.

Colonna, Fabio. *Purpura.* Rome: Jacobus Mascardus, 1616.

Comenius, Jan Amos. *Naturall Philosophie Reformed by Divine Light.* London: Thomas Pierrepont, 1651.

Craige, John. *John Craige's 'Mathematical Principles of Christian Theology',* ed. Richard Nash. Carbondale and Edwardsville: Southern Illinois University Press, for the *Journal of the History of Philosophy,* 1991.

Croft, Herbert. *Some Animadversions upon a Book Entitled the Theory of the Earth.* London: Charles Harper, 1685.

Croll, Oswald. *Philosophy Reformed and Improved in Four Profound Tractates … The other III discovering the wonderfull mysteries of the creation by Paracelsus, being his philosophy to the Athenians,* tr. Henry Pinnell. London: Lodowick Lloyd, 1657.

Cudworth, Ralph. *The True Intellectual System of the Universe.* London: Richard Royston, 1678.

Daniel, Gabriel. *A Voyage to the World of Cartesius.* London: Thomas Bennett, 1692.

Deane, Anthony. *Deane's Doctrine of Naval Architecture, 1670,* ed. Brian Lavery. Conway: Maritime Press, 1981.

[de Cordemoy, Géraud.] *A Discourse written to a Learned Friar, by M. Des Fourneillis, shewing that the Systeme of M. Des Cartes, and particularly his Opinion concerning Bruets, does contain nothing dangerous; and that all he hath written of both, seems to have been taken out of the First Chapter of Genesis.* London: Moses Pitt, 1670.

de Foigny, Gabriel. *La Terre Australe Connue*. Paris, 1676. Tr. as *A New Discovery of Terra Incognita Australis*. London, 1693. Modern edition: *The Southern Land, Known*, ed. David Fausett. New York: Syracuse University Press, 1993.

de Maillet, Benoît. *Telliamed: or Conversations between an Indian Philosopher and a French Missionary on the Diminution of the Sea*, tr. and ed. Albert V. Carozzi. Urbana: University of Illinois Press, 1968.

Dennis, John. *Miscellanies in Prose and Verse*. London: J. Knapton, 1693.

Derham, William. *Astro-Theology or a Demonstration of the Being and Attributes of God from a Survey of the Heavens*. 6th edn., London: W. Innys, 1731.

Descartes, René. *Principia Philosophiæ*. Amsterdam: Elzevier, 1644.

Descartes, René. *Oeuvres de Descartes: Correspondance*. 5 vols., Paris: Publiées par Charles Adam et Paul Tannery sous les auspices du Ministère de l'Instruction publique, 1897–1903.

Descartes, René. *The Principles of Philosophy*, tr. with explanatory notes by V. R. Miller and R. P. Miller. Dordrecht: Kluwer, 1983.

Eachard, John. *The Grounds and Occasions of the Contempt of the Clergy*. London: Nathaniel Brooke, 1670.

Eachard, John. *Some Observations upon the Answer to an Enquiry into the Grounds and Occasions of the Contempt of the Clergy*. London: Nathaniel Brooke, 1671.

'Eirenaeus Philalethes'. *Secrets Reveal'd, or an Open Entrance to the Shut-Palace of the King*. London: William Cooper, 1669.

Evelyn, John. *An Essay on the First Book of T. Lucretius Carus*. London: Gabriel Bedle and Thomas Collins, 1656.

Fabricius, Johannes Albertus. *Delectus Argumentorum et Syllabus Scriptorum qui Veritatem Religionis Christianæ ... Asseruerunt*. Hamburg: T. C. Felginer, 1725.

Flamsteed, John. *The Correspondence of John Flamsteed, the First Astronomer Royal*, ed. Eric Forbes, Lesley Murdin, and Frances Willmoth. 3 vols., Bristol: Institute of Physics, 1995–2002.

Gassendi, Pierre. *Opera omnia*. 6 vols., Lyons: Laurentius Anisson et al., 1658.

Gay, John. *Three Hours After Marriage*. London: Bernard Lintot, 1717.

Gilbert, William. *De Magnete, Magneticisque Corporibus, et de Magno Magnete Tellure, Physiologia Nova*. London: Peter Short, 1600.

Gilbert, William. *On the Loadstone and Magnetic Bodies.* Chicago: William Benton, 1952.

Glanvill, Joseph. *The Vanity of Dogmatizing.* London: Henry Eversden, 1661.

Glanvill, Joseph. *Lux Orientalis, or an Enquiry into the Opinion of the Eastern Sages, concerning the praeexistence of souls.* London: s.n., 1662.

Godwin, Francis. *The Man in the Moone*, ed. William Poole. Ontario: Broadview, 2009 [1638].

Godwyn, Morgan. *The Negro's and Indians Advocate.* London: for the author, 1680.

González de Mendoza, Juan. *History of the Great and Mighty Kingdom of China.* London: Edward White, 1588.

Grew, Nehemiah. *Musaeum Regalis Societatis.* London: for the author, 1681.

Grew, Nehemiah. *Cosmologia Sacra.* London: W. Rogers, S. Smith, and B. Walford, 1701.

Grotius, Hugo. *The Truth of Christian Religion in Six Books ... with the addition of a seventh book by Symon Patrick.* London: Richard Royston, 1683.

Hakewill, George. *An Apology or Declaration of the Power and Providence of God.* Oxford: William Turner, 1635.

Hale, Matthew. *The Primitive Origination of Mankind.* London: William Shrowsbery, 1677.

Hales, John. *Golden Remaines.* London: R. Pawlet, 1659.

Halley, Edmond. *Correspondence and Papers*, ed. E. F. McPike. Oxford: Clarendon Press, 1932.

H[allywell], C[harles]. *A Philosophical Discourse of Earthquakes.* London: Walter Kettilby, 1693.

Hartlib, Samuel. *Samuel Hartlib His Legacy of Husbandry.* London: Samuel Hartlib, 1655.

Hartlib, Samuel, collector. *The Hartlib Papers*, ed. Judith Crawford et al. 2nd edn., 2 CD-ROMs. Ann Arbor, MI: UMI Research Publication, 2002.

Helmont, J.-B. Van. *Oriatrike, or Physick Refined.* London: Lodowick Lloyd, 1662.

Hevelius, Johannes. *Selenographia.* Gdansk: for the author, 1647.

Hobbes, Thomas. *The Correspondence*, ed. Noel Malcolm. Oxford: Clarendon Press, 1994.

Hooke, Robert. *Micrographia.* London: John Martyn and James Allestry, 1665.

Hooke, Robert. *An Attempt to Prove the Motion of the Earth from Observations.* London: John Martyn, 1674.

Hooke, Robert. *Lectures de Potentia Restitutiva, or of Spring.* London: John Martyn, 1678.

Hooke, Robert. *Bibliotheca Hookiana.* London: Edward Millington, 1703.

Hooke, Robert. *Posthumous Works*, ed. Richard Waller. London: for the editor, 1705.

Hooke, Robert. *Philosophical Experiments and Observations*, ed. William Derham. London: W. & J. Innys, 1726.

Hooke, Robert. *The Diary of Robert Hooke M.A., M.D., F.R.S. 1672–1680*, ed. H. W. Robinson and W. Adams. London: Taylor and Francis, 1935.

Hooke, Robert. [Later Journal.] In *ESO* vol. 10, pp. 69–265, transcribed from BL MS Sloane 4024.

Huet, Pierre-Daniel. *Against Cartesian Philosophy [Censura Philosophiæ Cartesianæ]*, tr. Thomas M. Lennon. New York: Humanity Books, 2003.

Huygens, Christiaan. *The Celestial Worlds Discover'd, or Conjectures concerning the Inhabitants, Plants and Productions of the Worlds in the Planets.* London: Timothy Childe, 1698.

Hyde, Thomas. *Syntagma dissertationum.* 2 vols., Oxford: Clarendon Press, 1767.

Keckermann, Bartholomäus. *Systema Compendiosum Totius Mathematices hoc est Geometriæ, Opticæ, Astronomiæ et Geographiæ.* Hanover: P. Antonius, 1617.

Keill, John. *An Examination of Dr. Burnet's Theory of the Earth.* Oxford: at the Theatre, 1698.

[King, Edward.] *Morsels of Criticism, tending to illustrate some few passages in the Holy Scriptures.* London: J. Robson et al., 1788.

Kircher, Athanasius. *Mundus Subterraneus.* Amsterdam: Joannes Janssonius and Elizabeth Weyerstraten, 1665.

Kircher, Athanasius. *Arca Noë.* Amsterdam: Joannes Janssonius à Waesberge, 1675.

La Peyrère, Isaac. *Præ-Adamitæ.* Amsterdam: Elzevier, 1655.

La Peyrère, Isaac. *Men Before Adam*, tr. David Whitford. London: s.n., 1656.

Lawrence, Thomas. *Mercurius Centralis.* London: Richard Royston, 1664.

Le Clerc, Jean. *Twelve Dissertations out of Monsieur Le Clerk's Genesis.* London: R. Baldwin, 1696.

Leibniz, Gottfried Wilhelm. *Protogaea*, tr. and ed. Claudine Cohen and Andre Wakefield. Chicago: University of Chicago Press, 2008.

Locke, John. *An Essay Concerning Human Understanding*, ed. Peter H. Nidditch. Oxford: Clarendon Press, 1975 [1690].

Lodwick, Francis. *The Works of Francis Lodwick*, ed. Vivian Salmon. London: Longmans, 1972.

Lodwick, Francis. *A Country Not Named*, ed. William Poole. Tempe, Arizona: ACMRS, 2007.

Lord, Henry. *A Display of Two Forraigne Sects in the East Indies*. London: Francis Constable, 1630.

Lovell, Archibald. *A Summary of Material Heads which may be Enlarged and Improved into a Compleat Answer to Dr. Burnet's Theory of the Earth*. London: printed by T. B., 1696.

Lucretius, T. *Lucretius Carus the Epicurean philosopher his six books De natura rerum*, tr. Thomas Creech. Oxford: Anthony Stephens, 1682.

Lydiat, Thomas. *Emendatio temporum compendio facta*. Oxford: Felix Kyngston, 1609.

Mede, Joseph. *The Key of the Revelation*. London: Philip Stephens, 1643.

Mersenne, Marin. *Cogitata Physico-Mathematica*. Paris: Antonius Bertier, 1644.

Milton, John. *Paradise Lost*. London: Peter Parker et al., 1667.

Montaigne, Michel de. *The Essayes*, tr. John Florio. London: Edward Blount and William Barrett, 1613.

Montanus, Arnoldus. *Atlas Japannensis*, tr. John Ogilby. London: John Ogilby, 1670.

More, Henry. *The Immortality of the Soul*. London: William Morden, 1659.

More, Henry. *An Explanation of the Grand Mystery of Godliness*. London: William Morden, 1660.

Moxon, Joseph. *Sacred Geographie, or Scriptural Maps*. London: Joseph Moxon, 1691.

Newton, Isaac. *Principia mathematica philosophiæ naturalis*. London: [Edmond Halley and] The Royal Society, 1687.

Newton, Isaac. *Optickes*. New York: Dover, 1952 [1730].

Newton, Isaac. *The Correspondence, Volume II 1676–87*, ed. H. W. Turnbull. Cambridge: Cambridge University Press, 1960.

Nicholls, William. *A Conference with a Theist*. London: Francis Saunders, 1696.

Nicholls, William. *A Conference with a Theist. Part II*. London: Francis Saunders, 1697.

Nicolson, William. *Letters on Various Subjects*. 2 vols., London: Longman, Hurst, Rees, and Orme, 1809.

Oldenburg, Henry. *The Correspondence*, ed. A. R. Hall and M. B. Hall. 13 vols., Madison and Milwaukee: University of Wisconsin Press (vols. 1–9); London: Mansell (vols. 10–11); London and Philadelphia: Taylor and Francis (vols. 12–13), 1965–86.

Ortelius, Abraham. *Epistulae*, ed. J. K. Hessels. Cambridge: Cambridge University Press for the Dutch Church, 1887.

'P', 'L.' *Two Essays sent from Oxford to a Nobleman in London*. London: R. Baldwin, 1695.

Patrick, Simon. *A Commentary upon the First Book of Moses, called Genesis*. London: Richard Chiswell, 1695.

Pepys, Samuel. *Memoires relating to the State of the Royal Navy of England for Ten Years, Determin'd December 1688*. London: Benjamin Griffin, 1690.

Pepys, Samuel. *The Diary of Samuel Pepys: A New and Complete Transcription*, ed. Robert Latham and William Matthews. 11 vols., London: G. Bell, 1970–83.

Pepys, Samuel. *The Later Diaries*, ed. C. S. Knighton. Stroud: Sutton, 2004.

Pererius, Benedictus. *Commentariorum et Disputationum in Genesim, Tomi Quatuor*. Cologne: Elzevier, 1622.

Petty, William. *The Discourse … concerning the Use of Duplicate Proportion*. London: John Martyn, 1674.

Petty, William. *Another Essay in Political Arithmetick*. London: Mark Pardoe, 1683.

Petty, William. *The Petty Papers*, ed. the Marquis of Lansdowne. 2 vols., London: Constable, 1927.

Petty, William. *The Petty–Southwell Correspondence 1676–1687*, ed. the Marquis of Lansdowne. London: Constable and Co., 1928.

Pliny the Elder. *The Historie of the World*, tr. Philemon Holland. London: Adam Islip, 1601.

Plot, Robert. *The Natural History of Oxford-Shire*. Oxford: at the Theatre, 1677.

Poole, Matthew. *Synopsis Criticorum aliorumque S. Scripturae interpretum*. London: Cornelius Bee, 1669.

Pordage, Samuel. *Mundorum Explicatio*. London: Lodowick Lloyd, 1661.

Porta, Giovan Della. *Natural Magick.* London: Thomas Young and Samuel Speed, 1658.

Power, Henry. *Experimental Philosophy.* London: John Martyn and James Allestry, 1664.

Prideaux, John. *Hypomnemata logica, rhetorica, physica, metaphysica, pneumatica, ethica, politica, oeconomica.* Oxford: Leonard Lichfield, [1650].

Purchas, Samuel. *Purchas his Pilgrimage.* 4 vols., London: Henry Featherstone, 1626–7.

Ralegh, Sir Walter. *The History of the World.* London: Walter Burre, 1614.

Ray, John. *Observations Topographical.* London: John Martyn, 1673.

Ray, John. *The Wisdom of God Manifested in the Works of the Creation.* London: Samuel Smith, 1691.

Ray, John. *Miscellaneous Discourses concerning the Dissolution and Changes of the World.* London: Samuel Smith, 1692.

Ray, John. *Three Physico-Theological Discourses.* London: Samuel Smith, 1693.

Ray, John. *Further Correspondence of John Ray.* London: for the John Ray Society, 1928.

Ridley, Mark. *A Short Treatise of Magneticall Bodies and Motions.* London: Nicholas Okes, 1613.

Robinson, Tancred. *A Letter Sent to Mr. William Wotton, B.D.* [London]: s.n., 1697.

Robinson, Thomas. *The Anatomy of the Earth.* London: John Newton, 1694.

Robinson, Thomas. *New Observations on the Natural History of this World of Matter.* London: John Newton, 1696.

Sammes, Aylett. *Britannia antiqua illustrata.* London: for the author, 1676.

Sanderson, Robert. *Physicæ scientiae compendium.* Oxford: Richard Davis, 1671, 1690.

Sandys, George. *Ovid's Metamorphosis.* London: William Stansby, 1626.

Sarayna, Torellus. *De origine et amplitudine civitatis Veronæ.* Verona: Antonius Putelleti, 1540.

Scaliger, Joseph Justus. *Opuscula Varia Antehac Non Edita.* Frankfurt: Iacobus Fischer, 1612.

Scheibler, Christoph. *Philosophia compendiosa.* Oxford: Henry Curteine, 1639.

Scilla, Agostino. *La Vana Speculazione Disingannata dal Senso.* Naples: Andrea Colicchia, 1670.

Shadwell, Thomas. *The Virtuoso*. London: Henry Herringman, 1676.

Sharrock, Robert. *The History of the Propagation and Improvement of Vegetables*. Oxford: Richard Davies, 1672.

Sheringham, Robert. *De Anglorum gentis origine disceptatio*. Cambridge: John Hayes, 1670.

Simon, Richard. *A Critical History of the Old Testament*. London: Walter Davis, 1682.

Sorbière, Samuel. *Relation d'un voyage en Angleterre*. Paris: Louis Billaine, 1664.

Sorbière, Samuel. *A Voyage to England*. London: John Woodward, 1709.

Spinoza, Baruch. *A Treatise Partly Theological, and Partly Political*. London: s.n., 1689.

Sprat, Thomas. *The History of the Royal-Society of London for the Improving of Natural Knowledge*. London: John Martyn, 1667.

Steno, Nicolaus. *Prodromus*, tr. Henry Oldenburg. London: Moses Pitt, 1671.

Stier, Johann. *Praecepta doctrinae logicæ, ethicæ, physicæ, metaphysicæ, sphaericaeque, brevibus tabellis compacta una cum quaestibus physicae controversis*. Cambridge: Roger Daniel, 1647.

Stiernhielm, Georg. *Evangelia, ab Ulfila Gothicè*. Stockholm: Nicolaus Wankif, 1671.

Stillingfleet, Edward. *Origines Sacræ*. London: Henry Mortlock, 1662.

Stillingfleet, Edward. *Origines Sacræ*. 8th edn., London: Henry and George Mortlock, 1709.

Tachard, Guy. *A Relation of the Voyage to Siam*. London: J. Robinson and A. Churchil, 1688.

Taylor, Jeremy. *A Discourse of the Liberty of Prophesying*. London: Richard Royston, 1647.

Thompson, E. M., ed. *Letters of Humphrey Prideaux, sometime Dean of Norwich, to John Ellis, Under-Secretary of State, 1674–1722*. Camden Society, New Series, 15. London: Camden Society, 1875.

Twyne, John. *De rebus albionicis*. London: Richard Watkins, 1590.

Tymme, Thomas, tr. *The Practise of Chymicall and Hermeticall Physicke … written in Latin by Josephus Quersitanus, Doctor of Phisicke*. London: Thomas Creede, 1605.

Varenius, Bernhardus. *Descriptio regniæ Iaponis*. Amsterdam: Elzevier, 1649.

Varenius, Bernhardus. *Geographia generalis*. Amsterdam: Elzevier, 1650.

Verstegan, Richard. *A Restitution of Decayed Intelligence in Antiquities concerning the most noble and renowmed English nation.* London: John Norton and John Bill, 1605.

Vossius, Isaac. *Dissertatio de vera aetate mundi.* The Hague: Adriaan Vlacq, 1659.

Vossius, Isaac. *A Treatise concerning the Motion of the Seas and Winds.* London: Henry Brome, 1677.

Vossius, Isaac. *Variarum observationum liber.* London: Robert Scott, 1685.

Ward, Seth. *In Thomæ Hobbii philosophiam exercitatio epistolica.* Oxford: Richard Davis, 1656.

[War]D, [Set]H and [Joh]N [Wilkin]S. *Vindiciae Academiarum.* Oxford: Thomas Robinson, 1654.

Warren, Erasmus. *Geologia.* London: Richard Chiswell, 1690.

Webb, John. *An Historical Essay endeavoring a Probability that the Language of the Empire of China is the Primitive Language.* London: Nathaniel Brooke, 1669.

Webster, John. *Academiarum Examen.* London: Giles Calvert, 1654.

Webster, John. *Metallographia, or an History of Metals.* London: Walter Kettilby, 1671.

Whiston, William. *A New Theory of the Earth from the Original to the Consummation of Things.* London: Benjamin Tooke, 1696.

Whiston, William. *Memoires of the Life and Writings of Mr. William Whiston.* London: J. Whiston and B. White, 1753.

Wilkins, John. *A Discourse concerning a New World and another Planet.* London: John Maynard, 1640.

Wilkins, John. *An Essay concerning a Real Character, and a Philosophical Language.* London: John Martyn and Samuel Gellibrand, 1668.

Wilkins, John. *Of the Principles and Duties of Natural Religion: Two Books.* London: T. Basset et al., 1678 [1675].

Woodforde, Samuel. *A Paraphrase upon the Psalms of David.* London: Octavian Pulleyn, 1667.

Woodward, John. *An Essay toward a Natural History of the Earth and Terrestrial Bodies, especially Minerals.* London: Richard Wilkin, 1695.

Wotton, William. *Reflections on Ancient and Modern Learning.* London: Peter Buck, 1694.

Wotton, William. *A Discourse concerning the Confusion of Languages at Babel.* London: S. Austin and W. Bowyer, 1730.

Wren, Stephen, ed. *Parentalia.* London: T. Osborn and R. Dodsley, 1750.

Secondary Texts

Adams, F. D. *The Birth and Development of the Geological Sciences.* New York: Dover, 1954 [1938].

Albritton, Claude C. *The Abyss of Time: Changing Conceptions of the Earth's Antiquity after the Sixteenth Century.* New York: Dover, 2002 [1980].

Allen, D. C. *The Legend of Noah: Renaissance Rationalism in Art, Science, and Letters.* Urbana: Illinois University Press, 1949.

Ames-Lewis, Francis, ed. *Sir Thomas Gresham and Gresham College.* Aldershot: Ashgate, 1999.

Baily, Francis. *Account of the Rev John Flamsteed, the First Astronomer Royal.* London: Printed by order of the Lords Commissioner of the Admiralty, 1835.

Baker, J. N. L. 'The Geography of Bernhard Varenius.' *Transactions and Papers (Institute of British Geographers)* 21 (1955): 51–60.

Barnes, Alison. *Henry Winstanley: Artist, Inventor and Lighthouse-builder 1644–1703.* Saffron Walden: Saffron Walden Museum et al., 2003.

Barr, James. 'Why the World was Created in 4004 B.C.: Archbishop Ussher and Biblical Chronology.' *Bulletin of the John Rylands University Library* 67 (1985): 574–608.

Benítez, Miguel. 'Matériaux pour un inventaire des philosophiques clandestins.' *Rivista di Storia della Filosofia,* nuova serie, 3 (1988): 501–31.

Bennett, Jim. *The Mathematical Science of Christopher Wren.* Cambridge: Cambridge University Press, 1982.

Bennett, Jim. 'Christopher Wren's Greshamite history of astronomy and geometry.' In Francis Ames-Lewis, ed., *Sir Thomas Gresham and Gresham College* (1999), pp. 189–97.

B[ennett], J[im]. 'Sphere no. 11.' *Sphæra: The Newsletter of the Museum of the History of Science* 11 (2000), article 9.

Bennett, Jim, et al. *London's Leonardo: The Life and Work of Robert Hooke.* Oxford: Oxford University Press, 2003.

Bennett, Jim, and Scott Mandelbrote. *The Garden, the Ark, the Tower, the Temple: Biblical metaphors of knowledge in early modern Europe.* Oxford: MHS/The Bodleian Library, 1998.

Biswas, Asit K. 'Edmond Halley, F.R.S., Hydrologist Extraordinaire.' *Notes and Records of the Royal Society of London* 25 (1970): 47–57.

Blair, Ann. 'Mosaic Physics and the Search for a Pious Natural Philosophy in the Late Renaissance.' *Isis* 91 (2000): 32–58.

Bonfante, Giuliano. 'Ideas on the Kinship of the European Languages from 1200 to 1800.' *Cahiers d'Histoire Mondiale* 1 (1953–4): 679–99.

Briesemeister, William A. 'Some Three-Dimensional Relief Globes, Past and Present.' *Geographical Review* 47 (1957): 251–60.

Brown, Harcourt. *Scientific Organizations in Seventeenth-Century France (1620–1680)*. New York: Russell & Russell, 1967.

Bryden, D. J. 'The Instrument-Maker and the Printer: Paper Instruments Made in Seventeenth Century London.' *Bulletin of the Scientific Instrument Society* 55 (1997): 3–15.

Collier, K. B. *Cosmogonies of Our Fathers: Some Theories of the Seventeenth and Eighteenth Centuries*. New York: Octagon Books, 1968 [1934].

Conklin, G. N. *Biblical Criticism and Heresy in Milton*. New York: King's Crown Press, 1949.

Cook, Alan. 'Edmond Halley and the Magnetic Field of the Earth.' *Notes and Records of the Royal Society of London* 55 (2001): 473–90.

Cormack, Leslie B. 'Good Fences Make Good Neighbors: Geography as Self-Definition in Early Modern England.' *Isis* 82 (1991): 639–61.

Cormack, Leslie B. *Charting an Empire: Geography at the English Universities 1580–1620*. Chicago: University of Chicago Press, 1997.

Darley, Gillian. *John Evelyn: Living for Ingenuity*. New Haven and London: Yale University Press, 2006.

Davies, G. L. *The Earth in Decay: A History of British Geomorphology 1578–1878*. London: Macdonald and Co., 1969.

Debus, Allen G. *The Chemical Philosophy: Paracelsian Science and Medicine in the Sixteenth and Seventeenth Centuries*. 2 vols., New York: Science History Publications, 1977.

Dekker, Kees. *The Origins of Old Germanic Studies in the Low Countries*. Leiden: Brill, 1999.

de la Bédoyère, Guy. *Particular Friends: The Correspondence of Samuel Pepys and John Evelyn*. Woodbridge: Boydell, 2005.

Dick, Steven J. *Plurality of Worlds: The Origins of the Extraterrestrial Life Debate from Democritus to Kant*. Cambridge: Cambridge University Press, 1982.

Dobbs, B. J. T. 'Newton's Alchemy and his Theory of Matter.' *Isis* 73 (1982): 511–28.

Dobbs, B. J. T. 'Stoic and Epicurean doctrines in Newton's system of the world.' In Osler 1991: 221–38.

Dobbs, B. J. T. *The Janus Faces of Genius: The Role of Alchemy in Newton's Thought*. Cambridge: Cambridge University Press, 1991.

Drake, Ellen Tan. *Restless Genius: Robert Hooke and his Earthly Thoughts*. New York: Oxford University Press, 1996.

Farrar, Frederick. *History of Interpretation*. London: Macmillan, 1886.

Feingold, Mordechai. *The Mathematician's Apprenticeship: Science, Universities and Society in England 1560–1640*. Cambridge: Cambridge University Press, 1984.

Feingold, Mordechai et al. *Before Newton: The Life and Times of Isaac Barrow*. Cambridge: Cambridge University Press, 1990 [pbk. 2008].

Feingold, Mordechai. 'Of Records and Grandeur.' In *Archives of the Scientific Revolution*, ed. Michael Hunter (Woodbridge: Boydell, 1998), pp. 171–84.

Feingold, Mordechai. 'Mathematicians and Naturalists: Sir Isaac Newton and the Royal Society.' In *Isaac Newton's Natural Philosophy*, ed. Jed Z. Buchwald and I. Bernard Cohen (Cambridge, Mass.: MIT Press, 2001), pp. 77–102.

Feingold, Mordechai. 'Science as a Calling? The Early-Modern Dilemma.' *Science in Context* 15 (2002): 79–119.

Feingold, Mordechai. 'The Origins of the Royal Society Revisited.' In *The Practice of Reform in Health, Medicine and Science 1500–2000*, eds. Margaret Pelling and Scott Mandelbrote (Aldershot: Ashgate, 2005), pp. 167–83.

Firth, Katharine R. *The Apocalyptic Tradition in Reformation Britain, 1530–1645*. Oxford: Oxford University Press, 1979.

Force, James E. *William Whiston: Honest Newtonian*. Cambridge: Cambridge University Press, 1985.

Force, James E. and R. H. Popkin, eds. *The Books of Nature and Scripture*. Dordrecht: Kluwer, 1994.

Frank, Robert G. *Harvey and the Oxford Physiologists*. Berkeley: University of California Press, 1980.

Freedman, Joseph S. 'The Career and Writings of Bartholomew Keckermann, d. 1609.' *Proceedings of the American Philosophical Society* 141 (1997): 305–64.

Frisinger, H. Howard. *The History of Meteorology to 1800*. New York: American Meteorological Society, 1977.

Funkenstein, Amos. *Theology and the Scientific Imagination.* Princeton, NJ: Harvard University Press, 1986.

Gabbey, Alan. 'Henry More and the Limits of Mechanism.' In Hutton 1989: 19–35.

Garber, Daniel and Michael Ayers, eds. *The Cambridge History of Seventeenth-Century Philosophy.* 2 vols., Cambridge: Cambridge University Press, 1998.

Gaudant, Jean. 'Jean-François Séguier (1703–1784), premier historiographe de la paléontologie.' *Comptes Rendus Palevol* 4 (2005): 295–310.

Glacken, C. J. *Traces on the Rhodian Shore: Nature and Culture in Western Thought from Ancient Times to the End of the Eighteenth Century.* Berkeley: University of California Press, 1967.

Golinski, Jan. '"Exquisite Atmography": Theories of the world and experiences of the weather in a diary of 1703.' *British Journal for the History of Science* 34 (2001): 149–71.

Goodrum, Matthew R. 'Atomism, Atheism, and the Spontaneous Generation of Human Beings: The Debate over a Natural Origin of the First Humans in Seventeenth-Century Britain.' *Journal of the History of Ideas* 63 (2002): 207–24.

Grafton, Anthony. *Forgers and Critics: Creativity and Duplicity in Western Scholarship.* Princeton, NJ: Harvard University Press, 1990.

Grafton, Anthony. 'Traditions of Invention and Inventions of Tradition in Renaissance Italy: Annius of Viterbo.' In Grafton, *Defenders of the Text* (Cambridge, Mass.: Harvard University Press, 1991), pp. 76–103.

Grafton, Anthony, 'Scaliger's Chronology: Philology, Astronomy, World History.' In Grafton, *Defenders of the Text* (Cambridge, Mass.: Harvard University Press, 1991), pp. 104–44.

Grafton, Anthony. *Joseph Scaliger: A Study in the History of Classical Scholarship. II: Historical Chronology.* Oxford: Clarendon Press, 1993.

Green, John C. *The Death of Adam: Evolution and its Impact on Western Thought.* Iowa: Iowa State University Press, 1959.

Gunther, R. T., ed. *Early Science in Oxford.* 15 vols., Oxford: privately printed, 1923–67.

Harris, Victor. *All Coherence Gone: A Study of the Seventeenth-century Controversy over Disorder and Decay in the Universe.* Chicago: University of Chicago Press, 1949.

Harrison, Peter. 'The influence of Cartesian cosmology in England'. In *Descartes' Natural Philosophy*, ed. Stephen Gaukroger, John Schuster and John Sutton (London: Routledge, 2000), ch. 8, 169–92.

Harrison, Peter. *The Fall of Man and the Foundations of Modern Science*. Cambridge: Cambridge University Press, 2007.

Haycock, David Boyd. *William Stukeley: Science, Religion and Archaeology in Eighteenth-Century England*. Woodbridge: Boydell, 2002.

Heilbron, J. H. *Elements of Early Modern Physics*. Berkeley: University of California Press, 1982.

Hessayon, Ariel and Nicholas Keene. *Scripture and Scholarship in Early Modern England*. Aldershot: Ashgate, 2006.

Hill, Christopher. 'Till the Conversion of the Jews'. In Hill, *Collected Essays*, vol. 2 (Brighton: Harvester, 1986), pp. 269–300.

Hodgen, Margaret T. *Early Anthropology in the Sixteenth and Seventeenth Centuries*. Philadelphia: University of Pennsylvania Press, 1964.

Humphreys, A. L. 'Marcle Hill, Hereford.' *Notes & Queries* 11 (1915): 151–3.

Hunter, Michael. 'The Royal Society and the origins of British archaeology.' *Antiquity* 65 (1971): 113–21, 187–92.

Hunter, Michael. *John Aubrey and the Realm of Learning*. London: Duckworth, 1975.

Hunter, Michael. *Science and Society in Restoration England*. Cambridge: Cambridge University Press, 1981.

Hunter, Michael. *Establishing the New Science: the Experience of the Early Royal Society*. Woodbridge: Boydell, 1989.

Hunter, Michael. *The Royal Society and its Fellows, 1660–1700: The morphology of an early scientific institution*. 2nd edn., Chalfont St Giles: BSHS, 1994.

Hunter, Michael. '"Aikenhead the atheist": the context and consequences of articulate irreligion in the late seventeenth century'. In Hunter, *Science and the Shape of Orthodoxy: Intellectual change in late seventeenth-century Britain* (Woodbridge: Boydell, 1995), pp. 308–32.

Hutton, Sarah, ed. *Henry More (1614–1687): Tercentenary Studies*. Dordrecht: Kluwer, 1989.

Hutton, Sarah. 'Science, Philosophy, and Atheism: Edward Stillingfleet's Defence of Religion'. In Popkin and Vanderjagt 1993: 102–20.

Inwood, Stephen. *The Man Who Knew Too Much: The Strange and Inventive Life of Robert Hooke 1735–1703*. London: Macmillan, 2002.

Israel, Jonathan I. *Radical Enlightenment: Philosophy and the Making of Modernity 1650–1750*. Oxford. Oxford University Press, 2001.

Ito, Yushi. 'Hooke's Cyclic Theory of the Earth in the Context of Seventeenth Century England.' *British Journal for the History of Science* 21 (1988): 295–314.

Jacob, M. C. and W. A. Lockwood. 'Political Millenarianism and Burnet's *Sacred Theory*.' *Science Studies* 2 (1972): 265–79.

Jagger, Graham. 'Joseph Moxon, F.R.S., and the Royal Society.' *Notes and Records of the Royal Society of London* 49 (1995): 193–208.

Jardine, Lisa. *On a Grander Scale: The Outstanding Career of Sir Christopher Wren*. London: HarperCollins, 2003.

Jones, W. Powell. 'Science in Biblical Paraphrases in Eighteenth-Century England.' *Publications of the Modern Language Association* 74 (1959): 41–51.

Jue, Jeffrey. *Heaven Upon Earth: Joseph Mede (1586–1638) and the Legacy of Millenarianism*. Dordrecht: Springer, 2006.

Kendrick, T. D. *British Antiquity*. London: Methuen, 1950.

Kidd, Colin. *The Forging of Races: Race and Scripture in the Protestant Atlantic World, 1600–2000*. Cambridge: Cambridge University Press, 2006.

Kimble, G. H. T. *Geography in the Middle Ages*. London: Methuen, 1938.

Klaaren, Eugene M. *Religious Origins of Modern Science: Belief in Creation in Seventeenth Century Thought*. Grand Rapids, Mich.: William B. Eerdmans Publishing Company, 1977.

Kliger, Samuel. 'The "Goths" in England: An Introduction to the Gothic Vogue in Eighteenth-Century Aesthetic Discussion.' *Modern Philology* 43 (1945): 107–17.

Kollerstrom, Nicholas. 'The Hollow World of Edmond Halley.' *Journal of the History of Astronomy* 23 (1992): 185–92.

Korshin, Paul J. 'Queuing and waiting: the Apocalypse in England, 1660–1750.' In Patrides and Wittreich 1984: 240–65.

Lamprecht, Sterling P. 'The Rôle of Descartes in Seventeenth-Century England.' *Studies in the History of Ideas* 3 (1935): 181–240.

Levine, Joseph. *Dr. Woodward's Shield: History, Science, and Satire in Augustan England*. Ithaca, NY: Cornell University Press, 1991.

Lewis, Rhodri. 'Of "Origenian Platonisme": Joseph Glanvill on the Pre-existence of Souls.' *Huntington Library Quarterly* 69 (2006): 267–300.

Lewis, Rhodri. *Language, Mind and Nature: Artificial Languages in England from Bacon to Locke*. Cambridge: Cambridge University Press, 2007.

Lewis, Rhodri. *William Petty on the Order of Nature: An Unpublished Manuscript Treatise.* Tempe, AZ: ACMRS, 2010.

LoLordo, Anna. *Pierre Gassendi and the Birth of Early Modern Philosophy.* Cambridge: Cambridge University Press, 2007.

McColley, Grant. 'The Seventeenth-Century Doctrine of a Plurality of Worlds.' *Annals of Science* 1 (1936): 285–430.

McConnell, Anita. *No Sea Too Deep: The History of Oceanographic Instruments.* Bristol: Hilger, 1982.

MacGregor, Arthur. *The Ashmolean Museum: A brief history of the Institution and its collections.* Oxford: The Ashmolean Library, 2001.

MacIntosh, J. J. 'Robert Boyle on Epicurean atheism and atomism.' In Osler 1991: 197–219.

Malcolm, Noel. 'Hobbes and the Royal Society.' In Malcolm, *Aspects of Hobbes* (Oxford: Clarendon Press, 2002), pp. 317–35.

Mandelbrote, Scott. 'Isaac Newton and Thomas Burnet: Biblical Criticism and the Crisis of Late Seventeenth-century England.' In Force and Popkin 1994: 149–78.

Mandelbrote, Scott. 'English Scholarship and the Greek Text of the Old Testament.' In Hessayon and Keene 2006: 74–93.

Mandelbrote, Scott. 'Isaac Newton and the Flood.' In Mulsow and Assmann 2006: 337–53.

Martínez, Florentino García and Gerard P. Luttikhuizen, eds. *Interpretations of the Flood.* Leiden: Brill, 1999.

Moody, Ernest A. 'John Buridan on the Habitability of the Earth.' *Speculum* 16 (1941): 415–25.

Muller, R. A. 'The Debate over the Vowel Points and the Crisis in Orthodox Hermeneutics.' *Journal of Medieval and Renaissance Studies* 10 (1980): 53–72.

Mulligan, Lotte. 'Self-Scrutiny and the Study of Nature: Robert Hooke's Diary as Natural History.' *Journal for British Studies* 35 (1996): 311–42.

Mulsow, Martin and Jan Assmann, eds. *Sintflut und Gedächtnis.* Munich: Wilhelm Fink Verlag, 2006.

Murrin, Michael. 'Revelation and two seventeenth century commentators.' In Patrides and Wittreich 1984: 124–46.

Nash, Richard. *John Craige's 'Mathematical Principles of Christian Theology'.* Carbondale and Edwardsville: Southern Illinois University Press, for the *Journal of the History of Philosophy,* 1991.

Newman, William R. and Lawrence M. Principe. *Alchemy Tried in the Fire: Starkey, Boyle, and the Fate of Helmontian Chymistry*. Chicago: University of Chicago Press, 2005.

Nicolson, Marjorie Hope. *Mountain Gloom and Mountain Glory: The Development of the Aesthetics of the Infinite*. Ithaca, NY: Cornell University Press, 1959.

Oldroyd, David R. 'Geological Controversy in the Seventeenth Century: 'Hooke *Vs* Wallis' and its Aftermath.' In *Robert Hooke: New Studies*, ed. Michael Hunter and Simon Schaffer (Woodbridge: Boydell, 1989), pp. 207–33.

Osler, Margaret J., ed. *Atoms, Pneuma, and Tranquillity: Epicurean and Stoic Themes in European Thought*. Cambridge: Cambridge University Press, 1991.

Packer, J. W. *The Transformation of Anglicanism 1643–1660: with special reference to Henry Hammond*. Manchester: Manchester University Press, 1969.

Pagden, Anthony. *The Fall of Natural Man: The American Indian and the origins of comparative ethnology*. Cambridge: Cambridge University Press, 1982.

Pahl, Gretchen Graf. 'John Locke a Literary Critic and Biblical Interpreter.' In *Essays Critical and Historical Dedicated to Lily B. Campbell* (Berkeley and Los Angeles: University of California Press, 1950), pp. 139–57.

Park, Katharine and Lorraine Daston, eds. *The Cambridge History of Science vol. 3: Early Modern Science*. Cambridge: Cambridge University Press, 2006.

Parry, Graham. *The Trophies of Time: English Antiquarians of the Seventeenth Century*. Oxford: Oxford University Press, 1995.

Pasini, Mirella. *Thomas Burnet: una storia del mondo tra ragione, mito e rivelazione*. Florence: Pubblicazioni del Centro di Studi del Pensiero Filosofico del Cinquecento e del Seicento in Relazione ai Problemi della Scienza, 1981.

Patrides, C. A. 'Renaissance Estimates of the Year of Creation.' *Huntington Library Quarterly* 26 (1963): 315–22.

Patrides, C. A. and Joseph Wittreich, eds. *The Apocalypse in English Renaissance Thought and Literature: Patterns, Antecedents, and Repercussions*. Ithaca, NY: Cornell University Press, 1984.

Pavlov, A. P. 'Robert Hooke, Un évolutionniste oublié du XVII siècle.' *Palaeobiologica* 1 (1928): 203–10.

Poole, William. 'Seventeenth-century Preadamism, and an Anonymous English Preadamist.' *The Seventeenth Century* 19 (2004): 1–35.

Poole, William. 'The Genesis Narrative in the Circle of Robert Hooke and Francis Lodwick.' In Hessayon and Keene 2006: 41–57.

Poole, William. 'Antoine-François Payen, the 1666 Selenelion, and an unnoticed letter to Robert Hooke.' *Notes and Records of the Royal Society of London* 61 (2007): 251–63.

Poole, William. 'Sir Robert Southwell's Dialogue on Thomas Burnet's Theory of the Earth: "C & S discourse of M Burnetts Theory of the Earth" (1684).' *The Seventeenth Century* 23 (2008): 2–104.

Popkin, Richard H. *Isaac La Peyrère (1596–1676): His Life, Work and Influence.* Leiden: Brill, 1987.

Popkin, Richard H. 'The Rise and Fall of the Jewish Indian Theory.' In *Menasseh Ben Israel and his World*, ed. Yosef Kaplan, Henry Méchoulan, and Richard Henry (Leiden: Brill, 1989), pp. 63–82.

Popkin, Richard H. *The History of Scepticism from Savonarola to Bayle.* Revised and expanded edn., Oxford: Oxford University Press, 2003.

Popkin, Richard H. and Arjo Vanderjagt, eds. *Scepticism and Irreligion in the Seventeenth and Eighteenth Centuries.* Leiden: Brill, 1993.

Pumfrey, Stephen. *Latitude and the Magnetic Earth.* Cambridge: Icon, 2002.

Quennehen, Elizabeth. 'À Propos des *Préadamites.*' *La Lettre Clandestine* 3 (1994): http://lancelot.univ-paris12.fr/lc3-5c.htm

Quennehen, Elizabeth. 'Un Noveau Manuscrit des *Préadamites.*' *La Lettre Clandestine* 4 (1995): http://lancelot.univ-paris12.fr/lc4-2i.htm

Ramsey, Rachel. 'China and the Idea of Order in John Webb's *Historical Essay.*' *Journal of the History of Ideas* 62 (2001): 483–503.

Rappaport, Rhoda. 'Hooke on Earthquakes: Lectures, Strategy and Audience.' *British Journal for the History of Science* 19 (1986): 129–46.

Rappaport, Rhoda. *When Geologists were Historians, 1665–1750.* Ithaca, NY: Cornell University Press, 1997.

Raven, Charles. *John Ray: Naturalist.* Cambridge: Cambridge University Press, 1950.

Rees, Graham. 'The Fate of Bacon's Cosmology in the Seventeenth Century.' *Ambix* 24 (1977): 27–38.

Richet, Pascal. *A Natural History of Time*, tr. John Venerella. Chicago: University of Chicago Press, 2007.

Robinson, Ira. 'Isaac de la Peyrère and the Recall of the Jews.' *Jewish Social Studies* 40 (1978): 117–30.

Roller, Duane H. D. *The 'De Magnete' of William Gilbert*. Amsterdam: Menno, 1959.

Romm, James S. 'Lucian and Plutarch as Sources for Kepler's *Somnium*.' *Classical and Modern Literature* 9 (1988–9): 97–107.

Romm, James S. 'A New Forerunner for Continental Drift.' *Nature* 367 (3 Feb 1994): 407–8.

Rossi, Paolo. *The Dark Abyss of Time: The History of the Earth and the History of Nations from Hooke to Vico*. Chicago: Chicago University Press, 1984.

Rudwick, Martin J. S. *The Meaning of Fossils: Episodes in the History of Palaeontology*. 2nd edn., Chicago: University of Chicago Press, 1985.

Sailor, Danton B. 'Moses and Atomism.' *Journal of the History of Ideas* 25 (1964): 3–16.

Schaffer, Simon. 'Halley's Atheism and the End of the World.' *Notes and Records of the Royal Society of London* 32 (1977): 17–40.

Scherz, Gustav, ed. *Nicolaus Steno and his Indice*. Copenhagen: Munksgaard, 1958.

Schnapper, Antoine. 'Persistance des Géants.' *Annales* 41 (1986): 177–200.

Scholder, Klaus. *The Birth of Modern Critical Theology*. London: SCM Press, 1990.

Seaton, Ethel. *Literary Relations of England and Scandinavia in the Seventeenth Century*. Oxford: Clarendon Press, 1935.

Stedall, Jacqueline A. *A Discourse Concerning Algebra: English Algebra to 1685*. Oxford: Oxford University Press, 2002.

Stephens, Walter. 'When Pope Noah Ruled the Etruscans: Annius of Viterbo and his Forged Antiquities.' *Modern Language Notes* 119 (2004): 201–23.

Taylor, E. G. R. '"The English Atlas" of Moses Pitt, 1680–83.' *The Geographical Journal* 95 (1940): 292–9.

Taylor, E. G. R. 'The English Worldmakers of the Seventeenth Century and their Influence on Earth Sciences.' *The Geographical Review* 38 (1948): 104–12.

Thrower, Norman J. W., ed. *The Compleat Plattmaker: Essays on Chart, Map, and Globe Making in England in the Seventeenth and Eighteenth Centuries*. Berkeley: University of California Press, 1978.

Thrower, Norman J. W. 'Edmond Halley and Thematic Geo-Cartography.' In Thrower 1978: 195–228.

Trevor-Roper, Hugh. 'The Paracelsian Movement.' In Trevor-Roper, *Renaissance Essays* (London: Secker and Warburg, 1985), pp. 149–99.

Tyacke, Nicholas, ed. *The History of the University of Oxford IV: Seventeenth Century Oxford*. Oxford: Oxford University Press, 1997.

Tyacke, Sarah. *London Map-Sellers, 1660–1720*. Tring: Map Collector Publications, 1978.

van den Berg, Jan. 'Glorious revolution and millennium: the "apocalyptical thoughts" of Drue Cressener.' In *Church, Change and Revolution*, ed. J. van den Berg and P. G. Hoftijzer (Leiden: Brill, 1991), pp. 130–44.

Vermij, Rienk. 'The Flood and the Scientific Revolution: Thomas Burnet's System of Natural Providence.' In Martínez and Luttikhuizen 1996: 150–66.

Vogel, Klaus A. 'Cosmography.' In Park and Daston 2006: 469–96.

Walker, D. P. *The Decline of Hell: Seventeenth-Century Discussions of Eternal Torment*. London: RKP, 1964.

Wallis, Helen M. 'Geography is Better than Divinitie. Maps, Globes, and Geography in the Days of Samuel Pepys.' In Thrower 1978: 1–43.

Ward, Charles E. 'Religio Laici and Father Simon's History', *Modern Language Notes* 61 (1946): 407–12.

Warner, Deborah. 'Terrestrial Magnetism: For the Glory of God and the Benefit of Mankind.' *Osiris* 9 (1994): 67–84.

Warntz, William. 'Newton, the Newtonians, and the *Geographia Generalis Varenii.' Annals of the Association of American Geographers* 79 (1989): 165–91.

Wear, Andrew. *Knowledge and Practice in English Medicine, 1550–1680*. Cambridge: Cambridge University Press, 2000.

Webster, Charles. 'Water as the Ultimate Principle of Nature: The Background to Boyle's Sceptical Chymist.' *Ambix* 13 (1966): 96–107.

Webster, Charles. *The Great Instauration: Science, Medicine and Reform 1626–1660*. Oxford: Peter Lang, 2002 [1975].

Webster, Charles. *From Paracelsus to Newton: Magic and the Making of Modern Science*. New York: Dover, 2005 [1982].

Westfall, Richard S. *Never At Rest: A Biography of Isaac Newton*. Cambridge: Cambridge University Press, 1980.

Williams, Arnold. *The Common Expositor: An Account of the Commentaries on Genesis 1527–1633*. Chapel Hill: University of North Carolina Press, 1948.

Willmoth, Frances. 'John Flamsteed's letter concerning the natural causes of earthquakes.' *Annals of Science* 44 (1987): 23 70.

Wittreich, Joseph. 'Bibliography.' In Patrides and Wittreich 1984: 369–440.

Woodward, David A. 'English Cartography, 1650–1750: A Summary.' In Thrower 1978: 159–93.

Index